D0364323

Ulster University
LIBR

European Welfare Policy

Also by Vic George

Modern Thinkers on Welfare (edited with R. Page)

Welfare and Ideology (with P. Wilding)

Social Policy Towards 2000 (edited with S. Miller)

Poverty Amidst Affluence: Britain and the United States (with I. Howards)

Wealth, Poverty and Starvation

The Impact of Social Policy (with P. Wilding)

Socialism, Social Welfare and the Soviet Union (with N. Manning)

Poverty and Inequality in Common Market Countries (edited with R. Lawson)

Ideology and Social Welfare (with P. Wilding)

Social Security and Society

Motherless Families (with P. Wilding)

Foster Care: Theory and Practice

Social Security: Beveridge and After

Also by Peter Taylor-Gooby

Markets and Managers (edited with Robyn Lawson)

Dependency Culture (with H. Dean)

Social Change, Social Welfare and Social Science

The Private Provision of Public Welfare (with Elim Papadakis)

Public Opinion, Ideology and the Welfare State

Social Theory and Social Welfare (with J. Dale)

Political Philosophy and Social Welfare (with R. Plant and H. Lesser)

European Welfare Policy

Squaring the Welfare Circle

Edited by

Vic George

and

Peter Taylor-Gooby

Selection, editorial matter and Introduction © Vic George and
Peter Taylor-Gooby 1996

Individual chapters (in order) © Vic George; Roger Lawson;
Linda Hantrais; Arthur Gould; Peter Taylor-Gooby; Mauro
Niero; Peter Stathopoulos; Elisabet Almeda and Sebastia
Sarasa; Vic George; Peter Taylor-Gooby 1996

All rights reserved. No reproduction, copy or transmission of
this publication may be made without written permission.

No paragraph of this publication may be reproduced, copied or
transmitted save with written permission or in accordance with
the provisions of the Copyright, Designs and Patents Act 1988,
or under the terms of any licence permitting limited copying
issued by the Copyright Licensing Agency, 90 Tottenham Court
Road, London W1P 9HE.

Any person who does any unauthorised act in relation to this
publication may be liable to criminal prosecution and civil
claims for damages.

First published 1996 by
MACMILLAN PRESS LTD
Houndmills, Basingstoke, Hampshire RG21 6XS
and London
Companies and representatives
throughout the world

ISBN 0–333–60916–6 hardcover
ISBN 0–333–60917–4 paperback

A catalogue record for this book is available
from the British Library.

10   9   8   7   6   5   4   3   2   1
05 04 03 02 01 00 99 98 97 96

Printed in Malaysia

Contents

Acknowledgements

The authors and publishers wish to thank the following for permission to use copyright material: The Controller of HMSO for Tables 1.9, 9.3 from *Social Trends 1994* and Table 5.2 from 'Households Below Average Income', DSO; International Social Security Association for Table 1.7 from Whiteford and Bradshaw, 'Benefits and Incentives for Lone Parents: A Comparative Analysis', *International Social Security Review*, 47, 3–4/94, table 1, p. 71; Office for Official Publications of the European Communities for Tables 9.2, 9.3, 9.4 for data produced by Eurostat from the Labour Force Survey (as reprinted in *Employment in Europe*, 1994, *A Social Portrait of Europe*, 1991 and *Poverty Statistics in the Late 1980s*); Organisation for Economic Co-operation and Development for Tables 1.1, 1.2, 1.3, 1.4, 1.5, 1.6, 1.8, 1.10, 9.1, 10.1 for data from OECD sources and *OECD Economic Studies*, No. 17, 1991, and *Economic Outlook*, No. 55, 1994. Copyright © OECD. Every effort has been made to trace all the copyright-holders, but if any have been inadvertently overlooked the publishers will be pleased to make the necessary arrangement at the first opportunity.

List of Tables

List of Contributors

Elisabet Almeda is a Researcher in Gender issues in the Department of Public Administration, Pompeu Fabra University, Barcelona, Spain.

Vic George is Professor of Social Policy and Social Work, University of Kent, Canterbury, UK.

Arthur Gould is a Senior Lecturer in Social Policy, University of Loughborough, UK.

Linda Hantrais is Professor of Modern Languages and Director of the European Research Centre, University of Loughborough, UK.

Roger Lawson is a Senior Lecturer and Head of the Department of Social Policy and Sociology, University of Southampton, UK.

Mauro Niero is Professor of Social Welfare, University of Venice, Italy.

Sebastia Sarasa is Professor of Public Policy, Pompeu Fabra University, Barcelona, Spain.

Peter Stathopoulos is Professor of Social Planning and Social Policy, Technological Educational Institute, Athens, Greece.

Peter Taylor-Gooby is Professor of Social Policy, University of Kent, Canterbury, UK.

Introduction

Several recent reports by the European Community and the OECD view social and economic policy as inseparable. They consider active social policies as not only conducive to economic growth but as necessary prerequisites to it. On the other hand, they stress that low or zero rates of economic growth inevitably make the achievement of social policy goals very difficult, if not impossible. It is the balance and the right mix of social and economic policies that is the crux of the matter for a vigorous welfare state.

In this volume, we consider the social policies of seven European countries during the past fifteen years within their broader economic, political and social environment. They are all now members of the European Union, but with rather different government approaches to economic and social policy. They range from Sweden with its reputation as the prototype of a fully developed welfare state to Greece with a welfare state in the making. The seven countries are also divided between the more affluent countries of Northern Europe – Sweden, Germany, France and the UK – where family patterns are unstable and the less affluent countries of the Mediterranean rim – Italy, Spain and Greece – where families tend to be more cohesive. The family and the community play a greater part in welfare provision in the latter than in the former group of countries.

The concern of the book is to examine the social policy experiences of these countries; to understand the demographic, social and economic pressures for increased welfare spending; and to reach some tentative conclusions on the possible future developments in welfare provision. The book shares the view of many writers that the 1980s and 1990s are a rather special period in the development of the welfare state. A number of factors coalesce to produce a political environment that, on one hand, makes for the containment or the reduction of state welfare spending and, on the other, for the expansion of voluntary and private effort. Apart from issues concerning the volume of state welfare, this period has also seen the beginnings of a trend away from unquestioned decision-making structures and towards greater public accountability in welfare services. Thus the 1980s and the 1990s may well mark the beginning of a new era in the history of the welfare state.

The book begins with a review of trends in the economy, labour market, the family, demography, taxation and welfare spending during the post-war period in our seven countries (Chapter 1). It then reviews the experience of the seven countries during the years 1980–95 and casts a glance at their likely development in the remaining years of this century (Chapters 2–8). Chapter 9 examines the pressures affecting the demand for welfare today and in the immediate future. While demographic, family and social factors play their part, it is unemployment which directly and indirectly is the major pressure point. Chapter 10 looks at the political responses of the seven countries.

There is a limited tendency towards convergence in spending levels (as lower spending Mediterranean countries with left-wing governments increase provision and Northern governments retrench) and in the broad structure of provision (as Bismarckian social insurance systems are subsidised from direct taxation and are extended to include at least some groups among the 'new poor' who are not strictly entitled on the basis of work records). So far so good for the protagonists of Maastricht! How far this trend will go in eroding the disparity between welfare systems based essentially on social insurance and those which place much greater reliance on direct state tax is unclear. Nowhere are welfare reforms adequate to meet the needs of those who have been penalised as a result of the current changes in family life and patterns of employment. So far political ideology has had a real but limited effect on welfare reform in recessionary times, although the evidence of Chapter 1 indicates that the test for the stability of welfare systems has not yet arrived. The exception is the UK, where a right-wing government has achieved substantial welfare cuts.

We are immensely grateful to all our contributors without whose work the book would not have been possible. We are also grateful to Jan Terpstra of the University of Nijmegen, the Netherlands; to Ramesh Mishra of the University of York, Canada; and to Paul Wilding of the University of Manchester, UK, for valuable comments on several chapters. As editors, we are jointly responsible for any errors and any weaknesses of the book.

Social policy debates will assume increasing importance within the European Union because of the increasing pressures for welfare expansion, the uncertainties surrounding the future of economic growth and the new ideas of how welfare should be provided and administered. The need for comparative studies of European social policies is greater than ever before and we hope this volume will make some contribution in the understanding of the forces that affect the development of policy in different countries.

Vic George
Peter Taylor-Gooby

1

The Future of the Welfare State

VIC GEORGE

A society preoccupied with private production and aggressive sale of consumer goods, however magnificent, is a society that starves its public sector. (Wilensky and Lebeaux, 1958, p. xi)

Governments in all advanced industrial societies today are hard pressed to find solutions to a series of interrelated economic, fiscal, social and cultural problems facing the welfare state. It is not so much a crisis in the sense that it is an acute condition that a neat surgical operation can soon put right, otherwise the whole welfare state edifice will collapse. Rather it is a chronic condition that will persist for some time and the way out will be through protracted incrementalism rather than comprehensive planning. It is as much a political and an ideological as well as an economic problem and its solution will vary, to a lesser or greater extent, between governments of different political orientations.

Governments have always had to face an array of problems of different kinds. What is unique about the present situation is that the number, nature and severity of these problems demand solutions that are often beyond the scope of the traditional forms of welfare provision. It is for this reason that the ever-expanding, universalist and bureaucratically run welfare state of earlier decades is gradually being contained, modified and replaced by new forms of welfare provision.

This chapter attempts to provide first the historical background of how this situation has come about. It, therefore, reviews briefly trends in economic growth, productivity, employment, unemployment and inflation; it documents demographic, family and social trends; it discusses the rise in

1

public and social expenditure; and it analyses the changing perspectives on the welfare state during the post-war period.

The chapter, secondly, examines the ways which governments have used so far and are likely to use in the future to deal with the major of these problems – reconciling demands and resources in the public sector from both the supply and the demand side of social provision. It summarises the methods governments can use to raise more funds as well as the policies they can adopt to reduce demand for services.

Thirdly, the chapter discusses the main processes in contemporary welfare capitalist societies that pose serious challenges to the volume, sources and nature of welfare provision. These go beyond issues of finance and they coalesce to form a major force for radical change in the nature of the welfare state. They are likely to lead to a welfare state that is very different from both the universalist welfare state of Beveridge and the minimal state of Hayek.

The Post-War Development of the Welfare State

Debates during the past fifty years on the desirability, viability and the future prospects of the welfare state can be divided into two stages, each representing a particular period: the optimistic outlook of the years 1950–75 when the ideas of the broad left were dominant, followed by the questioning and pessimistic approach of 1975–90 when the new right ideology became supreme. Each of these two welfare outlooks was embedded in and was a partial reflection of different socio-economic environments.

The Years of Welfare Optimism, 1950–75

Most industrial societies witnessed a substantial reorganisation and expansion of their social services during the immediate post-war years. It was a welfare reconstruction that was backed by considerable political consensus. The dominant expressed public view was that the state had the economic ability, administrative capacity and the moral duty to provide a range of services that would ensure a National Minimum, as the Beveridge report in the UK, the Marsh report for Canada, the report of the Van Rhijn Commission in the Netherlands and Laroque's writings in France demostrate. There was a general desire to work hard, to rebuild and never to return to the economic depression of the 1930s.

Public spending was seen in positive terms: it would not only help create a socially cohesive society and ensure a minimum standard for all but it would also encourage economic growth. Keynes gave public expenditure an economic respectability that would stand it in good stead in the future. Moreover, the ambition of governments was that the range and standard of these services should be continually improved. There were, of course, discordant voices, mainly from the right, but these were marginalised and had no influence on government policies. Undoubtedly, the political forces favouring the creation of a universalist welfare state were in the ascendancy during this period.

The material conditions for this strongly pro-welfare political alliance were decidedly positive. On the demand side, demographic factors were not seen as unfavourable, unemployment rates were extremely low and family break up rates were not significant. On the supply side, rates of economic growth were consistently high, inflation was low, national indebtedness was not considered an issue, public expectations for the range and quality of services were modest and, in several countries, people were used to high taxes during the war. All this was particularly the case for the years up to 1970 for after that dark clouds began to gather menacingly over the economies of many countries. It is this confluence of ideological and material factors that made these years the Golden Era of the welfare state. The argument is not that the quality and range of services were necessarily superior to today's, but rather that the perception of the services and the outlook for their future development were decidedly positive and optimistic.

Table 1.1, as well as most of the other tables in this chapter, covers the six countries that are the concern of this book, as well as Denmark and the Netherlands to give a wider European picture and the USA because of its pivotal position in world affairs. It shows quite clearly how favourable the economic factors were up to 1970 and how these began to deteriorate after that in the OECD countries as a group. A more detailed look at the figures reveals that almost all country trends conformed to this pattern. Growth rates of GDP were lower and price rises were higher during 1970–5 than during 1960–70 in every country. Similarly, though unemployment rates for 1970–5 were modest by today's standards, they were higher than for the previous decade.

Table 1.2 shows some of the trends in public expenditure, that is all government outlays including servicing the national debt; and social expenditure, that is mainly on social security, health and the personal social services. The general picture is one of rising trends for all countries

TABLE 1.1   Economic indicators, 1960–75 (percentages)

	Annual average growth of real GDP		Annual average growth of prices		Annual average unemployment rates	
	1960–70	1970–75	1960–70	1970–75	1960–70	1970–75
Total OECD	4.8	3.1	3.2	8.8	n/a	3.8
Denmark	4.9	2.0	5.9	9.3	1.2	2.4
France	5.6	3.8	4.0	8.8	1.5	3.1
Germany	4.7	1.9	2.7	6.1	0.8	1.3
Greece	7.7	5.2	2.1	12.5	n/a	2.3
Italy	5.6	2.4	3.9	11.5	3.2	5.9
Netherlands	5.3	3.4	4.0	7.2	1.1	1.7
Spain	7.5	5.5	6.1	12.5	1.5	2.4
Sweden	4.6	1.2	4.1	8.0	1.2	1.8
UK	2.8	1.9	4.1	13.2	1.6	2.8
USA	3.4	2.2	2.8	6.8	4.5	6.1

Source: OECD (1973), country tables; OECD (1978), no. 24, pp. 126–7; OECD (1990), no. 47, June and R.19 p. 199.

for both public expenditure and social expenditure. It is, however, social expenditure that grew sharply during this period and particularly in Denmark, the Netherlands, Sweden and the USA where the figures doubled, a rate of increase above that of the growth of the economy.

It is these high increases and fears of further escalation that gave rise to the anti-welfare New Right critique which gained increasing acceptance, particularly in the UK and USA, even though it had no effect on public expenditure levels until the late 1970s. Interestingly enough, the figures for the UK and USA were lower than those of other industrial countries in the table, though their rates of economic growth for the same period were lower. It suggests that objective conditions by themselves do not necessarily determine government behaviour. They have to be politically interpreted and this depends on a host of other factors that vary from country to country at any one time.

The Years of Welfare Pessimism, 1975–90

Many of the New Right criticisms of the welfare state that came to command increasing support from the late 1970s onwards had been voiced before. They now began to be seen as relevant because economic condi-

TABLE 1.2   *Trends in public and social expenditure as a percentage of GDP, 1960–75*

	Public expenditure			Social expenditure	
	1960	*1970*	*1975*	*1960*	*1975*
Total OECD	28.5	32.3	38.0	10.1	18.1
Denmark	24.8	40.2	48.2	9.0*	24.2
France	34.6	38.5	43.4	13.4	17.7
Germany	32.0	38.6	48.9	18.1	26.2
Greece	17.4	22.4	26.7	7.1	8.6
Italy	30.1	34.2	43.2	13.1	21.0
Netherlands	33.7	45.5	55.9	11.7	29.6
Spain	13.7	22.2	24.7	7.8	11.8**
Sweden	31.1	43.3	48.9	10.8	21.2
UK	32.6	38.8	46.6	10.2	15.6
USA	27.8	31.6	43.6	7.3	14.5

* This figure is taken from OECD (1988), table 1, p. 10 and may not be comparable with the other figures in the table.
**Gabrero, G. (1992), table 1, p. 24.
Source: OECD (1982), no. 32, December table R8, p. 161; OECD (1990), no. 47, June, table R15, p. 195; OECD (1994a), table 1a, p. 57.

tions in many countries began to deteriorate. In several countries, rates of economic growth began to slow down, inflation was rising, government borrowing was on the increase and public opposition to direct taxation was becoming more visible. The New Right strictures of welfare began to make sense not only to middle- and upper-class groups but also to many in the well-paid sections of the working class which had gradually come to see the market as a major provider of their individual and family welfare. In other words, the post-war pro-welfare political alliance began to weaken not only because of the current problems of the welfare state but also as a result of its past successes. Part of the New Right ideology gained currency not only by political parties of the right and the centre but by parties of the left as well. Clearly, this situation varied somewhat from country to country depending on the details of the prevailing economic and political conditions. Nevertheless, the anti-welfare forces were gaining ground in all countries, though at different speeds and patterns.

The welfare state, claimed the New Right, undermined economic growth, political legitimacy and the traditional way of community and family life. High levels of public expenditure undermine rates of economic growth, claims the New Right, for at least two reasons: they involve high levels of taxation which in turn act as disincentives for hard work, savings and investment – a widely expressed view; and more particularly, they pull human and capital resources away from wealth creating into public services and thus set in train the process of 'de-industrialisation' (Bacon and Eltis, 1976). As a British government white paper succinctly put it a few years later: 'Public expenditure is at the heart of Britain's present economic difficulties' (HM Treasury, 1979, p. 1).

As for the adverse effects of welfare on political legitimation, the argument was that as welfare states 'overloaded' themselves with responsibilities of all kinds, their ability to deal effectively with problems declined in equal measure. The result was that public confidence in government inevitably suffered. As a British political commentator put it, 'just as the range of responsibilities of Governments has increased, so, to a large extent independently, their capacity to exercise their responsibilities has declined' (King, 1975, p. 288). Similarly, an American commentator concluded more graphically: 'There is mounting evidence that government is big rather than strong; that it is fat and flabby rather than powerful; that it costs a great deal of money but does not achieve much' (Drucker, 1969, p. 3). Nothing short of a drastic reduction in both government activity and expenditure would change the situation.

The economic and the political strictures of the welfare state were equally common in both Britain and the USA. The social criticism, however, was much more an American feature of anti-welfarism and was directed particularly at the payment of benefits to the unemployed and the lone parents. Such a system of benefits, according to Banfield, 'causes the breakup of a great many families' (Banfield, 1969, p. 94); it 'enables a great many people who should work to escape work' (p. 95); it 'offers an incentive to wholesale lying and cheating' (p. 94); and it 'tends to destroy honesty and fair dealing in all relations of life' (p. 97). There was no other solution but to lower substantially the generosity of benefits even though many of the poor would suffer. It was the lesser of two evils.

An equally powerful attack on the welfare state, though for different reasons, was mounted by Marxist writers in the mid-1970s. At the centre of this attack was the Marxist view that the welfare state is a contradictory and hence unstable economic and political formation. It had developed as far as it was possible within a capitalist economy but was now facing a 'fiscal crisis' (O'Connor 1973), a 'legitimation crisis' (Habermas, 1976) and a general 'systems crisis'. It would either develop into a socialist society or degenerate into chaos. There were those

Marxists, however, who believed that welfare provision was so essential to capitalism that no government would dare reduce it substantially let alone abolish it.

Another attack from the left came from those who saw the welfare state as being repressive, stigmatising and controlling. Services were provided in ways that reduced people's independence and strengthened the existing forms of ideological domination (Hewitt, 1992). Others produced empirical evidence that the welfare state was not vertically redistributive and was not even abolishing poverty. Added to these were the feminist and the ecological critiques which argued for different types of social provision. Finally, there was the critique from both the left and the right that the welfare state was dominated by bureaucrats and professionals who used it for their own ends rather than for the benefit of the public. In brief, the universalist welfare state was being subjected to unremitting criticism by both its supporters and its enemies.

Let us now look at the development of the welfare state from the mid-1970s onwards. Table 1.3 provides a summary of the main economic indicators. It shows that GDP growth during 1975–80 was lower than that of the 1960s, rather similar to that of the previous five years and it declined further during the 1980s and early 1990s. Prices rose faster during 1975–80 than previously but, with the exception of Greece, were reigned back during the 1980s. Unemployment, however, continued to rise both during the second half of the 1970s as well as during the 1980s in each of the countries covered by the table, as well as for the whole of the OECD group of countries. For those who were in secure jobs, the 1980s were a prosperous decade since prices were held down but for those out of work, and particularly the long-term unemployed, low inflation was not such a great achievement.

In brief, the economic environment of the 1980s was unfavourable and in many countries hostile to the economically painless expansion of the welfare state that was a feature of previous decades. The significance of employment levels to the welfare state cannot be overestimated. Low levels of unemployment are conducive to low levels of government expenditure, high levels of public revenues, usually high rates of economic growth and often to public confidence and optimism in the future of their country. High levels of unemployment have the opposite effects. Hard economic decisions had to be made during the 1980s by governments of all political complexions and these must also be seen in the context of demographic and family trends which added further pressure on resources.

TABLE 1.3   *Economic indicators, 1975–93 (percentages)*

	Annual average growth of real GDP		Annual average growth of prices		Annual average unemployment rates	
	1975–80	*1980–93*	*1975–80*	*1980–93*	*1975–80*	*1980–93*
Total OECD	3.6	2.5	10.0	5.4	5.3	7.5
Denmark	2.5	1.8	10.4	5.0	6.4	9.6
France	3.1	1.9	10.5	5.5	5.4	9.6
Germany	3.4	2.1	4.1	2.9	3.0	7.2
Greece	4.4	1.5	16.4	18.5	2.0	7.5
Italy	4.8	2.1	16.8	8.7	7.3	10.8
Netherlands	2.2	1.7	6.0	2.8	3.6	9.0
Spain	1.8	2.5	18.6	8.2	7.4	18.9
Sweden	1.3	1.1	10.5	7.1	1.6	3.1
UK	1.9	1.9	14.4	6.0	5.1	9.6
USA	3.4	2.4	8.9	4.4	6.8	7.1

Source: OECD (1990), no. 47, June, table R.1, p. 181 and table R.19, p. 199; OECD (1993), no. 54, December, table A1, p. 126, table A15, p. 140 and table A18, p. 143; OECD (1994), no. 55, June, table 15, p. A18.

Perhaps the most significant of all economic indicators is the growth rate of productivity. Table 1.4 presents the trend for the whole period, 1960–1990. What is important is not only that productivity growth rates declined in all the countries in the table and in the whole of the OECD, but also that there is no evidence of any consistent or significant change in the direction of these trends. True, productivity was still rising in the 1980s, albeit at exceedingly modest rates, and some countries improved their record slightly in relation to the depressed rates of the late 1970s, but for others the trend was in the opposite direction. It can rightly be claimed that what matters most is productivity in the manufacturing sector rather than in the whole economy and by this yardstick the trend is less discouraging than that shown in Table 1.4.

The relative level of productivity growth rate of a country is an indication of the degree of competitiveness of its business and industry in the international market. Coupled with high unemployment, low productivity rates result in reduced rates of economic growth in advanced industrial societies. Accompanied by high wage rises, they tend to be associated with reduced rates of profitability. In this way, declining productivity growth rates not only can reduce the economic capacity of a country to

TABLE 1.4   *Percentage changes in annual rates of productivity,* * *1960–92*

Country	1960–73	1973–79	1979–92
Total OECD	3.0	0.6	0.9
Denmark	2.7	1.1	1.4
France	3.9	1.7	1.4
Germany	2.6	1.8	1.0**
Greece	5.8	2.1	0.5
Italy	4.4	2.1	1.1
Netherlands	3.4	1.8	0.9
Spain	3.3	0.9	1.7
Sweden	2.0	0.2	0.7
UK	2.6	0.6	1.6
USA	1.6	–0.4	0.4

* Figures refer to the combined labour and capital productivity rates.
** Refers to West Germany only.
Source: *Economic Outlook,* No. 55 OECD (1994), no. 55, June, annex table 57, p. A63.

meet rising levels of public expenditure, but they can also increase hostility to the welfare state among the business community. Since 1980, however, it has been wage levels rather than profits that have suffered. In all EU countries as well as in the US, 'wages adjusted for inflation have risen by less than productivity and profits have taken a greater share of value-added' (EU, 1994d, p. 11).

Table 1.5 summarises the trends in public and social expenditure. It shows that both types of expenditure continued to rise though at a slower pace than before with the notable exception of Greece where social expenditure exploded in the 1980s. This general decline in the upward pace of social expenditure took place in a decade when demand for social provision was on the increase in all countries, particularly as a result of the sharp rise in unemployment rates. It is a clear reflection of the restrictive government policies in the social services, and particularly social security benefits, pursued in many countries, as the following chapters will show.

The rise in the percentage of public expenditure during the early 1990s, shown in Table 1.5, is as much the result of the slowing down in the rise of GDP per annum as of the expansion of expenditure in real terms. Though figures for social expenditure for 1993 are not available at the time of writing, they would confirm the statement made about public expenditure. Despite the rise in expenditure, it will be very difficult, if not impossible, to find examples in any of the countries covered by this book,

TABLE 1.5   *Trends in public and social expenditure as a percentage of GDP, 1980–93*

	Public expenditure			Social expenditure	
	1980	1990	1993	1980	1990
Total OECD	37.1	39.1	42.0	19.6	21.5
Denmark	56.2	58.3	62.3	26.8	27.8
France	46.1	49.8	54.9	22.5	26.5
Germany	47.9	45.1	50.0	25.7	23.5
Greece	33.1	53.3	52.7	11.1	20.9*
Italy	41.9	53.2	56.2	21.2	24.5
Netherlands	54.9	54.1	55.8	28.3	28.8
Spain	32.2	41.8	46.9	16.8	19.3*
Sweden	60.1	59.1	71.3	25.9	33.1
UK	43.0	39.9	43.5	16.4	22.3
USA	31.8	33.3	34.4	13.4	14.6

* The figure for Greece refers to 1989; figures for Spain are provisional.

Source: OECD (1993), no. 54, December, table A23, p. 148; OECD (1994a), no. 55, June, table 26, p. A29; OECD (1994b), tables 1a, 1b and 1c, pp. 57–61.

where standards of services or levels of benefits were improved in the 1990s. This is a good example of the claim that statistical trends, if taken at face value, can be very misleading.

The factors that make for more demand for social service provision are many and varied: unemployment, the growth in the size of the elderly population, the rise in the number of lone parent families, rising public expectations for better services, technological medicine, recognition of disability as a public issue, and so on. We have already provided the data for unemployment and here we shall document two others: the rise in the number of elderly persons and of lone parents.

Table 1.6 provides the demographic data for 1960, 1990 and the projections for 2020. As expected, it shows a rise in the proportions of those aged 65 and over as well as 75 and over in all the countries. In addition, the proportion of those retiring from work before the official retirement age has increased while the proportion of those staying on at work after retirement age has declined. There are some minor country differences as well as gender differences but the general conclusion must be that a greater proportion of resources in terms of health, pensions and social care will be taken by this age group in the future.

TABLE 1.6   *Percentage of population aged 65 or over, 1960–20*

| | 65 or over | | | 75 or over | | |
	1960	1990	2020	1960	1990	2020
Denmark	n/a	15.5	19.5	n/a	6.9	8.2
France	11.6	14.0	19.7	4.3	6.8	8.2
Germany	10.6	15.3	22.2	3.4	7.4	10.6
Greece	8.1	13.7	19.9	3.0	6.0	9.2
Italy	9.1	14.4	22.8	3.0	6.3	10.7
Netherlands	8.6	12.8	18.6	2.8	5.3	7.4
Spain	n/a	13.2	18.3	n/a	5.4	7.9
Sweden	11.8	17.8	20.8	4.1	6.8*	9.0
UK	11.7	15.6	18.0	4.2	6.8	12.4
USA	9.2	12.8	16.2	3.1	5.0*	6.0

* Refers to 1986.
Source: EU (1993a), table 1.1, p. 13; OECD (1988), tables 4 and 5, p. 11; OECD (1994a), table 15, pp. 112–13.

The situation is made worse by the high rates of unemployment among those nearing retirement age because of the practice by governments and employers to retire people earlier in order to provide jobs for younger age groups. At the other end of the age continuum, the share of young people will decrease. It is a complex issue and its implications for social policy are not as straightforward as it is sometimes assumed. We will return to it in the final chapters of the book. Suffice it to say here that the state of the economy has been and will remain the paramount factor in welfare developments. The real economic issue is not so much the rise in the proportion of the elderly but whether there is full-time employment for the working age population and whether European economies can compete successfully in the international market.

The rise in the proportion of lone parents has been primarily the result of greater employment opportunities for women and the sexual revolution that has taken place during the period covered by this book. Historical data are very sparse while contemporary comparative data are rather suspect because they are based on slightly different definitions. Nevertheless, Table 1.7 shows that there has been a substantial rise in the proportion of one parent families in most of the countries. It also shows that Northern European countries have much higher rates than the Mediterranean countries, a reflection of economic and cultural factors, as well as of the fact that many one parent families reside with

TABLE 1.7   *Percentage of lone parents 1980 and 1990*

	1980	1990
Denmark	12	18
France	7	13
Germany	9	12
Greece	n/a	5
Italy	4	7
Netherlands	8	10
Spain	3	5
Sweden	18	19
UK	12	19
USA	22	25

Source: Whiteford and Bradshaw (1994), table 1, p. 71.

close relatives and are therefore not included in the statistics in countries such as Spain and Greece. Though data are not available for all countries, evidence from the UK and the USA suggests that the rise was faster during the 1970s and 1980s than during the previous two decades. In the USA the figures for 1950, 1960, 1970, 1980 and 1990 were 7 per cent, 8 per cent, 13 per cent, 19 per cent and 25 per cent respectively (Kriesberg 1970 pp. 82–86; Ellwood 1988 figure 3.7 p. 60). In the UK, there are no reliable figures for 1950 and 1960 but estimates suggest 4.4 per cent and 5 per cent respectively (George and Wilding, 1972, p. 6). Reliable figures for later years are as follows: 8.6 per cent for 1971, 12.1 per cent for 1981 and 17.9 per cent for 1991 (Haskey, 1993, table 3, p. 30).

The immediate cost implications of large numbers of one parent families to the state in terms of social security benefits are obvious in countries with even modest provisions. In countries where a high proportion of lone parents support themselves through full-time or part-time employment, costs appear elsewhere in the form of high child care costs. Equally important, though less obvious, are the long-term indirect costs to society resulting from the very depriving conditions in which many children in these families are brought up. It is an area of social policy which is shrouded in emotionalism that makes rational planning both very difficult and very different from one country to another. The range of provision varies considerably between countries with relatively generous provisions such as Sweden and others such as Greece and Spain providing no social security benefits on a national basis.

Another major change that has taken place over the years that merits documentation is the rise in the proportion of women at work and particularly in part-time employment. The share of women in the labour force in the European Union rose from 32 per cent in 1970 to 37 in 1980 and 41 in 1991 (EU, 1993b, figure 17, p. 56). It has immense implications for family living standards, for child care, for the care of the very elderly and other groups, the nature of the social security system and indeed the whole network of family relationships. It is a change that needs to be addressed urgently by governments for both economic, social and gender reasons. Table 1.8 shows that the employment ratios of women are approaching those of men in Denmark and Sweden but they lag well behind in the Mediterranean countries.

What general conclusions can be drawn from the above statistical evidence? First, the level of both public and social expenditure in 1990 was higher than at any time since the end of the last world war. It is this simple statistic that leads many to conclude that, despite many cuts and changes, the welfare state is surviving quite well the New Right onslaught and the economic recession (Le Grand, 1990; Glennerster, 1992). Others, however, define the welfare more broadly to include employment rates, rights at work and so on, or they look at public expenditure levels in relation to rising needs in society and inevitably

TABLE 1.8   *Annual employment/population ratios,* * *1980–90/91 (percentages)*

	Male			Female		
	F-T	*P-T*	*Total*	*F-T*	*P-T*	*Total*
Denmark	74.3	6.8	81.2	39.9	28.5	68.5
France	67.9	2.1	70.0	39.0	10.6	49.6
Germany	74.5	1.5	76.0	34.0	14.4	48.4
Greece	71.7	2.1	73.8	32.7	3.6	36.3
Italy	70.2	2.1	72.3	30.8	3.4	34.2
Netherlands	63.3	9.3	72.6	17.6	23.8	41.4
Spain	63.1	1.2	64.3	25.5	3.6	29.1
Sweden	77.1	5.4	82.5	42.5	33.3	75.8
UK	73.4	3.5	76.9	31.5	24.3	55.8
USA	69.0	7.8	76.8	43.9	15.8	59.7

F-T = Full-time; P-T = Part-time.
* The employment ratio is the number of persons in employment as a percentage of the population aged 15–64.
Source: OECD (1994b), table 16, p. 115.

reach different and more pessimistic conclusions (Mishra, 1990; Wilding, 1992; Gould, 1993; George and Miller, 1994).

Second, the growth in social expenditure has been slightly faster than the growth in public expenditure in general, mainly because of the rise in demand rather than the improvement in the quality of services. In fact in some areas – benefits for lone parents and the unemployed – the value of benefits deteriorated in many countries during the 1980s with the result that the rise in social expenditure during the 1980s and early 1990s was slower than in previous years, despite the increase in demand (EU, 1994a, pp. 33–5).

Third, the size of the national debt has increased in most countries as it was one of the ways governments used freely to finance public services that were expanding faster than their revenues. Thus the net public debt as a percentage of GDP for the group of OECD countries rose from 21.3 per cent in 1978 to 39.4 per cent in 1993 with substantial variations between member countries. The highest recorded rise was for Italy where the corresponding figures were 52.3 and 112.6 respectively (OECD, 1993, no. 54, December, table A30, p. 155).

Fourth, despite the public service cutbacks of the 1980s, there has been no social unrest. The public has accepted them, thus suggesting that the social legitimation function of social service provision may not be as significant as theories of welfare assumed. At the same time, public support for the welfare state in general remains high, though guarded and even hostile in some areas (Taylor-Gooby, 1991, pp. 106–36; Ferrera, 1993). There are also doubts as to how meaningful data on this issue are, bearing in mind the rather anti-taxation sentiments of voters at general elections in several countries. The issue of public attitudes to taxation is complex and central to our study and we will return to it later in the chapter.

Fifth, there does not seem to be a consistent correlation between the levels of public or social expenditure, on one hand, and the political nature of governments, on another. Socialist France in the 1980s, for example, exhibited trends of economic growth, social and public expenditure that were not significantly different from those of Germany which was ruled by Conservative governments. What matters to the welfare of people, however, is not so much these aggregate levels of expenditure but the actual pattern of service delivery. Two countries may be spending the same proportion of their GDP on a social service but the distributional effects of the two services may be quite different. Moreover, the Capital/Labour concorde on welfare provision in conservative Germany had firmer roots than its equivalent in socialist France. Briefly, the political label of the government by itself is not a good guide to welfare developments. A similar absence of correlation can be observed between levels of government expenditure and general living standards in the country. The percentage of both public and social expenditure in the USA during the 1980s and 1990s was lower than that of both Spain and Greece whose general living standards are much lower.

Finally, the evidence suggests that no clear and uniform methods to the problem of squaring the welfare circle emerged in the 1980s. All countries tried to contain or reduce the rise in social expenditure but not through any generally agreed methods. Rather, what characterised government policies was a 'variety of response to common problems' (Moran, 1988, p. 414). Welfare states are still faced with the problem of how to match resources and demand in the social field and it is this that the next section will discuss. The following country chapters will look at this issue in some detail. Here, we merely outline some of the possible ways in which governments are likely to deal with this problem.

Squaring the Welfare Circle

Clearly the measures that governments are likely to use can be divided into two groups: those designed to raise more resources and those intended to reduce demand. We examine each in turn. What combination of these measures governments in different countries will use will depend on the interplay between the prevailing economic and political factors, as well as the influence exercised by EU policies and directives on national governments.

First, it is generally accepted that the best way to raise more funds for welfare expenditure is through improved rates of economic growth. It is the one method that has general popular backing and will almost certainly guarantee electoral longevity to the party that achieves it. The trouble is that, as the tables above showed, advanced industrial societies are at present locked into an economic pattern of low levels of economic growth and high rates of unemployment. There is no evidence that this is likely to change dramatically for the better in the next few years. So at least for the short term, this painless way of funding expanding demands for welfare provision does not look very promising. There is also evidence which strongly suggests that even when rates of economic growth increase, joblessness will persist as a result of the new employment patterns.

Second, even with low levels of economic growth, advanced industrial societies possess the wealth to finance better services if governments and public were willing to meet it through increased taxation. Indeed, taxes are now consuming a higher proportion of GDP in all countries than they did in 1981, as Table 1.9 shows. The figure for Germany will be higher now after the unification of the country which involved substantial expenditure at a time of low economic growth. The same applies to the figure for the UK as a result of the government's reluctant raising of taxes on fuel in 1994 in order to help balance its books. It is the same story for France because of the introduction of the new tax, Contribution Sociale Generalisse, in 1990.

Objections to tax rises are based on ideological grounds – it limits the liberty of individuals to spend their income as they think best – on economic grounds that they undermine work, savings and investment incentives and hence economic growth – and on political beliefs about their electoral implications. The ideological claim is a matter of personal choice while the claim of the economic ill-effects of taxation and public expenditure is difficult to substantiate, as a comparison between Tables 1.3 and 1.4, on one hand, and 1.9, on the other, shows. An OECD study in 1975 concluded that 'taxation does not have a large and significant effect on the total supply of work effort'

TABLE 1.9   *Direct taxes (DT), indirect taxes (IT) and social security contributions (SSC) as a percentage of GNP, 1981 and 1991*

	1981				1991			
	DT	IT	SSC	Total	DT	IT	SSC	Total
Denmark	26.8	19.0	1.0	46.8	30.5	18.1	1.6	50.4
France	8.9	15.1	17.7	41.8	10.0	14.8	19.4	44.2
Germany	12.3	12.9	16.2	41.3	12.1	13.0	16.0	41.1
Greece	5.0	13.1	8.9	26.9	6.6	19.0	11.1	36.7
Italy	11.1	9.0	11.5	31.5	14.8	12.1	13.3	40.1
Netherlands	15.0	11.8	18.4	45.2	17.1	12.8	17.8	47.7
Spain	7.5	7.4	12.3	27.1	10.4	10.9	12.5	33.8*
Sweden	21.5	14.5	15.1	51.0	20.5	18.5	15.7	54.7
UK	15.0	16.4	6.2	37.7	14.1	14.3	6.4	36.3**
USA	14.1	8.1	6.4	28.7	12.9	8.4	7.7	29.0

* Refers to 1990.

**This includes 1.5 from the Community Charge which was a Poll Tax and hence neither a DT or IT.

Source: Central Statistical Office, February 1994, table 3, p. 99 and table 4, pp. 100–3.

(Godfrey, 1975, p. 126), a conclusion that was confirmed by a later study in 1985 (Saunders and Klau, 1985 p. 166). A more recent paper by the European Union, which compared levels of social expenditure in member countries with their trade competitiveness and the level of their unemployment rates, concluded that 'it seems that a high level of social protection is not an obstacle to economic development' (EU, 1994a, p. 86). Even more forceful in its endorsement of the positive effects of social policy on economic growth was the most recent OECD report on social policy.

> Because the elderly need not fear serious deprivation, their adult children are freed to work, raise their children, and to take advantage of opportunities and to make contribution to society that might otherwise be denied them; the unemployed are provided with income not only for survival, but also to permit time to search for a job appropriate to their skills, or to acquire new skills; public intervention in education and support for children is an investment in tomorrow's resources, and in everyone's future; provisions for health care are an investment in the productive capacity of human resources. Together, these and other benefits of social policies contribute to a more efficient and a more just society. (OECD, 1994b, p. 10)

Whatever the evidence may suggest, many governments have accepted the view of the negative effects of direct taxation and social expenditure on economic growth, with the result that over the past decade or so they have been trying either to reduce rates of direct taxation and public expenditure or to hold them steady. They have also convinced large sections of the public of the undesirability of high taxation rates so that raising taxes has, in many countries, become tantamount to electoral suicide. All in all, there does not seem to be any political desire in any country to go down this road of funding further rates of public expenditure and it appears that this route will remain closed for the foreseeable future. Some governments have tried to get round this problem by merely raising rates of indirect taxation. The OECD paper on social policy acknowledges all this but adds that earmarked taxes may be politically more viable. 'Evidence from some countries suggests that taxpayers may be more willing to accept tax increases that pay for specific programmes which meet with their approval, rather than increases that support the general purposes of government' (OECD, 1994a, p. 13).

The introduction of CSG in France in 1990 is a case in point and there may well be other instances of new earmarked taxes. It has to be acknowledged, however, that earmarked taxes present other problems: they are less flexible than general taxes and they have a tendency to foster self-interest.

In some ways fears of taxation work disincentives are the issue of yesterday. What worries governments more these days of free international mobility of capital is the possibility of capital flight and hence of investment from those countries with high to those with low capital taxes and low labour costs. The issue of taxation demonstrates how powerful multinational companies have become in the internal affairs of any country.

Third, governments can finance increased activity through higher rates of borrowing. All governments borrow and modest national debts pose no real difficulty to government policy since they are easily repayable. When national debts, however, assume high levels and they become a long-term method of financing government activity, particularly to fund current expenditure rather than investment in the country's infrastructure, they can eventually become unsustainable. It is not so much that high public debts can be inflationary but rather that they simply consume a high proportion of the national income in interest repayments. Therefore, this option is now possible for some countries and not for others, as Table 1.10 indicates. Countries like Italy and Greece will sooner or later have to reduce their national debt burden and if they cannot do it through economic growth, they will be obliged to address it otherwise including, perhaps, reductions of public expenditure. This is the policy that the IMF metes out to third world and East European countries and occasionally to more

TABLE 1.10   *Net public debt and debt interest payments as a percentage of GDP, 1979, 1990 and 1993*

	Net public debt			Debt interest payments	
	1979	*1990*	*1993*	*1979*	*1990*
Denmark	1.8	23.5	33.0	3.5	7.2
France	13.8	25.0	35.7	1.4	3.1
Germany	11.5	22.6	31.8	1.7	2.6
Greece	27.7	86.7	106.1*	2.2	11.2
Italy	55.6	98.2	112.6	5.3	9.7
Netherlands	21.8	59.4	59.6	4.2	6.7
Spain	5.9	30.7	42.3	0.7	3.6
Sweden	−19.9	−3.7	19.6	4.1	5.8
UK	47.9	28.9	41.2	4.4	3.4
USA	19.2	31.2	39.3	2.8	5.2

* Refers to Gross Debt.
Source: Oxley and Martin (1991), tables 1 and 2, pp. 148 and 159; *OECD Economic Studies*, No. 17 (1991) and OECD (1994a), table 33, p. A36 for 1993 col.

affluent countries, such as the UK during the Labour government's office in 1976. Despite all this, the volume of national debt has continued to rise in all countries.

The sale of nationalised assets is the fourth method that governments can use to raise further revenues. This has been used by governments in the UK far more than by any other government, though there is a noticeable trend for others to follow suit. Thus during the 1980s, the proceeds from privatisation in the UK amounted to 11.9 per cent of the average annual GDP, whereas for other countries the sale started later and brought in far less money. France, for the period 1983–91, brought in 1.5 per cent of GDP; Sweden 1.2 per cent and Germany a mere 0.5 per cent (Stevens, 1992, p. 6 in Bos, 1993, p. 100). Obviously, both economic and ideological factors associated with Thatcherism explain the high profile of denationalisation in Britain. Income from such a source, however, can only be a one off transaction and to the extent that the sold enterprises were profitable or reduced industrial costs, governments may lose more than they gain in revenue in the long term. There are, of course, numerous arguments and counter-arguments about the relative profitability of nationalised versus private enterprises which are beyond the scope of this section. This seems such an easy and obvious source of revenue that it is likely to attract the attention of even governments which are ideologically opposed to denationalisation.

The fifth possible way of raising further funds is by introducing new or increasing existing charges for the use of services. There are obvious administrative difficulties with this approach as well as the danger that such charges may deter people in genuine need from making use of the service, particularly if such charges are high. If, on the other hand, the charges are very low the financial gain for the government can be negligible bearing in mind the high administrative costs of this approach. It is an approach more in line with the ideology of the right because it is usually coupled with the idea that it acts as a rationing deterrent against unnecessary and excessive use of services. No doubt, it will be used more by governments but it is unlikely to raise much in funds unless its very nature is changed. If, for example, all state services were open to everyone as now but either most or all users had to pay *something* according to their means and this was applied to education, health and the personal social services, then it would be a different situation. It would revolutionise the finances of welfare states but, apart from other considerations, such a change carries severe political risks and it is unlikely to be adopted by any government.

These are the main methods of increased revenue raising though there must be others including unexpected wealth bonuses, such as the oil discoveries for the UK and Norway, which are not possible to take into account beforehand. In dealing with their public expenditure budgets, governments will also look for ways in which they can reduce expenditure either through reducing the number of state service users or through lowering the cost or the standard of services.

The first of these methods is the transfer of the entire or most of the financial and administrative responsibility for social service provision to non-state agencies such as employers. The government role is then limited to providing merely the legal framework for service provision. An example of this approach is the transfer of most of the responsibility for sickness and maternity benefits in the UK to employers during the 1980s. Society still continues to spend the same or a similar proportion of its wealth on the services but it is not done through state agencies. It is not always, however, a mere accounting device. Occasionally, it can have adverse effects on some groups of beneficiaries, usually the weak groups in the labour market. There are obvious limits to this approach since it is unlikely that employers or other agencies are likely to accept the financial responsibility for more service provision.

The second method of reducing public expenditure is to encourage an increasing proportion of the public to choose private rather than state services. This can be done through tax concessions to those who opt for private services as it is the case for occupational pensions or health services for some population groups in the UK and in other countries. It is a method that has immense implications for the scope and the nature of the welfare state. Carried to its logical conclusion, this approach will inevitably result in a two-tier welfare state with high quality private services for the better paid and low quality state services for the others. By the very nature of things, those who opt out of services will not be prepared to pay high taxes in order to provide state services that are of equal standard to those in the private sector that they and their families use. It is true that this approach can be quite costly in the sense that the government forgoes large amounts in revenue, but this is seen by both its advocates and large sections of the public as different from the usual type of government expenditure.

A third way is to stiffen eligibility criteria for service entitlement. It is an approach that is usually reserved for unpopular groups of beneficiaries, such as lone parents or the unemployed. Several industrial countries have adopted such policies recently in relation to both groups. Even the much discussed workfare scheme for the unemployed may not save all that much money for governments. It is an approach that has high emotional content but exceedingly low financial returns for governments. A related approach is that of targeting, that is providing benefits or services to lower income groups only. Proponents of this view claim that such a policy will enable governments to provide better services or benefits to the low income groups than those they receive today. The real question mark is whether other groups will react by refusing to pay the necessary taxes with the result that the level of benefits or services will decline over time. It also needs to be added that the notion of targeting assumes that state services are provided in order to reduce poverty only. It ignores the economic, social and political functions of public policy.

Fourth, governments can attempt to reduce expenditure by lowering the standard or diluting the quality of services. In some cases, facts speak for themselves as when governments change the indexation method for social security benefits from increase in average earnings to rise in prices. There is no doubt that when this is done, as in the UK in 1980, the real value of benefits inevitably falls albeit gradually but over a long period of time quite considerably. Similarly, where the entitlement period to unemployment benefit is reduced, as in Germany, the result is obvious enough. In the service sector, however, a small increase in the pupil/teacher ratio or the doctor/patient ratio may or may not constitute a dilution of service standards, according to research evidence. There are severe limits to this approach particularly nowadays when consumers are very quality minded and their definition of quality is not always the same as that of the experts. Try as they may, governments cannot get away from the basic fact that social services are labour intensive and shedding of labour cannot be achieved with the same ease as in the manufacturing sector.

A fifth method that has been quite effective is to depress the relative wages of state employees in relation to those of other workers or reduce the number of state employees. Though such comparisons are problematic, they none the less suggest that 'for a wide range of countries, public sector wages have declined relative to the private sector for a considerable period'. In addition, 'employment growth in the public sector slowed substantially during the 1980s compared to the 1970s' (Oxley and Martin, 1991, p. 165). This process has continued in the 1990s, probably at an even faster pace, in some countries. It is an approach that appeals to some governments for it not only reduces public expenditure but it also presents them as crusaders against bureaucracy which the public loves to hate.

Seventh, several countries have introduced new management techniques designed to curb expenditure and/or to get better value for money (Ormond, 1993; Taylor-Gooby and Lawson, 1993). The first of these is the introduction of annual budgets for several services, with the result that the overarching criterion that decides the volume of service is not so much need or demand but the availability of funds in the budget. Coupled with this is the use of quasi-markets in the social services in order to encourage competition, improve efficiency, increase consumer responsiveness and hence raise the quality of service and expand the volume of the service delivered. This latter, however, can only be guaranteed to take place if there are no annual budgets for services. Other techniques introduced were the notion of targets for departments and their employees as well as the idea of citizen's charters in various public services. This is not the place to review these procedures but suffice it to say that only the idea of annual budgets can have the certain effect of reducing expenditure. The effect of the other measures on service costs can vary and it can be both upward as well as downward.

Finally, from both the right and the left there has recently been a keen interest in involving the community in the running of public services for a variety of reasons, including the belief that it can reduce expenditure. Thus emphasis on care in the community for the elderly, the mentally ill, the disabled and other groups has been driven partly by the belief that it will be less costly than residential care. Government ideas of involving parents in the day to day running of schools – supervising children in the playground, helping with some teaching for the very young and so on – has also an element of cost saving in the thinking behind it. On the whole, there does not appear to be much cost saving in these ideas though some of them are worth having for other reasons.

These are some of the ways in which governments will attempt to square their welfare circle. The process has already begun and there are as many similarities as differences between the various national responses. But the problems facing the welfare state are not just financial. There are also other issues and these combine to create a new situation which demands radical changes in the welfare state. It is these that we now proceed to discuss.

The Future of the Welfare State

There are certain moments in the history of a country when a number of significant economic, social, political, ideological and other factors coalesce to create a new challenging situation, 'a new macro-constellation', where existing forms of social provision no longer work (Alber, 1988, p. 201). The end of the last century and the immediate post-war years were such periods; the post 1980s is another (Ferrera, 1993b, p. 108). In between these critical moments, welfare reform is not only incremental but also within the same ideological paradigm. During these critical moments reform may be incremental but it is moving from the old to the new ideological welfare paradigm. It is not so much that the slate is wiped clean and a new start is made for this is an impossibil-ity. Rather a gradual shift over a number of years is made from the old to the new welfare system. As the recent EC White Paper on social policy put it: 'It is clear that the profound changes currently affecting our soci-eties means that the complex interaction of policies that make up social policy will need to develop in new ways in the future' (EU, 1994c, p. 1).

What then are these challenges to the welfare state? The first and perhaps the most important is that demands and needs for its services are growing faster than its resources. For example, the rise in social protection expenditure during the period 1980–92 for the twelve EC member coun-tries was 40.6 per cent per head in real terms, while the rise in GDP per head was 26.5 per cent in real terms (EU, 1994b, p. 1). A similar picture emerges in relation to the larger group of OECD countries (Boltho, 1993). This does not necessarily lead to the conclusion that governments in affluent countries cannot afford to meet rising social expenditure demands as is the case in third world countries. Expansion of welfare provision is possible if there is political support for it – if the public agreed that less resources would come directly to them and more would go to the social field, thus being prepared to vote for governments that had to raise taxes. Another indication of the economic ability of affluent countries to finance an expanding social service sector is the fact that apart from state expendi-ture there is a great deal of private expenditure in these services. In econ-omic terms, both state and private welfare consume national resources.

But despite the fact that the level of social provision in affluent societies is the result of primarily ideological rather than economic factors, expan-sion of expenditure is not unlimited. The modest rise in living standards of recent years has to be seen along with the declining employment rate in the European Community so that today it stands at 'less than 60% of the working-age population' (EU 1994c, p. 9); the fact that rises in rates of labour productivity in all advanced industrial societies, including Japan, were considerably and consistently lower for the years 1974–90 than for the period 1961–73, as Table 1.4 showed (Englander and Gurney, 1994,

Table 1, p. 31); the fact that governments have other duties besides social protection; and the insatiable public demand for consumer goods. These considerations strongly suggest that continued expansion of welfare provision is most unlikely.

The second challenge facing the welfare state stems from the very different social environment in which it now operates compared to that of the post-war era. People are more affluent, better educated, healthier, live longer, they demand better quality services, and they want to have a greater involvement in the services that they receive. It is a social environment for a more participatory and a better quality welfare state in terms of service standards and the provision of choice. But herein lies the contradiction: a better quality and a more participatory welfare state requires more funds and since these are unlikely to come from rapid economic growth in the near future, they would need to come from other sources, mainly higher taxation, which is rather unlikely as it was pointed out above. Pro-welfare state governments could use this situation to improve the transparency of social service provision – to provide the public with clear accounts of how public expenditure is spent and how much more will be needed in order to implement demands for a more participatory and user-friendly welfare state.

Third, family patterns have changed so considerably. It is not simply that there are more marriages, remarriages, extra-marital births, divorces and more lone parent families. Far more important, there is growing demand for greater equality between the sexes and for a less sexist form of welfare state – one that takes seriously into account women's contribution to society as workers and mothers and which responds with appropriate welfare provisions (Hantrais, 1994). But a non-sexist welfare state would be more expensive than the traditional male dominated forms of welfare provision. For example, social security benefits paid to women on account of their mothering or caring work would require extra funds than at present. Similarly, generous maternity and paternity leave will be costly to employers.

Fourth, working patterns are very different. The full-time male factory breadwinner that was the norm of the post-war era is now a thing of the past. Part-time work is more widespread today, women's work is now an integral part of working life, moving in and out of employment is normal, and very soon working from home will be an established form of earning a living. All these changes have major implications for trade unionism, for the distribution of power in society and for class conflict over wages, employment rights and welfare issues in society. At the same time, they also require major adjustments from such welfare institutions as the education or social security system.

Fifth, the economy of every country now is far more at the mercy of international capital and particularly transnational corporations (TNCs). Production, investment, financial services, transport and communication have all become international and global in character. TNCs plan their investment, production and distribution on a global basis. Even though they 'have a national base, their activities are predominantly geared to maximising their international competitive position and profitability such that individual (national) subsidiaries operate in the context of an overall corporate strategy. Investment and production decisions therefore may not always reflect local or national conditions' (Held and McGrew, 1993, p. 268). They can transfer production or assembly of many commodities to countries with lower labour costs; they situate their financial centres in countries with low taxation costs; and they can place severe political limits to all governments. A recent United Nations Report showed that two-thirds of TNCs are based in fourteen wealthy countries, though 40 per cent of their investment was in developing countries mostly in Asia and Latin America. Above all, 'the workplace is being shaped by TNCs, with trade unions and national governments largely impotent to prevent the biggest companies setting their own agenda in terms of jobs, industrial relations and training' (Elliott, 1994, p. 11).

Cheaper industrial production in Japan with its more advanced technology and in those developing countries which are dominated by TNCs and which have low labour costs poses a serious challenge to the economies and hence to welfare provision of European countries. This challenge is in the direction of cost containment and market principles playing a greater role in state welfare than before. Indeed, Gould claims that 'a new convergence is taking place between capitalist welfare systems because of the dynamics of international capitalism on the one hand and demographic changes on the other' (Gould, 1993, p. 248). It is a convergence away from universalistic services designeed to meet needs towards the 'affordable welfare state' with fixed annual budgets to contain costs (George and Miller, 1994, p. 17).

Sixth, the working class solidarity that was one of the major driving forces behind the growth of the welfare state during the post-war era in many countries has now been replaced with a more fragmented social formation, as a result of the processes just outlined. Moreover, several occupational groups within the working class tend to align themselves with middle- and upper-class groups in welfare debates. In addition, new groups have emerged outside the class structure that make their own special demands on the state: feminist demands already referred to, demands by ethnic groups for strong anti-racist policies, environmentalists for more sustainable forms of development, and so on. In such a situation, the anti-welfare forces in society have gained considerable ground with the result that they exert far more influence on welfare state debates and policies than they did previously. Even in countries such as Sweden where Labour and Capital had reached an uneasy consensus on welfare provision, the situation is changing rapidly and welfare expenditure is now under close scrutiny. In Mishra's words, we are witnessing 'the decline of neo-corporatism or tripartism as a mode of conflict management' and welfare support (Mishra, 1993, p. 25) without replacing it with a viable alternative.

Seven, increased economic affluence has led to insatiable consumerism that poses a threat to the whole environmenmt. People seek their fulfilment through increased consumption, ignoring Hirsch's graphic aphorism: 'If everyone stands on tiptoe, no one sees better' (Hirsch, 1977, p. 5). Economic affluence and consumerism have, in turn, nurtured a more individualistic culture that stresses far more the rights rather than the obligations of individuals towards others. It is not that individualism has replaced collectivism for these two values always coexist in society. Rather, it is that the balance has tipped towards the former and this needs to be rectified before pro-welfare governments can implement any ambitious plans of restructuring, particularly if they involve increased levels of expenditure. Galbraith's notion of 'the culture of contentment' favouring the affluent majority at the expense of the impoverished minority may be a gross caricature of welfare beliefs in advanced industrial societies, but it does contain an element of truth substantial enough to be taken seriously by pro-welfare political leaders and governments (Galbraith, 1992). Thus the late leader of the Labour Party in the UK, John Smith, insisted that democratic socialists should argue their case for reform not only on its intellectual merit but also 'on the basis of its moral foundation' (Smith, 1993, p. 137). The suggestion that the recent decline in rates of economic growth has spawned a new culture of 'diminished expectations' (Krugman, 1994, p. 231) is premature, for the stranglehold of ever-rising consumerism remains as strong as ever.

Finally, there is growing uneasiness that, despite rising levels of public expenditure, the seriousness of such problems as poverty, crime, drug addiction and so on has either not declined or has increased substantially. Explanations and solutions vary reflecting different political ideologies. There are those on the right who consider welfare not the solution but the cause of many of these social problems (Murray, 1984). Even among the supporters of the welfare state, however, who reject the above view there is no confidence of how best to deal with such problems. Though they are not the result of existing forms of welfare provision, they coexist with it and not unnaturally questions are being raised as to whether different types of public provision would not deal with them better than those we have used so far. It is a more diffuse challenge to the traditional welfare state but no less serious than many of the others discussed above.

Predicting the future development patterns of the welfare state is always an extremely difficult task but the chapters that follow will provide further evidence of the possible pathways. We will return to this issue in the concluding chapters. Suffice it to say here that on the strength of past evidence certain trends are likely to be common to all countries: a continuing attempt to contain the costs of public provision; a greater role for the voluntary and private sector; an increased stress on better management in the public sector; more emphasis on different forms of participation; and a greater emphasis, more rhetorical than real, on giving the public more choice in welfare. The welfare state of the future is likely to be different but the public demand for better services – public, private and voluntary – will remain both unabated and unmet, for the message of the quotation at the beginning of the chapter is as true today as it was when first made by Galbraith and summed up by Wilensky and Lebeaux.

References

Alber, J. (1988) 'Is There a Welfare Crisis?', *European Sociological Review*, vol. 4, no. 3, December, pp. 181–203.

Beacon, R. and Eltis, W. (1976) *Britain's Economic Problem: Too Few Producers* (London: Macmillan).

Banfield, E.C. (1969) 'Welfare: A Crisis without "Solutions"', *Public Interest*, no. 16, Summer, pp. 89–101.

Boltho, A. (1993) 'Western Europe's Economic Stagnation', *New Left Review*, no. 201, September/October.

Bos, D. (1993) 'Privatisation in Europe: A Comparison of Approaches', *Oxford Economic Policy Review*, vol. 9, no. 1, Spring, pp. 95–111.

Bradshaw, J., Ditch, J. and Homes, H. (1993) 'A Comparative Study of Child Support in Fifteen Countries', *Journal of European Social Policy*, vol. 3, no. 4, pp. 255–71.

Central Statistical Office (CSO) (1994) 'Taxes and Social Security Contributions: An International Comparison, 1981–1991, *Economic Trends*, no. 484, February, pp. 92–103.

Drucker, P.F. (1969) 'The Sickness of Government', *Public Interest*, no. 14, Winter, pp. 3–23.

Elliott, L. (1994) 'Elite Companies Rule World Trade', *The Guardian*, 31 August, p. 11.

Ellwood, T.E. (1988) *Poor Support: Poverty in the American Family*, New York: Basic Books.

Englander, E.S. and Gurney, A. (1994) 'Productivity in Perspective', *The OECD Observer*, no. 188, June/July, pp. 30–2.

EU (1991) *A Social Portrait of Europe* (Brussels: Commission of the European Communities).

EU (1993a) *Older People in Europe: Social and Economic Policies* (Brussels: Commission of the European Communities).

EU (1993b) *European Social Policy: Options for the Union,* Green Paper (Brussels: Commission of the European Communities).

EU (1994a) *Social Protection in Europe* (Brussels: Commission of the European Communities).

EU (1994b) 'Eurostat: Population and Social Conditions', no. 5 (Brussels: Commission of the European Communities).

EU (1994c) *European Social Policy – A Way Forward for the Union*, A White Paper (Brussels: Commission of the European Communities).

EU (1994d) *Employment in Europe 1994* (Brussels: Commission of the European Communities).

Ferrera, M. (1993a) *EC Citizens and Social Protection* (Brussels: European Commission).

Ferrera, M. (1993b) *Modelli di Solidarieta*, Bologna: il Mulino.

Gabrero, G. (1992) 'Between Welfare State and Social Assistance in pain, 1980–1992', paper for the Conference on Comparative Research in Welfare States in Transition, Oxford, 9–12 September.

Galbraith, J.K. (1992) *The Culture of Contentment* (London: Penguin).

George, V. and Miller, S. (eds) (1994) *Social Policy Towards 2000: Squaring the Welfare Circle* (London: Routledge)

George, V. and Wilding, P. (1972) *Motherless Families*, (London: Routledge and Kegan Paul).

Glennerster, H. (1992) *Paying for Welfare: The 1990s* (Hemel Hempstead: Harvester Wheatsheaf).

Godfrey, L. (1975) *Theoretical and Empirical Aspects of Taxation in Labour Supply* (Paris: OECD).

Gould, A. (1993) *Capitalist Welfare Systems* (London: Longman).

Habermas, J. (1976) *Legitimation Crisis* (London: Beacon Press).

Hantrais, L (1994) 'Family Policy in Europe', in Page, R. and Baldock, J. (eds) *Social Policy Review*, no. 6, Social Policy Association, University of Kent, Canterbury.

Haskey, J. (1993) 'Trends in the Numbers of One-parent Families in Great Britain', *Population Trends*, no. 71, Spring, pp. 26–34.

Held, D. and McGrew, A. (1993) 'Globalisation and the Liberal Democratic State', *Government and Opposition*, vol. 28, no. 2, Spring, pp. 261–85.

HM Treasury (1979) *The Government's Expenditure Plans 1980–81*, Cm 7746, (London: HMSO).

Hewitt, M. (1992) *Welfare, Ideology and Need* (Hemel Hempstead: Harvester Wheatsheaf).

Hirsch, F. (1977) *Social Limits to Growth* (London: Routledge & Kegan Paul).

King, A. (1975) 'Overload: Problems of Governing in the 1970s', *Political Studies*, vol. XXIII, nos 2 and 3, pp. 284–96.

Kriesberg, L. (1970) *Mothers in Poverty* (Chicago: Aldine).

Krugman, P. (1994) *The Age of Diminished Expectations* (Cambridge, Mass.: MIT Press).

Le Grand, J. (1990) 'The State of Welfare', in Hills, J. (ed.) *The State of Welfare*, (Oxford: Oxford University Press).

Mishra, R. (1990) *The Welfare State in Capitalist Society* (Hemel Hempstead: Harvester Wheatsheaf).

Mishra, R. (1993) 'Social Policy in the Postmodern World', in Jones, C. (ed.) *New Perspectives on the Welfare State in Europe* (London: Routledge).

Moran, M. (1988) Review article: 'Crises of the Welfare State', *British Journal of Political Science*, vol. 18, pp. 397–414.

Murray, C. (1984) *Losing Ground: American Social Policy, 1950–1980*, (New York: Basic Books).

O'Connor, J. (1973) *The Fiscal Crisis of the State* (London: St Martin's).

OECD (1973) *Labour Force Statistics, 1960–1971* (Paris: OECD).

OECD (1978) *Economic Outlook*, no. 24, December (Paris).

OECD (1982) *Economic Outlook*, no. 32, December (Paris).

OECD (1988) *The Future of Social Protecting*, Paris.

OECD (1990) *Economic Outlook*, no. 47, June (Paris).

OECD (1992) *Economic Outlook*, no. 51, June (Paris).

OECD (1993) *Economic Outlook*, no. 54, December (Paris).

OECD (1994a) *Economic Outlook*, no. 55, June (Paris).

OECD (1994b) *New Orientations for Social Policy* (Paris: OECD).

Ormond, D. (1993) 'Improving Government Performance', *The OECD Observer*, No. 184, October/November, pp. 4–9.

Oxley, H. and Martin J.P. (1991) 'Controlling Government Spending and Deficits', *OECD Economic Studies*, no. 17, Autumn, pp. 145–89.

Saunders, P. and Klau, F. (1985) 'The Role of the Public Sector', *OECD Economic Studies*, no. 4.

Smith, J. (1993) 'Reclaiming the Ground – Freedom and the Value of Society', in Bryant, C. (ed.) *Reclaiming the Ground – Christianity and Socialism* (London: Spire).

Taylor-Gooby, P. (1991) *Social Change, Social Welfare and Social Science* (Hemel Hempstead: Harvester Wheatsheaf).

Taylor-Gooby, P. and Lawson, R. (eds) (1993) *Markets and Managers* (Hemel Hempstead: Harvester Wheatsheaf).

Walker, A., Alber, J. and Guillemard, A-M. (eds) (1993) *Older People in Europe: Social and Economic Policies* (Brussels: Commission of the European Communities).

Whiteford, P. and Bradshaw, J. (1994) 'Benefits and incentives for Lone Parents: A Comparative Analysis' *International Social Security Review*, vol. 47, nos 3/4, pp. 69–91.

Wilding, P. (1992) The 'Public Sector in the 1980s', in Manning, N. and Page, R. (eds) *Social Policy Review*, no. 4, Social Policy Association, University of Kent, Canterbury.

Wilensky, L. H. and Lebeaux, C.N. (1958) *Industrial Society and Social Welfare* (New York: Free Press).

2

Germany: Maintaining the Middle Way

ROGER LAWSON

> The Germans ... have constructed a civilisation in which social cohesion and prosperity are interdependent. If the model founders before the demands of globalisation, there is little hope for the rest of us. Spot-market barbarism will reign. (Hutton, 1995, p. 11)

In an essay on German public policy, Manfred Schmidt (1989) began by asking what was distinctive about it. His initial response was that the Germans had a strange claim to distinctiveness. In contrast to the *Sonderweg*, or exceptional course, pursued by their predecessors between 1870 and 1945, they had taken a path towards relative normalcy. 'What is distinctive about West Germany's public policy', wrote Schmidt, 'is that it has ceased to be dramatically distinctive.' However, the main thrust of his insightful analysis was that there nevertheless remained something different about the Federal Republic's public policy profile. By building on historic traditions surrounding the German state and at the same time learning from the catastrophes of the twentieth century, the Germans had chosen 'a middle way ... between the extremes of Scandinavian social democratic welfare capitalism and political economies in which centre-right, or rightist tendencies, dominate'.

This chapter takes up this theme as it applies to social policy over the past two decades. The main sections of the chapter illustrate how successive governments, especially Chancellor Kohl's conservative coalitions, have responded to the profound economic and social changes since the 1970s, as well as the pressures of unification, with an unusual mix of policies. Efforts to cut back on social expenditures have been combined with a

continued emphasis on a strong state presence in social policy. The
chapter begins with a brief account of the middle way in social policy
prior to the economic downturn of the mid-1970s.

The Middle Way in Social Policy

In studying German social policy, one quickly becomes aware of strong
elements of historical continuity, especially in German expectations of
their governments. Like their predecessors in the nineteenth and early
twentieth centuries, Germans across the political spectrum have placed
considerable emphasis on the state's responsibility for steering, regulating
and codifying society in the interests of social welfare. As one observer
puts it, there has been in the Federal Republic 'a predisposition to accept
the desirability of public regulation on a consistent and equal basis of a
wide range of activities which in other countries are left entirely unregu-
lated ... a continuing sense of the state's necessity for individual well-
being' (Johnson, 1973, p. 19).

In the Bismarckian tradition, social and labour programmes have also
been used more consciously in the Federal Republic than in most other
countries as a means of regulating conflict and maintaining social peace.
They can be seen, too, as part of a larger historic quest in German society
for security, predictability and stability, as well as economic efficiency
(Schmidt, 1989, p. 69).

These themes have been clearly evident in the policies pursued by the
conservative Christian Democrats (CDU) and their Bavarian partners, the
Christian Social Union (CSU), the dominant political force in the Federal
Republic for much of the period since the 1940s. The notion of the 'social
market economy' associated with the CDU/CSU stems in part from the
activities of their distinctive Social Christian wing. Itself influenced by
Christian, mainly Catholic, trade unionists, this section of the party has
been committed to expansive social protection and to policies promoting
job security and codetermination in enterprises. Like the first Chancellor,
Konrad Adenauer, the social wing has argued that the Bismarckian tradition of social protection is one of the few state traditions Germans should
'hold on to ... and be proud of'. However, the CDU/CSU has also contained a powerful neo-liberal wing committed to a strong market economy
and to fostering an individualistic, democratic culture firmly anchored in
political and economic liberalism. It has profoundly influenced German
economic policy, most of all by an overriding emphasis on controlling

anti-inflationary pressures and promoting orderly housekeeping in fiscal and monetary policy. In social policy, the neo-liberals have been an important constraining influence against more egalitarian trends, particularly through their insistence that social interventions should be 'market-conforming'.

It was under such influences that West Germany's 'social state' (the term 'welfare state' had negative connotations after Nazism) took shape between the 1950s and 1970s. After an initially cautious phase, the Christian Democrats embarked on a series of social reforms that raised social expenditures as a percentage of GDP to among the highest of all OECD nations. What characterised German social policy, however, was not the high levels of expenditure but the distinctive social priorities. The combination of liberalism, conservative reformism and Catholic social ethics was felt in a number of ways, but most importantly in an unusual policy profile that placed great stress on social security transfer payments and played down the role of directly provided public social services. Moreover, rather than establishing national minimum standards for all citizens, the core of the social state consisted of a range of social insurance schemes that were both work oriented and contained strong elements of compulsory self-help. They were designed to provide the bulk of the workforce with a high degree of security and predictability, by maintaining an individual's relative position in the income hierarchy or the social status acquired through work. The schemes were also largely financed by contributions from employees and employers, while much of their administration was decentralised and distanced from both federal and Länder (regional state) bureaucracies.

In the period up to the mid-1970s, these measures were underpinned by full employment and by a growing 'social partnership' between trade unions and employers. Under the latter the unions traded off wage moderation against high standards of job security and training and new forms of participation. All this proved highly effective in raising the general living standards and 'security of life' of the workforce, considerably more so for example than Britain's combination of Beveridge-based social programmes and traditional wage bargaining. It also created a homogeneous block in society strongly committed to the social insurance nucleus of the social state. To Germany's white collar employees and skilled workers, as well as ordinary blue collar workers, 'to be part of a comprehensive system of public transfers ... [was] almost as routine as a paycheck' (Heidenheimer *et al.*, 1983, p. 223). Another important factor underpinning the system was Germany's recourse to migrant 'guestworker' labour to overcome labour shortages, particularly in sectors with low wage, unskilled, dirty and monotonous jobs that Germans were increasingly unwilling to take. Prior to the mid-1970s, the social effects of migration included not just the upgrading and advancement of German workers, but the access of many poorer native Germans to high standards of social security and job protection. At the same time, since their recruitment was almost universally seen as a short-term, temporary expedient, the claims of 'guestworkers' on social benefits were initially minimal.

The other side of the German social state was its comparatively modest commitment to public social services. For most Germans, social insurance gave access to health care, but most medical goods and services (apart from certain public hospitals) were provided by private suppliers. Likewise, in housing, after a burst of state activism in the aftermath of the war, state support was confined to subsidising a limited supply of social housing, providing housing allowances for low income families, and certain rent regulation and tenant protection (Alber, 1988). For people with health and social needs not adequately covered by these provisions, the principle of 'subsidarity' operated. Strongly influenced by Catholic social theory, subsidarity stressed the primary importance of self-help and the caring functions of the family and then gave precedence to voluntary organisations over state agencies. Its effect in practice was that charitable organisations, including the social arms of the major churches and the labour movement's Worker's Welfare Association, came to play a more important role in the provision of social services than in most other welfare states. There has been, and remains, much that is impressive in the way they have conducted their affairs, not least in shaping social aware-ness and motivating people to commit themselves to voluntary work. However, the charity net had gaps, particularly for people whose needs were primarily financial. They found themselves dependent on mainly localised social services, often operating stringent means tests and with a distinctly inferior status. The most prominent of these was the social assis-tance service (*Sozialhilfe*) run by local authorities, and providing last-resort subsistence relief as well as a number of services. Until the 1970s, this was a largely hidden sector of German social policy. There were no notable welfare rights movements and only a few local studies, most of them emphasising pressures on the poor to keep silent about their poverty and not claim assistance.

The German social state also had a distinctive stance on both educa-tional and family policy. In education, which was almost entirely the responsibility of the Länder governments, the themes of security, stability and economic efficiency were given more prominence than equality. The much vaunted traditions of apprenticeship training continued in the Federal Republic, creating a highly skilled workforce and indeed a sense that there was 'a community of skills' in German society. However, prior to the late 1960s, the goals of social equality and social mobility held low priority. Efforts to develop comprehensive schools met widespread resistance, while both working-class and female access to higher education were limited. Conservative family values, themselves in part a reaction to the Nazi abuse of the family, were clearly evident in family policy. The belief was widely held, particularly in CDU/CSU circles, that the most effective family rights were constitutional guarantees designed to protect the institution of marriage and the integrity of family ties. Other measures, such as positive financial support for children or the provision of pre-school facilities, were viewed with suspicion and remained comparatively underdeveloped. Women's rights, particularly, were circumscribed by these educational and family policies, as well as by social and labour policies geared primarily to the male breadwinner and leading to low levels of public employment.

For a brief period prior to the mid-1970s other influences began to shape German social policy as the Social Democrats (SPD) entered government. In 1966, the SPD formed a 'grand coalition' with the CDU/CSU and then in 1969 became the main partner in a coalition with the liberal Free Democrats. On the whole, the Social Democrats were reluctant to depart too swiftly from the German welfare traditions. The broad social policy profile remained the same, but assumed a more egalitarian character as reforms sought to improve the prospects of women, increase educational opportunity, enlarge social housing and generally focused more on raising minimum standards of welfare. Moreover, following the Swedish model and as part of a shift towards 'social Keynesianism', German labour market and training programmes were reorganised into a more positive and ambitious 'active labour market policy'. As a result, by the mid-1970s, the German social state seemed to have entered a more inclusionary and expansive phase with poverty reduced to a problem of *Randgruppen*, peripheral groups on the margins of society.

Containing the Social State, 1975–95

Although this volume focuses mainly on the pressures on governments in the 1980s and 1990s, in the Federal Republic the year 1975 marks a

✗

clearer watershed in social policy than 1980. In responding to the economic downturn of the mid-1970s, following the first oil crisis and breakdown of the Bretton Woods system, the German government moved more swiftly than other governments to control public expenditures. West Germany was the first major industrial state in the 1970s in which social expenditures as a share of GDP fell, and they continued to fall until reunification in 1990. Significantly, this process began under the SPD-led government headed by Helmut Schmidt which remained in power until 1982. It accelerated, but only slightly, after Chancellor Kohl's CDU/CSU led coalition assumed office in 1982. Behind these trends lie controversial policy changes, but it is important not to be misled by them. By comparative standards Germany has continued to be a big spender on welfare. Much of the development of the past two decades can be seen as an effort to maintain and adapt the basic principles of the social state in the face of economic, demographic and social forces often pulling in different directions.

Responses to Economic Change, 1975–90

In Germany, as elsewhere, at the root of the problem of 'squaring the welfare circle' since the 1970s lie the profound changes in global trade and production and the severe pressures on economies to modernise and adapt to fierce competition and new technologies. As in the earlier postwar years, German reactions to these pressures in the 1970s and 1980s were distinctive. They involved an unusual balancing act between policies on the one hand restricting welfare expenditures and tolerating rising unemployment, and on the other hand emphasising the important role of state social policy in making modernisation and its attendant hardships acceptable. The restrictive tendencies stemmed partly, as the SPD-led government was forced to recognise in the mid-1970s, from the insistence of the Bundesbank and much of the civil service on tight monetary discipline to stabilise currency and prices. However, there was also in Germany a wide popular expectation — reflecting past experiences — that strict control of inflation should be accorded priority in economic policy. The consequences for social policy were particularly evident when there were global inflationary pressures in the mid-1970s and first half of the 1980s. Both the Schmidt and Kohl governments responded with annual austerity budgets cutting back on social benefits, allowing unemployment to rise, and reducing company taxation and state contributions to social insurance. The cuts affected a wide range of welfare recipients. They included delays in uprating pensions, the means testing of certain family benefits and cut-backs in health insurance, unemployment benefits and labour market programmes. However, the sharpest cuts, especially under the Kohl government, were in the educational, housing, labour market and social assistance provisions that were expanded as part of the more inclusionary policies of the late 1960s and early 1970s.

The broader reshaping of the economy in this period also profoundly affected employment and social policy. Although at times sluggish in their response to technological innovations, German industries adapted aggressively to international competition, by increasing their export orientation and slimming down, especially in structurally weak sectors. They received strong support from successive governments, mainly via fiscal policy but including support for encouraging older workers to retire and for modernising apprenticeship and training schemes. Germany succeeded as a result in maintaining a resilient and efficient industrial base, in which the proportion of its workforce in manufacturing employment was substantially higher than in any other OECD nation. In 1991 it was 40 per cent, compared with 34 per cent in Japan, 28 per cent in the UK, France and Sweden and 25 per cent in the USA. However, there was another side to this. Non-productive interests tended to be marginalised, which meant *inter alia* that the scope for the expansion of social welfare occupations continued to be restricted. Germany was a laggard, too, in creating new 'post-industrial' jobs. Moreover, the German economy began to divide more sharply into a modern and a marginal sector, with important consequences for social policy. The latter sector contained growing numbers of German as well as foreign workers with low wages and low skills, weak trade union protection, and a high risk of unemployment or of irregular work in the grey areas of the economy where employers could evade social and labour laws.

These trends provoked heated debate and controversy. In the late 1970s and early 1980s, they severely weakened the SPD-led government. Various new social movements emerged, often under the umbrella of the Green Party, lobbying, demonstrating and sometimes resorting to direct action to protest against the emphasis on 'productive' interests (Ginsburg, 1992). At the same time, concerns grew within the CDU/CSU and FDP and in industry with the scale of transfer payments and the 'ungovernability' of the social state. Despite this, however, there remained considerable support for a positive state presence in social policy. In striking contrast to the Thatcher and Reagan administrations, Chancellor Kohl's government continued to stress the need for 'a *strong* state, not the reduction but the

X *redirection* of state intervention... The present goal is only to organise that intervention in a more effective, less costly and above all, less politically disruptive manner' (Esser, 1986, p. 207). This also meant that there was still scope for improving social protection, especially when productivity rose and unemployment fell, as happened in the second half of the 1980s. The Kohl government responded by extending unemployment benefits for older workers, introducing a new parental leave allowance, and improving pension entitlements for women. Most of the Länder raised social assistance benefits at this time. Significantly, too, the government made little effort to promote privatisation in social policy, partly no doubt because public opinion surveys showed the overwhelming majority of Germans to be deeply suspicious of private insurance. The surveys — and also the demonstrations of the 1980s – revealed how the large number of potential welfare recipients in Germany formed a strong bulwark against cuts, particularly in social insurance benefits. A further important factor was the continued influence of trade unions, which they maintained through a canny process of 'conflictual cooperation' with government and industry.

Demographic and Social Changes

Demographic and social forces have added to these dilemmas in social policy. Mainly because of a sharp decline in birth rates but also as a result of migration, Germany has experienced marked shifts in its population. In the nation as a whole, including the new eastern Länder, the numbers of children and young people under 18 fell from 21.3 million in 1971 to 15.5 million in 1991. In the same period, the numbers aged 60 and over rose from 15.5 million to 16.4 million, but with a proportionately much larger increase among the older elderly. Not surprisingly, the main preoccupations of policy-makers associated with these trends have been the problems of maintaining the costly state pensions introduced in the 1950s and of containing rapidly rising health care costs. As already indicated, the late 1970s and 1980s saw a number of delays in the uprating of pensions and various other trimming measures. After a decade of discussion, these were consolidated in 1992 in an important reform aimed at safeguarding the state pension system against demographic trends over the next decade. Paralleling this have been cost-containment measures in health care, particularly in laws enacted in 1988 and 1993. This introduced new elements of 'self-responsibility', mainly direct payments by patients for certain services, and sought also to rationalise medical provision and cut hospital costs. The Kohl government has also responded more positively to the new needs and dependencies of many of the elderly, and in doing so has sought broad agreement with the SPD opposition and trade unions. The 1992 pension reform included measures proposed by the unions for improving women's pension rights. More importantly, after a long gestation period initiated by a broad alliance of the social wing of the CDU/CSU with the SPD, unions and voluntary organisations, the government introduced a new social care insurance in 1994 (see next section).

To an extent the problems of an ageing population have been eased by another trend largely unanticipated in the early 1970s, the growth of a new ethnic minority population. The Germans responded to the first oil crisis in 1973 with a ban on foreign recruitment and efforts to encourage repatriation. Paradoxically, however, these policies had the opposite effects. They encouraged a move towards permanent settlement among the existing foreign workers, produced a new wave of family migration and led, from the late 1970s onwards, to a shift from 'economic' migration to the 'political' migration of asylum seekers and refugees. Germany's *Ausländer* ('foreigners') rose to over 6 million, or 8 per cent of the population, in the early 1990s. Without the foreign workforce whole areas of German industry and many public services would be in serious difficulty, and the fiscal pressures on the social state much more severe. In 1989, for example, foreigners paid DM 12.8 billion in contributions to state pension funds. Mainly because of their demographic structure, they claimed only DM 3.7 billion in actual pensions.

However, the social state has been affected by migration in other, very different ways. Germany illustrates a failure, by no means confined to Germany, among those in politically responsible positions to develop a viable, long-term conception of policy towards immigrants and minorities. The very real problems of integration have been left to a large extent to voluntary organisations, more progressive local authorities, and ultimately to ordinary Germans to sort out, especially those in the poorest neighbourhoods. Although in theory foreigners have enjoyed identical social rights to those of German citizens, in practice these have been severely circumscribed by their lesser civil rights and, above all, because without the right to vote they have lacked political clout. One consequence has been the emergence since the 1970s of distinct 'underclass' attributes (structural and juridical rather than behavioural) among the minority population (Lawson 1994). German public opinion surveys also show how many Germans view immigrants as a source of the problems facing the welfare state and associate them with the abuse of certain benefits. At the same time, the social state's natural supporters, in the CDU/CSU as well as SPD, have found their constituents increasingly divided on the immigration and race issue.

Contradictions and inconsistencies are also evident in German responses to the various forces that have been weakening and fragmenting older social and family structures and traditional forms of solidarity. As elsewhere, German family life has changed profoundly since the 1970s, partly through declining birth rates and growing numbers of lone parent and 'remarried' families. The proportion of lone parent families tripled from 5 per cent in 1970 to around 15 per cent in the early 1990s. More distinctively German has been the sharp decline in traditional multigenerational families living together and the surprising large proportion of children, in more than 50 per cent of families in the 1990s, being brought up alone, without brothers or sisters. Faced with these trends, German policies on the family and gender issues, and also educational and housing policies, have remained notable for their lack of coherence and underlying conservatism. Issues relating to lone parenthood have been barely confronted at the Federal government level, while various child benefits and tax allowances were chopped and changed, and sometimes reintroduced, in the budgets of the late 1970s and 1980s. Women have made some significant advances in the German educational system and in training programmes. But occupational segregation and wage discrimination have left the growing numbers of women seeking work with incomes significantly lower than those of men.

Unification and Recession in the 1990s

Germany's dramatic reunification after the fall of the Berlin Wall in 1989 and the collapse of communism elsewhere in Eastern Europe have added a significant new dimension to the problems and prospects of the social state. As happened after 1945, Germany has faced a paradoxical situation, in which efforts to introduce a market economy in the former GDR and to remove the bureaucratic apparatus of communism have themselves required a high degree of political control over the economy and society. The steady reduction of public expenditures and efforts to reduce taxation in the 1970s and 1980s have been reversed as massive subsidies have been directed towards the imploding East German economy and the disastrous ecological and infrastructural heritage of communism. Personal dependency on state support has grown markedly, particularly in the East where by 1994 over 4 million of the 10 million in the former

University
of Ulster
LIBRARY

GDR workforce were no longer in regular employment. In West Germany, too, joblessness rose sharply with the global recession of the early 1990s. This itself was made more fierce in Germany by competition from eastern neighbours where labour costs were often one-tenth of those in the Federal Republic.

For East Germans unification brought far-reaching changes in social and labour policies. In a move typifying the whole process of unification, virtually the entire socialist system of social support was replaced by West German legislation when 'social union' was implemented at the same time as economic and currency union in July 1990. The only significant feature distinguishing the new East German system was the introduction of certain transitional 'supplements' in social security. These were designed to guarantee minimum pensions and to raise other benefits to levels that would avoid mass dependence on means tested social assistance. Many commentators now accept that the speed with which social union was achieved meant that too little thought was given to practical aspects of the process as well as to features of the old GDR system which people regarded favourably (Ammermüller, 1994). Women in the East were particularly hit by legislation which did little to facilitate employment prospects and in some ways backtracked towards traditional dependencies. Generally, however, by the mid-1990s many features of the new system met with approval in the East. This was notably true of pensions, but included also areas of health, social care and housing where unification brought improvements in standards and facilities.

The main problems for East Germans stemmed not from social union, but from the destruction of employment following the collapse of the eastern economy. These were also the issues that most affected the social state in the West in the 1990s, because of the fiscal dilemmas they created. In its efforts to divert resources into eastern economic reconstruction and reskilling, the Kohl government has sought to avoid penalising industry and has maintained a conservative line on taxation and incentives. Its resulting strategies have been highly controversial. In 1992 employees' social insurance contributions were raised by 3 per cent and DM 90 billion were transferred from western social insurance funds to support eastern labour market programmes and pensions. A year later a 'solidarity contribution' was announced, essentially a tax hike on West Germans that again most affected people in a broad middle stratum of society. Most controversial, however, was the enactment of Sparpaket 1994, the most extensive package of cuts in social benefits of any post-war German government. The cuts, aimed at saving DM 100 billion, affected a whole range of benefits, including western labour market programmes, education, children's allowances, and many services provided by the Länder and local authorities. However, the bulk of the savings were in benefits for the poorest sections of society, including substantial cuts in payments to refugees and asylum seekers.

Unification had other effects on social policy. In the west, in particular, it produced a toughening of attitudes towards the 'undeserving' poor, which was one of the reasons why the government was able to implement its 1994 package. Those seeking to draw attention to western poverty and disadvantage were often told to look *nach drüben* ('over there') at the conditions of East Germans, and think again. Government responses to poverty tended also, more than in the past, to stress behavioural traits, including claims of widespread abuse of the 'social net'. Much more seriously, the poisonous racial flareups and antagonisms that began to plague Germany in the 1990s stemmed in part from a populist view that foreigners formed the hard core of the 'undeserving' poor.

Retrospect and Prospects of the Social State

German Social Policy in the Mid-1990s

How, then, did the social state in the mid-1990s compare with the social state of the mid-1970s? Despite the cuts, German social expenditures reached record levels by 1994, largely because of commitments to the new eastern Länder. As a share of GDP, they rose from 29 per cent in the former Federal Republic to over 34 per cent in 1994; in East Germany with its lower GDP they reached a staggering 70 per cent. Financing these expenditures bore heavily on private households, especially on individuals paying social insurance contributions. Compared with the 1970s, the amount contributed by German employers to the total costs of the social state (excluding education), although high by international standards, fell from around 33 per cent to 30 per cent in 1994. The federal and Länder authorities also contributed less out of general taxation: under 40 per cent in 1994 compared with 45 per cent twenty years earlier. By contrast, the share financed by employees' social insurance contributions rose steadily from just over 20 per cent in the early 1970s to 30 per cent in 1994. When combined with changes in income tax, where there was also a shift in the incidence of tax away from higher earners, the result was a marked increase in taxation for typical working families. Tax and social insurance deductions from the wage packet of an average earner rose from one-quarter of gross earnings in 1975 to over one-third in 1994.

In the 1990s the centrepiece of the social state is still the system of social insurance that was extended to the bulk of the workforce in the early years of the Federal Republic. Organisationally, it remains highly complex. A variety of different agencies, with differing structures and administrations, provide state pensions, health insurance, accident insurance, and unemployment and labour market benefits. State pensions retain divisions, first established in Imperial Germany, between schemes for white collar and blue collar workers, while there are status divisions in the structure of health insurance. Despite this, however, the past two decades have continued the trends of the earlier post-war period towards uniformity of entitlement and treatment across the various schemes. Indeed, for women in particular, these have accelerated.

For the majority of German workers and their families, these 'solidaristic' social insurance schemes, rather than company welfare or private insurance, continue to be the principal source of social security, health and welfare. Although the 1992 Pension Reform lowered pension levels by linking their calculation to net rather than gross earnings, state pensions remain generous by comparative standards, at least for employees with good work records. Likewise, health insurance provides access to high standards of health care, though following the reforms of the past decade more is now being paid for in direct patient charges. Germany's commitment to social insurance has been underlined by the introduction of the new social care scheme in 1994. Given the constraints of the 1990s, this ranks as a highly imaginative reform and is testimony to the continued pursuit of the middle way. The measure has created a whole new branch of social insurance, paid for by the insured workforce, and aimed primarily at the care of the elderly and severely disabled. It provides direct financial support for carers, including individuals caring for relatives, and a range of benefits designed mainly to promote community care by voluntary organisations and private agencies.

If in these respects social insurance principles remain firmly entrenched in Germany, they have also begun to founder under the impact of unemployment and other economic and social changes. The most striking contrast between the pattern of social provisions in the 1970s and 1990s is the much higher profile nowadays of *Sozialhilfe*, the social assistance services run by local authorities (largely under Länder control) that provide meanstested income support and access to health care and various social services for those with inadequate social insurance rights. In 1993, the numbers receiving *Sozialhilfe* totalled 4.6 million, double the numbers in 1980 and more than three times the early 1970s' levels. The proportion receiving regular income support who were unemployed rose from less than one per cent in 1970 to around one-third by the mid-1990s. The numbers of lone parents on these benefits also sharply increased. Significantly, too, surveys in the 1990s suggest that half of those eligible for this relief are not applying, because of feelings of shame and the stigma traditionally attached to public assistance (Schneider, 1993). These trends, which have put considerable pressure on Länder and local authority budgets, have strained the resources of the voluntary organisations mentioned earlier. Indeed, their traditional role in social provision has also begun to founder.

Weaknesses in the social state of the 1990s are evident in three other areas of social policy studied in this volume – family policy, education and housing. As has been emphasised, despite the rhetoric of politicians and innovations such as the introduction of Parental Allowances in 1987, Germany lacks a coherent family policy. The real value of allowances paid for children, in both the tax and benefit systems, has eroded since the 1970s through a failure to index benefits and as a result of means testing benefits. Apart from the first child, child benefits (which are not part of social insurance) are currently means tested. Germany has been a laggard, too, in the provision of nursery and day care facilities, though the new Kohl government has announced its intention to give all children a right to a place in a Kindergarten. Estimates suggest, however, that this will require more than 600 000 new places as well as a massive investment in new buildings and personnel.

More generally, Germany's educational system – with the exception of its training schemes – has resisted innovation and adaptation to changing times. It remains heavily regulated by traditional Länder bureaucracies, most of which have been reluctant to experiment in new curricula and have insisted on retaining traditional divisions between grammar schools and ordinary secondary schools. For 94 per cent of all German children the schoolday still ends at around 1 p.m., a fact which profoundly affects women's lives. One noticeable trend of the past two decades has been the opting out of the state system by the more affluent and disaffected: the numbers in private schools have risen from 290 000 in 1970 to 436 000 in 1992.

Most discussions of housing in the 1990s speak of 'crisis', particularly in the major German cities. This stems partly from the rapid growth in households seeking separate accommodation and from sharp rises in the costs of building materials. However, it also reflects uncertainty in housing policy, both about the division of responsibilities between the federal government and the Länder and about the most effective policy instruments. Governments since the 1970s have used means-tested housing allowances (*Wohngeld*) as a major instrument of housing policy for those with modest incomes, but the allowances have suffered with the pressures for retrenchment. The cuts have also affected the more direct financial aid and tax concessions provided for the building of social housing, though since reunification efforts have been made to expand this. State aid for housebuilding rose from DM 42 billion in 1991 to DM 64 billion in 1994.

Gainers and Losers, 1975–95

As this suggests, despite the efforts of German governments to mediate the effects of rapid economic and social change, there is plenty of evidence of a clear reversal of the more egalitarian trends of the 1970s. The principal gainers from the past two decades have been the rich, especially those with incomes from entrepreneurial activity and property. Between 1980 and 1991 the real disposable incomes of their households rose by 30 per cent, compared with a 6 per cent rise among manual workers' households, and a slight drop in real income among the unemployed. Paralleling this, the concentration of property ownership increased in this period. Germany has also experienced a widening 'two thirds/one third' cleavage between a broad middle mass of society, including many skilled and affluent workers as well as the more conventional middle class, and the various strata below. This is reflected in the bifurcation of the social state between social insurance and social assistance (Leibfried and Tennstedt, 1985). In effect, the 'productive core' of German society, the well-organised majority with expectations of regular, stable employment, have consolidated their hold on the social insurance system. Those in more precarious employment or increasingly detached from the labour force have found themselves excluded from many of these provisions and have been forced to depend for their livelihood on localised social assistance or on family support, or on illegal forms of 'self help'.

The most important factor behind these trends has been the steady rise in long-term unemployment. However, the most disturbing feature is the way Germany's large foreign population appears to have become more ghettoised and more dependent on social assistance in the aftermath of unification. Until the end of the 1970s, foreign workers and their families were less likely than native Germans to rank among the 'official poor' receiving social assistance, and their unemployment rates were generally below average. By the 1990s, they were more than twice as likely as Germans to be unemployed and three times as likely to resort to social assistance for survival. According to a detailed survey of poverty in united Germany, 16.7 per cent of foreigners had incomes below a poverty line set at 50 per cent of average household income, compared with 7.8 per cent in the population at large. However, when the definition of poverty was broadened to include housing and living conditions, education and training and various indicators relating to employment, well over a third of foreigners (37.2 per cent) were identified as suffering two or more major forms of deprivation. Among West Germans the proportion was 7.9 per cent and among east Germans 10.3 per cent (Hanesch *et al.*, 1994).

Another distinctive trend has been the disproportionate rise in poverty and social assistance rates among children and young people as well as the prime-age workforce. While the numbers of elderly people on income support from social assistance fell between 1975 and the early 1990s, in West Germany alone the numbers of children under 15 in families on assistance grew from just over 300 000 to around 1 million. Various studies leave little doubt that unemployment, particularly long-term unemployment, has been the major cause of child poverty. However, they also point to the weaknesses of German social policy in contending with the sharp rise in female-headed families. Comparative studies show a wider disparity between the incomes of lone-parent and two-parent families in Germany than in most European nations (*McFate et al.*, 1995). This, in turn, reflects the obstacles to women's rights that remain in the German social state. Women's movements have achieved notable successes since the 1970s, particularly in broadening educational opportunities and in certain social rights such as pensions. However, the proportion of women in paid employment has continued to grow more slowly than in other countries and women in West as well as East Germany have been more prone to unemployment than men.

The Future of the Social State – Um*b*au or Ab*b*au?

Chancellor Kohl's CDU/CSU-led coalition was returned to office, with a much reduced majority, in the general election in October 1994. The new government's policies remain firmly anchored in the German middle way. However, maintaining this course in social policy is now seen to require a much stronger commitment to a process of restructuring (*Umbau*) of the social state. The guiding principles informing German social policy, especially the core principles associated with social insurance, are not fundamentally challenged. *Umbau* also requires a more positive approach to certain responsibilities, especially a bolstering of family policies and more effective interventions for the long-term unemployed. However, its central feature for the Kohl government is a strategy of enhancing 'self-responsibility' in areas such as health care, combating abuse of social benefits, reducing bureaucratic overload and the 'tyranny' of experts, and, above all, containing and reducing social and labour costs. Its corollary in economic policy is a more determined stance in dealing with the challenges to Germany's competitiveness via a more aggressive strategy of modernisation, deregulation and tax reform. Significantly, these are not seen as confrontational policies. On the contrary, one of the first acts of the new government was to seek a new 'solidarity pact on employment', with government, industry and unions cooperating to draw up a package of measures to tackle the employment crisis and the modernisation of the social state.

Whether such a traditional middle way pact will emerge remains to be seen, since there are substantial obstacles in mid-1990s Germany. Foremost among these is a growing alliance of liberal and rightist politicians and sections of industry and the media, whose objective where the social state is concerned is *Abbau*, a dismantling or radical reduction of social commitments. The theme has figured for some time within the liberal Free Democratic party, where a number of politicians have called, for example, for the replacement of social insurance by minimum benefits supplemented by private insurance. More recently, it has been taken up by the industrial *Mittelstand*, innovative and risk-taking small- and medium-sized enterprises that have grown as a result of Kohl's modernisation programmes but find themselves constrained by social costs and regulations. However, the most significant development occurred in the weeks following the 1994 election, when two prominent representatives of German industry produced concrete proposals that were commonly interpreted as the first stage of *Abbau*. Klaus Murmann, the president of the main federal body representing employers' associations (BDA), called for a significant reduction in state pensions and sickness payments and greatly increased patient charges for medical care. The theme was then taken up by the president of another leading association representing industry and commerce (DIHT). Warning of the consequences of competition from low wage countries in eastern Europe, he added to the calls for benefit cuts further demands for changing wage-negotiation practices especially by removing minimum wage agreements.

Although the Kohl government was quick to distance itself from these speeches, they indicate the pressures it is likely to come under from some of its close allies. However, the problems of developing a pact on employment and the future of the social state are by no means confined to this. Radical demands of a different kind for restructuring the social state have been growing on the broad left and among voluntary and church organisations. The 1990s have seen a lessening of divisions that characterised the left on social issues in the 1980s, when many were attracted by the Greens' emphasis on ecological issues and radical self-help and empowerment. The ecological issues are still prominent, but generally the mood has shifted back towards redistributive policies and employment programmes more typically associated with the left. Behind this lies a sense, after five years of unification, that Germany needs to look afresh at some of the socially more effective aspects of the old GDR system: its benefits for women, its elimination of status distinctions in the workforce, use of polyclinics in health care, etc. More important still has been the mounting evidence of 'new poverty' and marginalisation in the 1990s, a lot of which has come from church sources as well as left-biased organisations. The main effect of this, apart from focusing attention on the employment crisis, has been to create a more coordinated front demanding a new approach to social security, with more emphasis on citizenship-based social incomes. New nationally organised basic incomes would replace localised social assistance.

Such demands are creating dilemmas for the SPD opposition in the Bundestag as well as the unions, whose role in supporting social insurance for the organised majority is implicitly criticised. SPD leaders have maintained a distance from the more radical demands, though their 1994 election programme called for substantial rises in family benefits and for social assistance for pensioners to be replaced by a national means-tested income support scheme. Improvements in women's social rights and child care were also given prominence as was ecological 'renewal'. However, the programme's main feature was a ten-point plan for making employment promotion a cornerstone of the future social state. The centrepiece of this was a set of 'active labour market' policies enlarging training and relocation measures and extending certain of the job creation schemes of the eastern Länder to the whole country. The programme also included measures aimed at promoting more part-time employment and expanding the service economy and post-industrial jobs.

What then are the prospects for the social state, say in the year 2000? Judging by the trends of the past decade, two concluding observations can be made. First, despite a breaking of ranks on the right and left and pessimism among some at a loss of social solidarity, there remains a broad consensus in Germany favouring an active state presence in social policy. Assuming the present coalition remains in power, this consensus will be steered by the CDU/CSU version of the policy of the middle way. This promises, and has already begun to deliver, improvements in family policy and women's rights, and more energetic efforts to combat long-term unemployment. CDU/CSU policy-makers express confidence that pensions are effectively protected against demographic trends over the next decade. There are now some fears, however, that the new social care insurance may run into difficulty because of the large unmet need the new scheme is exposing. More cuts in benefits are likely, particularly in health care, and, judging by the current climate, a further toughening of measures directed at the poor. Elements of workfare may well enter the agenda.

The other conclusion is that Germany's new social and regional divisions are unlikely to change unless more radical policies are adopted. An upturn in the economy may well improve employment prospects, particularly in the East, but much of the current unemployment is deeply structural. Combating social exclusion in the 1990s requires a greater willingness than the political and fiscal climate seem to allow to tackle fundamental deficiencies in education and housing. Above all, German politicians across the political spectrum remain reluctant to extend their definitions of citizenship to embrace their new minority and immigrant communities. Until they fully recognise the interdependence of social rights with political and civil rights, there is a real danger of a racialised underclass emerging, marginalised by the social state as well as the economy. The experience of the past decade suggests that this could, in turn, erode the normative consensus on which the social state has been built.

References

Alber, J. (1988) 'Germany', in P. Flora (ed.) *Growth to Limits* (Berlin: De Gruyter).

Ammermüller, M. (1994) 'Deutscher Einigungsprozeß', in Bundesministerium für Arbeit und Sozialordnung (ed.) *Sozialstaat im Wandel* (Bonn: Economica Verlag).

Esser, J. (1986) 'State, Business and Trade Unions in West Germany after the Political Wende', *West European Politics*, vol. 9, no. 2, pp. 198–214.

Ginsburg, N. (1992) *Divisions of Welfare* (London: Sage).

Hanesch, W. u.a. (1994), *Armut in Deutschland* (Hamburg: Rowohlt Verlag).

Heidenheimer, A., Heclo, H. and Tech Adams, C. (1983) *Comparative Public Policy* (New York: St Martin's Press).

Hutton, W. (1995) 'Britain Falls Short of the Mark', *The Guardian*, 13 March 1995.

Johnson, N. (1973) *Government in the Federal Republic of Germany* (Oxford: Pergamon Press).

Lawson, R. (1994) 'The Challenge of New Poverty. Lessons from Europe and North America', *International Politics and Society*, 2, pp. 163–74.

Leibfried, S. and Tennstedt, F. eds. (1985) *Politik der Armut und die Spaltung des Sozialstaats* (Frankfurt am Main: Suhrkamp).

McFate, K., Lawson, R. and Wilson, W.J. (eds) (1995) *Poverty, Inequality and the Future of Social Policy* (New York: Russell Sage).

Schmidt, Manfred (1989) 'Learning from Catastrophes: West Germany's Public Policy', in Castles, F. (ed.), *The Comparative History of Public Policy* (London: Polity Press).

Schneider, U. (1993) *Solidarpakt gegen die Schwachen: Der Rückzug des Staates aus der Sozialpolitik* (Münich: Knaur).

3

France: Squaring the Welfare Triangle

LINDA HANTRAIS

> The future of Social Security is largely dependent on the prevailing
> psychological climate. In this respect, two opposing and contradictory
> elements can be identified: on the one hand, the French are strongly
> attached to the institution; on the other, they are not sufficiently aware
> of the responsibility they have towards it. (Laroque, 1985, p. 32)

France is one of the countries in continental Europe where social protection is essentially based on corporatism and the insurance principle
derived from the triangular relationship between employers, employees
and the state. The social security system which had developed by the early
1980s as the centrepiece of social policy was comprehensive, complex and
pluralistic. The period of post-war expansion (*les trente glorieuses*) had
been brought to an abrupt close in the wake of the oil crises of the 1970s
and, as in other neighbouring countries, the deepening recession was
forcing French governments to adapt their policies in response to budgetary deficits and rising unemployment. From 1981 to 1993, except for a
brief hiatus between 1986 and 1988, France was ruled by left-wing governments at a time when most other European Union countries were governed from the right or centre right. The Socialist Party's election
manifesto of 24 January 1981 had bound them to seek new solutions to the
problems of unemployment, social inequality, access to health, housing
and education, and the rights of immigrants. In 1993 the electorate
expressed its disappointment with ten years of Socialism, enabling the
centre-right coalition to recapture power with a much more convincing
majority than in 1986.

The experience of the 1980s in France suggests that, at least at national level, politics may not really matter when it comes to solving intractable social problems. The fourteen years during which François Mitterrand held the supreme office in France as President demonstrated that neither right nor left have a magic political formula which can be applied to the persistent problems of unemployment, new forms of poverty and social inequality. This chapter examines how recent governments in France have sought to shape social policy in the face of socio-economic and demographic change and provides some pointers to policy developments through to the year 2000.

Social Protection in France at the Beginning of the 1980s

The policy-making process in France has been aptly described by Gary Freeman (1990, p. 190) as 'statist in style, corporatist in form and pluralistic in practice'. A central administration formulates policy, with presidents and prime ministers publicly announcing their commitment to specific measures, but the structures for implementing proposals are largely decentralised (particularly since the 1983 reform), corporatist and semi-autonomous, notionally under the control of elected representatives of employers, unions and the insured themselves. As a result, conflicts between interest groups are a characteristic feature of social policy and have been influential in shaping the development of the social services over the post-war period. A key issue in social administration has been the relationship between centralised public policy-making and locally operated services. This is true of the social security system, which is organised in three branches at national and local level, covering health and industrial accidents, old age, maternity and family affairs. It applies even more so in the case of social assistance where discretion at local level can lead to considerable discrepancies in the provision of services. Although education and unemployment do not fall within the remit of social security, they have been affected over the post-war period by the same problems of corporatism and pluralism and are closely intertwined with the other areas of social policy which are of interest here.

The French social security system, instituted in 1945–6 and gradually extended to cover all sectors of the population and all contingencies, is credited nowadays with being one of the most comprehensive but also one of the most complex in the EU. Attempts to create a unified system by eliminating variations in levels of contributions and benefits and the methods for collecting and distributing them from one occupational group to another encountered strong resistance, and some 500 or more different schemes emerged, each with its own administrative structures. The mutualist tradition was also maintained, affording some occupational groups the opportunity to gain access to additional benefits.

Health Care

By the beginning of the 1980s, despite several decades of right-wing government and a relatively weakly organised labour movement, France had a highly developed social system where the whole population was, in principle, covered by social insurance. Employment related contributions and benefits in cash and kind were managed by the relevant funds. In accordance with the insurance principle, during absences from work due to illness, wage related benefits were paid to employees in return for contributions. Medical expenses and the cost of medicines were reimbursed both for insured persons and their dependants at a level ranging from 70 per cent for doctors fees to between 40 and 100 per cent for medicines, according to the nature of the illness and the status of the patient: all expenses relating to pregnancy and a number of designated chronic diseases were covered in full. In the case of hospital care, the medical insurance funds paid hospitals direct and covered the full cost of surgery. Contributions paid to mutual societies or commercial insurance companies ensured additional cover for the majority of the population. Over the post-war period, despite its internal divisions (Wilsford, 1991), the medical profession had acted as a powerful lobby to protect the basic principles of the health service: freedom of patients to be treated by the doctor and the hospital of their choice; freedom of doctors to prescribe whatever medication and treatment they considered appropriate; direct payment of doctors' fees by patients. Doctors had thus maintained their independent status, but the cost of the services, and particularly of drugs, had increased continuously in response to both demand and supply side factors.

In the early 1980s it was, however, old age which had become the area of social security representing the largest share of social spending. The cost of health care was stabilising in relation to total social expenditure, but elderly people were relatively big consumers of medical care (Charraud *et al.*, 1984, pp. 381–5). Many of them were eligible to receive medical assistance or free medical treatment because of their low incomes, inadequate medical insurance and the nature of their illnesses: in 1980, almost 300 000 elderly people were receiving social assistance

(Waltisperger, 1984, p. 218). Although insurance schemes had been progressively extended until the whole population was eventually covered in 1978, they continued to offer different benefits from one occupational group to another. The disparities in old age were therefore greater than those during working life, due largely to the impact of corporatism and pluralism. A multitude of complementary and supplementary pension schemes had been maintained to the distinct advantage of the sectors of society with higher incomes.

Pensions, Benefits and Housing

Contributions from employers and employees had been used to fund pensions on the basis of the pay-as-you-go principle, with the result that, by the beginning of the 1980s, some funds, for example in mining, agriculture or the railways, where the number of workers had fallen steeply, were dealing with more beneficiaries than contributors. Transfers from the more robust funds were used to compensate and balance budgets in deficit. Complementary (superannuation) schemes had been compulsory since 1975 for all except employers in industry and commerce, and incentives were provided to encourage workers to take retirement at the age of 60 on health grounds. Credits were given to women for two years of insurance cover per child to compensate them for raising children. By the beginning of the 1980s almost 93 per cent of people aged over 60 were living in their own homes. Many of them were receiving community care in the form of home help and nursing, visits to day care centres, respite care or sheltered housing, largely paid for by the insurance funds (Laroque, 1985a, pp. 192–4).

Unlike other benefits, family allowances were universal, non-means tested and funded by employer contributions. They were managed by the Caisse Nationale des Allocations Familiales (CNAF) and paid at a flat rate, increasing with the age of children, up to 16 or longer for children still in full-time education. They covered maternity, lone parents, housing, child care and provision for children with special needs. The operation of the redistributive principle in family policy was constrained by two factors: in accordance with pro-natalist objectives, family allowances were available only from the second child and were paid at a higher rate for the third and subsequent children, regardless of parental income; tax relief for children was still an important source of savings for parents on higher incomes with large families and accounted for about a fifth of the sum paid out in allowances.

Housing was an integral part of family policy. Post-war governments had intervened in two main ways: first, by building social housing (*habitations à loyer modéré*), and second, by paying housing benefits to families in need, as part of family policy. Home ownership had been encouraged by mortgage subsidies, and by the 1980s housing benefit was available for low income families, including young couples without children (*aide personnalisée au logement*), confirming the gradual shift in support away from buildings to people.

Education

Another area of social provision closely associated with family policy, but which falls outside the remit of the social security system, is education. In France, the educational system has been an important component of the welfare and social equality debate, and governments have invested heavily in schooling and higher education. As a proportion of GDP spending on education had increased steadily over the post-war period, reaching 3.5 per cent by 1980 (Oeuvrard, 1984, p. 470). Despite the fall in the number of children in primary schooling since the end of the baby boom in 1964, the number of places in nursery schooling had increased, more young people were staying on at school after the leaving age of 16, and a growing proportion of each generation were obtaining the *baccalauréat* (over 25 per cent in 1980) and continuing their education or training. The numbers in higher education had almost doubled in little more than a decade, but the socio-economic distribution of students had changed very little. The teaching profession had become increasingly feminised, particularly in the lower levels; women were in the majority as teachers in secondary education and as students in universities (Hantrais, 1990). More emphasis was being placed on training: a levy of 1.2 per cent was raised on all firms with more than ten employees, enabling the development of extensive provision for in-service training and retraining.

Unemployment and Social Assistance

Unemployment had not been a major concern in France in the immediate post-war period and was not part of the social security system instituted in 1945–6. Despite the introduction of a compulsory insurance scheme in 1958 for all employees in industry and commerce under a national collective agreement, it remained outside the social security system, thus distinguishing France from other EC member states. By the beginning of the

1980s the whole of the private sector was covered; public sector workers continued to enjoy a guarantee of employment. The unemployed who fulfilled the eligibility requirement were entitled to receive 35 per cent of previous income for a maximum of 270 days. Benefits had progressively been extended, and rates had increased. By 1980 more than 65 per cent of unemployed people were receiving unemployment benefits under the scheme (Revoil, 1984, p. 200).

Since the French social security system was based on employment insurance, rather than the welfare principle, specific institutions were needed to provide non-contributory means-tested benefits for the groups excluded from insurance cover because they did not meet eligibility criteria. State funded social assistance was provided to ensure a minimum income to individuals, including long-term unemployed, elderly and disabled people who were not eligible for insurance benefits earned by their employment record or who had exhausted their statutory rights.

At the beginning of the 1980s eligibility for social assistance was determined by nationality or residence criteria and a means test. Different forms of assistance were provided locally at the level of the *départements*, corresponding to a variety of categories of need: medical and community care for mentally ill, disabled or elderly people; social housing and income supplements for families. In 1980 expenditure on social assistance accounted for 3.6 per cent of all social spending, a declining but still not insignificant amount (Waltisperger, 1984, p. 216). The cost of caring for children at risk and elderly people, particularly community care for the latter, had been increasing most rapidly in the 1970s, and this was expected to be a major area of need in the 1980s.

Socio-economic and Demographic Change in the 1980s

The 1980s were a time of rapid socio-demographic and economic change, which took place in France against a background of political upheaval. Economic indicators for the period suggest that the legacy of the left was disappointing on some counts. Although by the end of the decade inflation had been contained (reduced from 13.6 in 1980 to 3.4 in 1990), and the national debt, after peaking in 1983, had been reduced, election pledges to reduce unemployment had not been fulfilled: it rose from 1.5 million in 1980 (6.4 per cent) to over 2 million (9.1 per cent) in 1990. During the 1980s France and Luxembourg were the only northern EU member states to have seen their total spending on social protection benefits increase by more than 30 per cent (Eurostat, 1991b). By the end of the 1980s France was in fourth place amongst the twelve EU member states for its per capita spending on social protection and in third place, after Germany and the Netherlands, for the share of GDP devoted to social protection. Expenditure on education also rose from 3.5 per cent of GDP in 1980 to 6.7 per cent in 1990.

In keeping with the insurance principle, social security in France has continued to be funded primarily from employer and employee contributions. A feature of the system which is often identified as a source of problems for the French in the international arena is the relatively large proportion of funding levied on employment, resulting in a high social cost of labour and the dampening of wages. In 1980, with Italy, France was the EU member state where the proportion of receipts for social protection from employers' contributions was highest, and where the contribution from taxation was lowest, well below Italy (Eurostat, 1991b, table 4). Employers argue that the social cost of labour in France makes French goods and services uncompetitive and militates against job creation. When salary levels are included in the calculation of the cost of labour, however, France occupies an intermediate position, since its wage levels are considerably lower than those in Belgium, the Federal Republic of Germany and Denmark (Willard, 1984, pp. 192–3).

Spending on social security and education accounts for more than a quarter of Gross Domestic Product in France. With Luxembourg it had seen the largest increase amongst the northern EU member states for spending on health, old age and unemployment. The relatively high rate of increase in France can be explained by a combination of supply and demand factors: socio-economic and demographic changes coincided with a prolonged period of left-wing government committed to improving social protection.

The 1982 and 1990 population censuses provide a picture of changing demographic structures over the period under study. Three trends are particularly relevant to an understanding of the development of social policy in the 1980s: patterns of family building and women's employment, the ageing of the population and migratory movements.

Family Patterns and Women's Employment

France has a long tradition of concern about depopulation, and pronatalism has been an important component of French family policy since the beginning of the twentieth century. Trends in the 1980s could therefore be used to justify political action. Total period fertility rates continued to fall, but the age at which women were having children was rising steeply: in slightly over a decade it had increased by two years, explained by longer schooling, youth unemployment, a reluctance to embark on family life and the reduction of the risks associated with pregnancies at a later age. At the beginning of the 1990s, France had none the less maintained one of the highest total period fertility rates (1.80) in the European Union (Monnier and de Guibert-Lantoine, 1991, p. 955). It was close to the level in the UK (1.85) but behind Ireland (2.18), both countries that had not pursued active pro-natalist family policies. The reduction in the birth rate in France could not, however, be interpreted as an indication that parents did not want to have children: by the end of the decade only about 10 per cent of couples were remaining childless, compared with 20 per cent for the generations born at the beginning of the century. Rather it reflected the reduction in the number of large families: 80 per cent of women were having one, two or three children at most (Desplanques, 1993c, p. 23).

The 1980s are recognised as the decade that saw a very marked increase in the number of extra-marital births in France, from 1.4 per cent in 1980 to 30.1 per cent in 1990 (Eurostat, 1991a, table 3; 1992, table 2), again one of the highest levels in the EU, slightly above the UK (27.9) but well below Denmark (46.4). Extra-marital births are generally associated with increasing levels of non-marital cohabitation, which had risen to about 1.7 million couples in 1990, representing 12 per cent of all couples (Rabin, 1993, p. 24). Extra-marital births were found to be most common amongst women working in industry, retailing and clerical and related occupations, amongst women of French nationality and in the younger age groups. Two-thirds of children born outside wedlock in France were, however, recognised by their fathers at birth (de Saboulin and Thave, 1993, p. 320), and by their first birthday almost all children born outside wedlock had been recognised by both parents.

This does not mean that lone parenthood had not increased in France during the 1980s, but by the end of the decade most lone mothers with at least one child aged below 18 were living alone with their children as the result of divorce or separation (60 per cent), whereas a relatively small but growing proportion of single mothers were 'never-married' (26 per cent) (Lefaucheur, 1992). It is estimated that by the age of 16 a quarter of the children born in France between 1971 and 1975 were no longer living with their two parents: 20 per cent had experienced a lone-parent family and 13 per cent a recomposed family (Villeneuve-Gokalp, 1993, p. 323). The length of time spent in a lone-parent family decreased over the 1980s, but a growing number of children were likely to have undergone the experience of living in more than one family unit. By the early 1990s one child in four was living with stepbrothers and sisters. These changes in family structure were occurring at the same time as changes in women's working patterns. During the 1980s female economic activity rates decreased for women aged 16 to 24, explained to a large extent by longer education, but they continued to rise amongst women aged 25 to 54 (OECD, 1990). Rates peaked for the 25 to 34 age group when most women were involved in raising children. Women's employment patterns became more continuous over the same period, indicating that they were no longer leaving the workforce or taking a prolonged break from employment when they had children. Although part-time employment rates for women almost doubled over the decade, rising from 15.5 per cent in 1980 to 23.5 per cent in 1990 (Eurostat, 1993a, table 34), they were still well below the levels in Denmark, the Netherlands and the United Kingdom.

Ageing of the Population

Increasing female economic activity rates explain why, despite the demographic ageing of the population, the size of the workforce was maintained during the 1980s. In 1990, as a percentage of total population, the proportion aged over 60 was still relatively small, compared with other EU countries, due to the effect of the low birth-rates prior to and during the first World War and the number of deaths in the Second World War, followed by the baby boom which lasted well into the mid-1960s. Although the proportion in this age group had risen to 19 per cent in 1990, it was still amongst the lowest in northern Europe (Eurostat, 1993b, table 2). French women have the highest life expectancy in the EU, and they are overrepresented particularly in the older generations: at the age of 85 and above in the early 1990s, there were 281 women for every 100 men.

Migratory Movements

Trends in immigration also affect the age and gender balance. France has long been a country of immigration. Already in the 1930s more than 2.7 million foreigners were living in metropolitan France. In the post-war period French governments encouraged immigration as a means of bolstering the depleted labour force at a time of rapid economic growth. By 1990 the figure had reached 3.6 million (excluding foreigners who acquired French nationality), or 6.3 per cent of total population. Despite the suspension of immigration in 1974 for all but family members, this represented a rise of about 2 per cent since the previous census in 1982 (Labat, 1993, p. 37). Over the years the proportion of immigrants from non-European countries (including central and Eastern Europe) had increased, and by 1990 African and Asian immigrants outnumbered Europeans, with the largest groups coming from Algeria and Morocco. In 1982, European immigrants accounted for 50 per cent of the total, but over the decade the numbers from Italy, Portugal and Spain fell. Due to the reuniting of families, the foreign population became more feminised (79 women for 100 men in 1990). By 1990 more than 40 per cent of foreigners were concentrated in the Paris area, where non-European nationals were dominant. Other concentrations were to be found in the Rhône-Alpes, Alsace, Provence-Alpes-Côte d'Azur, Nord-Pas-de-Calais and Franche-Comté regions. While the average birth rate for non-European foreigners living in France remained higher than for French nationals, it fell quite steeply during the 1980s amongst North African women, as they tended to adopt French family building patterns, particularly amongst the younger generations. Patterns of internal migration also changed during the 1980s: the trend of the previous decade to leave the Paris region (Ile-de-France) slowed down. Young people aged 20–9 tended to move to the Paris area to study or in search of work, whereas the older age groups left the capital to return to the provinces. The attraction of the South-East of the country was maintained, whereas the areas undergoing rapid deindustrialisation lost population, in particular the Nord-Pas-de-Calais and Lorraine (Desplanques, 1993a, pp. 54–64). In sum, during the 1980s France had seen changes in family structure and female economic activity patterns which required new policy directions; the anticipated demographic ageing of the population, although less of an immediate problem than in some neighbouring European countries, was causing governments to look for new incentives to encourage couples to increase family size. Governments were also reflecting on the longer term implications for pension funds. New immigration flows had been halted since the mid-1970s, and the structure of the foreign population was changing, in theory alleviating some of the social problems which a high concentration of foreigners can provoke.

The Impact of Policy Changes on Different Population Groups

The French social security system celebrated its fortieth anniversary in 1985, and this was the occasion for stocktaking and scrutiny. While recognising the considerable achievements over the post-war period in extending protection to the whole population to cover ill-health, old age, accidents and family responsibilities, in looking back over the period, Pierre Laroque (1985b), the founding father of the French social security system, expressed his disappointment on two counts in particular. First, he was critical of the fact that corporatist rather than national solidarity had triumphed. Second, he was forced to admit that administrators had not succeeded in inculcating a sense of responsibility into users of the services which they were helping to fund, and this was also having an effect on providers. Laroque identified growing financial problems as an issue policy-makers were having to address in the 1980s. Although most funds had experienced difficulty in balancing receipts and expenditure over the post-war period, the 1970s had been marked by increasing unemployment and growth in the number of elderly people eligible to receive pensions. To some extent these changes had been compensated for by contributions from the increasing number of women entering the workforce, but women were also being affected by unemployment.

Over the post-war period the French had become very attached to their social security system and were not prepared to countenance any measures which might undermine the advantages gained from it. Politicians were not therefore inclined to pursue policies which would reduce benefits and were looking rather for ways of making the system more cost effective. Although the redistributive principle had been one of the objectives in the minds of the founders of the French social security system, priority was given to income security and corporatist solidarity rather than to social justice and national solidarity, as pointed out by Laroque. Redistribution therefore tended to be horizontal rather than vertical, as for example from smaller to larger families and to couples with young children, with the result that, despite the relatively high level of social spending, France rates amongst the most inegalitarian of the capitalist societies (Cameron, 1991, p. 85). Although means-tested benefits were gradually introduced, they were generally of fixed duration; the underlying expectation was that any deviation from the insurance principle would soon be remedied, the emphasis being on security rather than equality (Ambler, 1991, p. 12). During the 1980s this assumption had to be revised as more people experienced long-term unemployment, and new forms of poverty proved resistant to traditional solutions. Policies formulated towards the end of the period were increasingly designed to prevent social exclusion as a result of unemployment, ageing or family breakdown.

The 1980s should not, however, be seen as a homogenous block as far as the relationship between social change and policy are concerned. In the early years of the decade social spending increased more quickly than the national budget, peaking at 28.8 per cent of GDP in 1984 and 1985. From 1986 it fell and then rose again in 1990, though without reaching the 1985 level (Eurostat, 1991b, table 2).

The Principle of Redistribution

The policies pursued by the left-wing government in the early 1980s explain the rapid increase in social spending at the beginning of the decade. On taking office the left-wing government set about fulfilling its election pledges: the minimum wage was increased by 55 per cent and the minimum income for elderly people went up by 65 per cent for a person living alone and by 51 per cent for a couple; family allowances were uprated by 25 per cent, and housing benefits were increased for low income families; unemployment benefits were also raised. These policies were intended to redistribute incomes from the wealthier to the poorer sectors of society; their immediate effect was to push up social spending. By 1982 various measures were being taken to contain rising social costs: levels of unemployment benefit were reduced, as was the duration of benefits, and plans to reform family allowances were shelved. Contribution rates were increased for old age and unemployment, the ceiling on contributions was raised for all but old age. The ceiling on employers' contributions for health was completely removed in 1984, albeit in conjunction with a decrease in the basic insurance rate. Contributions were levied on replacement incomes for the unemployed and those taking early retirement. New or higher taxes were levied on pharmaceutical firms from their expenditure for advertising, on car insurance companies and alcohol. A 1 per cent levy was raised on all incomes in 1983, abandoned in 1985, then reintroduced from October 1990 as a general tax levy (*contribution sociale généralisée*) of 1.05 per cent designed to raise additional resources for family allowances while reducing the burden on wages.

The redistributional principle soon came into conflict with the need to balance the budget. In the previous decade governments had already begun to look for ways of curbing spending on health. In 1982 Pierre Bérégovoy, the new Minister for National Solidarity and Social Affairs, put a freeze on doctors' fee levels, the prices of pharmaceutical goods and, temporarily, on sickness benefit rates. In January 1983 a daily charge was introduced for hospital beds, and in 1984 an attempt was made to institute strict budgeting for hospitals (*dotation globale de fonctionnement*), excluding the private sector (*cliniques*). Medicines which were intended to treat benign conditions were reclassified. Reimbursements were reduced, and some of the cost was shifted to mutual societies and patients themselves. Attempts to reform hospital management structures and the medical profession were strongly opposed and eventually shelved. By 1985 the growth of health expenditure seemed to have been brought under control, although the centre-right government during its period in office between 1986 and 1988 found it necessary to implement a series of further cost cutting measures to prevent the budget deficit from plunging to new depths. While most of the measures taken were of a stop gap nature rather than structural, the net result of attempts to curb spending on health was to shift the cost slightly more towards the private insurance sector and onto patients. To this extent they reinforced divisions between different categories of citizens: those who could afford to contribute to private insurance or were able to bear the additional cost themselves and those who were entitled to no more than standard levels of cover.

Family Policy

Also in line with their redistributive objective, the left drew up a new family policy designed to reduce the disparities which had developed as a result of the favoured treatment given to large families. They therefore increased family allowances for the second child and reduced them for the third. Benefits for lone-parent families were raised. They stopped short of introducing a family allowance for the first child but instead extended and simplified the benefits paid for dependent children up to the age of 3 (*allocation jeune enfant*). The new allowance was paid for all children from five months before birth, for the month of birth and the three months following it, and then continued on a means-tested basis until the child's third birthday, in effect covering an estimated 80 per cent of children (Steck, 1985, p. 96). With the same objective, the tax advantage was reduced for higher income families by placing a ceiling on tax relief for each child and raising the ceiling on incomes for the family supplement in cases where both parents were working. A law adopted in 1984 gave the regional Caisses des Allocations Familiales the task of collecting unpaid alimony, initially for lone parents and subsequently for remarried or cohabiting mothers. By the end of the 1980s 38 per cent of family benefits were distributed on a means-tested basis.

Family policy in France has fluctuated between redistributive, familialist and pro-natalist objectives (Lenoir, 1991). Although absent in the early years of the Socialist government, pro-natalism resurfaced by the mid-1980s, and support for larger families was prominent in the policies formulated at the end of the decade. Another objective also came to the fore in the 1980s in measures designed to help parents combine work and family life. In 1985 paid parental leave was introduced for the third child up to his/her third birthday after a qualifying period of twenty-four months employment in the preceding thirty months. The already relatively generous (Moss, 1990) child care provision was substantially improved (Desplanques, 1993b), and allowances for childminding were extended to all parents employing an approved minder, a policy further developed by the centre right between 1986 and 1988. The difference in emphasis between left and right became less clear cut, as both political groupings were forced by changing family and employment structures to recognise the need for the state to support family diversity and the family–employment relationship.

The Elderly and the Unemployed

Policy for elderly people provides another example of differences in emphasis between left and right. While neighbouring countries such as Germany were already looking for ways of reducing the impact of demographic ageing, the French left-wing government was improving the conditions for those wanting to retire at the age of 60 after thirty-seven and a half years of employment. Lowering of the legal retirement age to 60 took effect in April 1983, and unemployment benefits were replaced by retirement pensions for those aged over 60 eligible to receive full pensions. Earlier retirement and improved pension arrangements meant that the amount paid out for pensions rose as a proportion of social spending over the first half of the decade and then stabilised by 1986 as the guarantee of full replacement income for those taking early retirement was gradually removed from 1983. Lowering of retirement age was a very popular move and had already been initiated prior to 1981. As shown by Anne-Marie Guillemard (1993), by the end of the 1980s about three-quarters of workers were 'retiring' before statutory pensionable age with considerable consequences in the longer term for pension funds. As sounder economic management took over, from 1984 the unemployment benefits system was altered so that employment related insurance benefits were paid for a fixed period followed by non-contributory benefits. Later the same year various schemes were set up to occupy unemployed young people (for example, *travaux d'utilité collective*). As unemployment rates continued to rise, other alternatives were sought to reduce the burden of unemployment benefits. Schemes were instituted to encourage employers to take on unemployed people, either by reducing social insurance payments or providing tax incentives.

One of the Socialists' more imaginative schemes, introduced in December 1988 after their return to power, was the *revenu minimum d'insertion* (RMI), a minimum income for unemployed people aged over 25 who agreed to undertake some form of training or work placement designed to help them re-enter the job market on a longer term basis. By the end of 1991 the RMI had been paid to almost two million individuals and their dependants, or 1.7 per cent of the population in metropolitan France (Poubelle and Simonin, 1993, p. 548). Almost 85 per cent of funding was provided by the state and the remainder by the *départements*. Most beneficiaries, contrary to expectations, were younger people living alone; almost half aged below 35 and 60 per cent without children; only 20 per cent were lone parents with children. Two-thirds of recipients had no qualifications, and most were from poor families. Only about half the beneficiaries from the scheme had secured a longer term income on leaving it. The RMI was not intended for people aged below 25, yet the group displaying the highest unemployment rates were young women under the age of 25. Higher full-time continuous female activity rates have been associated with high unemployment rates: consistently about five to six points above those for men in 1990 (Marchand, 1993, pp. 154–6), when 14.7 per cent of women were unemployed, compared with 8.3 per cent of men (INSÉÉ, 1993, appendix 1, table 3.6). In the 20 to 24 age group the level amongst women was almost double that for men. The importance given to education and training as a protection against unemployment during the 1980s did not ease entry into the labour market for women, nor did it reduce disparities between the sexes. In the early 1980s, the left had invested heavily in education in an effort to achieve the objective set by Jean-Pierre Chevènement in 1985 of enabling 80 per cent of a generation to reach the level of the *baccalauréat* by the year 2000. By 1991 more than 50 per cent of each generation were achieving the target level (Esquieu, 1993, p. 86). In addition almost a third of adult wage earners and over half of all job seekers were undergoing some form of training or retraining (Sauvageot, 1993, p. 115).

The Immigrant Population

Another social group which suffered in the 1980s was the immigrant population. Although immigration had been stopped in the 1970s, except for family members, and foreigners were ostensibly being integrated into French society, the 1980s saw the growth of a strong right-wing extremist movement (Front national) led by Jean-Marie Le Pen. Together with his supporters Le Pen managed to establish a political stronghold in some of the areas where foreign workers were concentrated, claiming that 2 million unemployed meant 2 million immigrants too many, despite evidence that foreign workers were largely continuing to occupy less well paid jobs and were more likely to be unemployed than French workers (Échardour and Maurin, 1993, pp. 504–11). Immigration thus surfaced as an important and divisive political issue, reflecting and exacerbating many of the social problems governments were having to address in the early 1990s.

During its term of office the left had been unable to produce the results promised in the areas where it had staked its reputation. Unemployment, the top priority in 1981, had risen, and social inequalities had not been reduced. Some studies suggested that the gap between high and low incomes may have widened over the decade (CERC, 1989). Welfare spending as a proportion of GDP had continued to rise, while in most other northern EU member states it was slowing down (Eurostat, 1991b). In the early 1990s, an estimated 5.5 million people were being shielded from poverty by welfare benefits, either as direct beneficiaries (3 million) or as dependants (Paugam *et al.*, 1993). Family benefits protected another 3 million and state subsidised benefits a further 1.5 million. Before the 1980s the homeless were tramps and social misfits, but by the early 1990s anything between 200 000 and 400 000 individuals were believed to be homeless, primarily as a result of long-term unemployment and debt.

The Future of Welfare in France

After a honeymoon period of almost a year the Balladur government elected to power in 1993 had come under fierce attack for its social policies: first for its attempt to reform the private school system, an area which had brought strong and violent protests in 1984 when the left had tried to introduce reforms; then over the proposal for a *contrat d'insertion professionnelle* (CIP), a job creation scheme which would have enabled employers to take on young unemployed people at 80 per cent of the statutory minimum wage (therefore nicknamed the *Smic jeune*). The proposal brought students, the unemployed and unions out onto the streets in a movement bearing some of the hallmarks of the 1968 student unrest, offering a reminder of the strong opposition that social reform encounters in France.

Public reactions to the socialist experiment of the 1980s, the early social policy failures of the centre-right government between 1986 and 1988, and again after barely a year in office in 1994, reflected the French electorate's disillusionment with its politicians, the policy-making process and the ability of party politics to find innovative solutions to persistent social problems. Despite its widely recognised shortcomings and their awareness of the need to make savings, the French remain strongly attached to their social system (Ferrera, 1993) and to the insurance principle on which it is based. They are therefore prepared to resist any reforms which might undermine it and affect individual entitlements. Yet they are also opposed to further increases in employee contributions, thus presenting governments with difficult political decisions. One area where public opinion is more receptive to shifting the burden of social costs away from employers and employees onto general taxation is family policy. The change had already begun in 1991 with the CSG being used to contribute to the funding of family allowances. A broadening of the base for social insurance contributions had also been set in motion.

Economic analysts paint a gloomy picture for welfare in the remainder of the decade if the socio-economic trends of the 1980s continue against a background of an ageing population. By the year 2000, with increasing life expectancy, predictions put the proportion of the population aged over 60 at between 20.3 and 20.5 per cent, depending upon fertility rates in the intervening period (Dinh, 1993, p. 34). By the year 2010 the proportions of the population aged under 20 and of working age (20 to 59) are expected to begin to decline. By the time the full impact of the ageing of the baby boomers is felt in the year 2020, more than 25 per cent of the population will be over 60. Between 1990 and the year 2050 the proportion of the population in this age group is expected to have doubled and that over 75 to have trebled. Most of these elderly people will be female since at the age of 60 women are likely to outlive their male counterparts by more than five years, and the provision of care for older people, and more especially for older women, presents an intractable problem.

As a result of demographic ageing, France will be facing many of the problems already encountered by its 'more advanced' neighbours, with the nation's wealth being increasingly redistributed from a contracting workforce to a growing non-working population (Darmon *et al.*, 1991). Redistribution of income and the reduction of unemployment are likely to remain pressing problems for the last years of the decade. The shift in income during the 1980s from the working population to the unemployed and to elderly people is likely to continue, and disparities within occupational groups are expected to persist, unless a way can be found of dealing with the new forms of poverty which have been resulting from long-term unemployment. Spending on health care is also expected to continue to rise, implying that insurance contributions will have to be raised, patients will have to pay a larger proportion of the costs themselves or accept lower standards of care. In the early 1990s controls on health spending seemed to be having some impact as efforts continued to reduce wastage and ensure greater efficiency, but economy drives have their limits. While more state intervention and control over spending on health would be difficult to promote for the reasons mentioned above, the possibility of greater involvement by the private sector cannot, however, be ruled out. As in other EU member states, private insurance through the extension of mutual societies has been playing an increasingly important role.

In the early 1990s the economic debate on how to pay for welfare in the future, or how to square the growth–competitiveness–employment triangle, was focusing on a number of options (Caracosta *et al.*, 1991), but none offered a solution for both the short and the longer term. In a system where social protection is funded from employment related insurance, it is difficult to reconcile growth based on high labour productivity and the associated high wage costs because of the impact on international competitiveness. Incentives such as reductions in insurance contributions for employers who take on unemployed workers may lessen the burden of unemployment benefits but only marginally increase income from contributions. The emphasis on the insurance principle, in combination with the shift towards the private sector, is likely to exacerbate inequalities producing a three-tiered system which accentuates divisions between different population groups: the employed in secure jobs, covered by comprehensive insurance schemes and earning additional cover from contributions to mutual societies and higher occupational pensions; those employed in less secure jobs without additional schemes to top up benefits; the long-term unemployed or never employed dependant on a minimum income or national assistance which fall through the insurance net.

Because politicians have their sights set on popularity ratings and the next elections, they are less concerned about the longer term impact of social policy measures, and in any case they are constrained by economic forces largely beyond their control. Measures such as the lowering of the age of retirement in 1983, the reduction in working hours and the extension of part-time working had a strong left-wing ideological content but did little to curb unemployment. The arguments in favour of a reduction of the working week and greater flexibility of work time organisation have also been rehearsed by the right-wing government elected in 1993. Other schemes for creating jobs and balancing the social security budget resurface periodically, irrespective of the government in power, providing further evidence that politics may not matter, at least in so far as policy formulation is concerned. It may matter more with regard to enactment and implementation but, even then, as demonstrated by the 1980s, other factors, such as international economic and political events, may be more influential than ideology.

References

Ambler, J.S. (1991) 'Ideas, Interests, and the French Welfare State', in Ambler, J.S. (ed.) *The French Welfare State: Surviving Social and Ideological Change* (New York/London: New York University Press), pp. 1–31.

Cameron, D.R. (1991) 'Continuity and Change in French Social Policy: The Welfare State under Gaullism, Liberalism, and Socialism', in Ambler, J.S. (ed.) *The French Welfare State: Surviving Social and Ideological Change* (New York/London: New York University Press), pp. 58–93.

Caracosta, L., Fleurbaey, M. and Leroy, C. (1991) 'Compétitivité, croissance et emploi: la France de l'an 2000 en perspective', *Économie et statistique*, no. 243, May, pp. 69–87.

CERC (1989) *Les Français et leurs revenus: Le tournant des années 80* (Paris: Éditions la Découverte).

Charraud, A., Devouassoux, J. and Morel, B. (1984) 'La consommation médicale: évolution et disparités', *La société française*. Données sociales 1984 (Paris: INSÉÉ), pp. 359–87.

Darmon, D., Hourriez, J-M. and L'Hardy, P. (1991) 'Consommation: l'effet du vieillissment', *Économie et statistique*, no. 243, May, pp. 89–104.

Desplanques, G. (1993a) 'Cinq millions de personnes ont changé de région entre 1982 et 1990', *La société française*. Données sociales 1993 (Paris: INSÉÉ), pp. 54–64.

Desplanques, G. (1993b) 'Garder les petits: organisation collective ou solidarité familiale', *La société française*. Données sociales 1993 (Paris: INSÉÉ), pp. 330–3.

Desplanques, G. (1993c) 'Un siècle de difficultés à assurer le remplacement des générations', *La société française*. Données sociales 1993 (Paris: INSÉÉ), pp. 16–23.

Dinh, Q.C. (1993) 'Combien d'habitants en France dans trente ans?', *La société française*. Données sociales 1993 (Paris: INSÉÉ), pp. 30–6.

Échardour, A. and Maurin, É. (1993) 'La main-d'oeuvre étrangère', *La société française*. Données sociales 1993 (Paris: INSÉÉ), pp. 504–11.

Esquieu, P. (1993) 'La vague lycéenne: un défi pour les années quatre-vingt-dix', *La société française*. Données sociales 1993 (Paris: INSÉÉ), pp. 84–90.

Eurostat (1983) *Basic Statistics of the Community*, 21st edn (Luxembourg: Office for Official Publications of the European Communities).

Eurostat (1987) *Basic Statistics of the Community*, 24th edn (Luxembourg: Office for Official Publications of the European Communities).

Eurostat (1991a) 'A European Community with a Population of 345 Million', Rapid Reports. Population and Social Conditions, no. 3.

Eurostat (1991b) 'Social Protection in Europe: Trends from 1980 to 1989', Rapid Reports, Population and Social Conditions, no. 4.

Eurostat (1992a) *Basic Statistics of the Community*, 29th edn (Luxembourg: Office for Official Publications of the European Communities).

Eurostat (1993a) *Labour Force Survey: Results 1991* (Luxembourg: Office for Official Publications of the European Communities).

Eurostat (1993b) 'Older People in the European Community', Rapid Reports, Population and Employment, no. 1.

Ferrera, M. (1993) *EC Citizens and Social Protection: Main Results from a Eurobarometer Survey* (Brussels: Commission of the European Communities).

Freeman, G.P. (1990) 'Financial Crisis and Policy Continuity in the Welfare State', in Hall, P.A., Hayward, J. and Laroque, H.P. (1985) *Quarante ans de Securite sociale*. Review francais des affaires sociales, vol. 39, special issue, July–September.

Guillemard, A-M. (1993) 'Older Workers and the Labour Market', in Walker, A., Alber, J. and Guillemard, A-M., *Older People in Europe: Social and Economic Policies*. The 1993 Report of the European Observatory (Brussels: Commission of the European Communities), pp. 68–99

Hantrais, L. (1990) *Managing Professional and Family Life: a Comparative Study of British and French Women* (Aldershot/Vermont: Dartmouth).

INSÉÉ (1991) *Comptes et indicateurs économiques*. Rapport sur les comptes de la Nation 1990, INSÉÉ résultats, nos 36, 37, 38, June (Paris: INSÉÉ).

INSÉÉ (1993) *La société française*. Données sociales 1993 (Paris: INSÉÉ).

Labat, J-C. (1993) 'La population étrangère et son évolution', La société française. Données sociales 1993 (Paris: INSÉÉ), pp. 37–45.

Laroque, M-F. (1985a) 'La protection sociale des personnes âgées', *Revue française des affaires sociales*, 39 (special issue), July–September, pp. 179–95.

Laroque, P. (1985b) 'Quarante ans de Sécurité sociale', *Revue française des affaires sociales*, 39 (special issue), July–September, pp. 7–35.

Lefaucheur, N. (1992) 'France', in Roll, J. (ed.), *Lone Parent Families in the European Community*. The 1992 Report to the European Commission (London: European Family and Social Policy Unit), pp. 27–8.

Lenoir, R. (1991) 'Family Policy in France since 1938', in Ambler, J.S. (ed.) *The French Welfare State: Surviving Social and Ideological Change* (New York/London: New York University Press), pp. 144–86.

Marchand, O. (1993) 'Les groupes sociaux face au chômage: des atouts inégaux', *La société française*. Données sociales 1993 (Paris: INSÉÉ), pp. 153–61.

Monnier, A. and Guibert-Lantoine, C. de (1991) 'La conjoncture démographique: l'Europe et les pays développés d'Outre-mer', *Population*, vol. 46, no. 4, pp. 941–61.

Moss, P. (ed.) (1990) 'Childcare in the European Community 1985–90', *Women of Europe Supplements*, no. 31, August.

OECD (1990) *Labour Force Statistics, 1968–88* (Paris: OECD).

Oeuvrard, F. (1984) 'Le système éducatif', Données sociales 1984 (Paris: INSÉÉ), pp. 470–82.

Paugam, S., Zoyem, J-P. and Charbonnel, J-M. (1993) 'Précarité et risque d'exclusion en France', Documents du Centre d'Étude des Revenus et des Coûts, no. 109 (Paris: CERC), pp. 7–169.

Péano, S. (1993) 'Dépenses et décisions dans le système éducatif', *La société française*. Données sociales 1993 (Paris: INSÉÉ), pp. 78–83.

Poubelle, V. and Simonin, B. (1993) 'Le RMI: un million d'allocataires en trois ans', *La société française*. Données sociales 1993 (Paris: INSÉÉ), pp. 548–56.

Rabin, B. (1993) 'Un enfant sur trois naît hors mariage', *La société française*. Données sociales 1993 (Paris: INSÉÉ), pp. 24–9.

Revoil, J-P. (1984) 'L'indemnisation du chômage et de la pré-retraite', Données sociales 1984 (Paris: INSÉÉ), pp. 196–207.

Saboulin, M. de and Thave, S. (1993) 'La vie en couple marié: un modèle qui s'affaiblit', *La société française*. Données sociales 1993 (Paris: INSÉÉ), pp. 314–21.

Sauvageot, C. (1993) 'L'Éducation nationale forme aussi des adultes', *La société française*. Données sociales 1993 (Paris: INSÉÉ), pp. 114–19.

Steck, P. (1985) 'Les prestations familiales de 1946 à 1985. Ruptures ou constances?', *Revue franÿaise des affaires sociales*, 39 (special issue), July–September, pp. 63–98.

Villeneuve-Gokalp, C. (1993) 'La recomposition du paysage familial après la séparation des parents', *La société franÿaise*. Données sociales 1993 (Paris: INSÉÉ), pp. 322–9.

Waltisperger, D. (1984) 'L'aide sociale', Données sociales 1984 (Paris: INSÉÉ), pp. 215–9.

Willard, J-C. (1984) 'Coûts salariaux et charges sociales', Données sociales 1984 (Paris: INSÉÉ), pp. 188–95.

Wilsford, D. (1991) 'The Continuity of Crisis: Patterns of Heath Care Policymaking in France, 1978–1988', in Ambler, J.S. (ed.), *The French Welfare State: Surviving Social and Ideological Change* (New York/London: New York University Press) pp. 94–143.

4

Sweden: The Last Bastion of Social Democracy

ARTHUR GOULD

> As late as 1989, Sweden seemed immune to worldwide political
> trends in a conservative or neo-liberal direction, and the hegemony of
> Swedish social democracy seemed to be as secure as it had ever been.
> (Pontusson, 1992, p. 305)

If the crisis of welfare expenditure for many European countries occurred
during the early and middle 1980s, in Sweden it came towards the end of
the decade. As economic growth declined and unemployment and public
sector debt increased, neither the Social Democrats nor their successors in
the Bourgeois centre right coalition have found it easy to adjust to the
changing world around them. The very forces, expectations and interests
created by the world's most impressive system of state welfare made it
even more difficult to reduce and reform. After three years of flirtation
with free market politics, the electorate has returned the party of the strong
state.

The Swedish Model

The difficulty that Sweden has faced since the late 1980s is understandable
given the significance of the People's Home. As two American observers
pointed out, the social democratic project had become the national project
(Heclo and Madsen, 1986). The consistent election of Social Democratic
governments from 1932 to 1976 had resulted in a welfare state in which
social policy had a high priority. By the end of the 1970s, Sweden was

regarded as a prototype of a modern society (Tomasson, 1970). Its capitalist economy had grown at an impressive rate throughout the postwar years; the standard of living of ordinary Swedes was amongst the highest in the world; while the state's commitment to an active labour market policy, high social security benefits and affluent public services was second to none. When the Social Democrats tried to push reforms in a clearer, socialist–egalitarian direction at the same time as the economy was experiencing the problems of the post–1973 oil crisis, the electorate moved to the right.

The Bourgeois coalitions of 1976 and 1979, however, not only failed to bring about any significant changes to the public sector but demonstrated an inability to run the economy. With the return of the Social Democrats in 1982 (and in the subsequent elections in 1985 and 1988) the economy recovered; the welfare reforms of the 1960s and 1970s were consolidated; and full employment was maintained. Moreover, the power of trade unions within Sweden's liberal corporatist institutions had been strengthened not only by the passing of the Codetermination Law of 1976 but with the introduction of the wageearner funds in 1983. These reforms were seen by some on the left as an indication that the Swedes were on the their way to becoming the first country to achieve socialism by democratic means (Stephens, 1979). Others insisted that Swedish welfarism operated within the confines of a capitalist economy and that its egalitarianism was exaggerated. It was difficult to deny, however, that the range of programmes that continued into the 1980s was impressive in comparison with those in other European countries.

Throughout the 1980s, the recipients of social insurance benefits continued to experience high living standards. The retired elderly continued to receive either a supplement to their basic pensions or an additional earnings related element which gave them an income replacement ratio of around 70 per cent. In addition, housing benefits and subsidised social services made Swedish pensioners as well off in retirement as they had been when earning.

Social services for other groups such as the handicapped were also impressive. Moreover, the new social services legislation, which came into effect in 1982, established the rights of those in need to services and benefits. Although this led to more people claiming social assistance, few observers could detect obvious signs of material poverty in the Swedish population. With subsidised child care, also provided by local social services departments, and a system of parental leave, backed by parental insurance – again at an income replacement level of 90 per cent – and a growing number of jobs in the public sector, Swedish women were able to seek work in ever increasing numbers. Not only were 80 per cent of adult women in the workforce but their pay rates relative to that of men was in the order of 85 per cent.

Sickness benefits of 90 per cent of income and modest charges for prescriptions, visits to the doctor and for stays in hospital meant that illness held no fear for the sick. Sweden devoted around 9 per cent of its GNP to health care (public and private), second only to the US, but boasting considerably better health indices. As in Britain but unlike the USA, the private sector in health care was relatively small.

Unemployment remained low and unemployment benefits high for those in the trade union managed (although largely statefunded) unemployment schemes. Most workers could expect to find a job easily and for those who could not, the Labour Market Board provided an impressive range of training and job creation opportunities.

Young people attended through state comprehensives – *grundskolor* – from the age of 7 to 16. Less than 1 per cent went to private schools. Classes were unstreamed and assessment based upon coursework. A national curriculum was followed which emphasised social as well as academic objectives. Most young people stayed on after the school leaving age to attend the three year gymnasia from which a high proportion transferred to some form of higher education. During the 1970s education had expanded according to the principles of recurrent education, a philosphy which stressed the need for learning to be relevant, democratic and a lifelong project (Boucher, 1982). Adults who had lost out on education when they were young were able to obtain grants to improve their basic education. Others attended subsidised study circles and folk high schools for self-improvement and to better their employment opportunities. The right to educational leave, passed in 1975, enabled adults to take advantage of educational opportunities without losing their jobs. Some used this right to attend full-time classes, others took a few hours off each week to improve their negotiating skills and knowledge of labour relations on courses funded by their trade unions (Gould, 1983). Immigrant workers had the additional right to 240 hours paid educational leave to learn Swedish.

None of this was cheap, of course. The Swedes paid very high taxes (see Table 1.9) to maintain a public sector which employed over 30 per cent of the workforce and spent 60 per cent of the country's GDP. This system had been established by a corporatist political system which depended upon the close cooperation of employers, trade unions and government. None of these parties was weak. The employers included some of the world's best known multinational companies – Volvo, SAAB, Electrolux, Ericssons, SKT – while the LO, the federation of manual trade unions, represented 90 per cent of all manual workers. Even white collar workers were 80 per cent unionised. Since 1938 the centralised federations of employees had negotiated a basic pay deal with SAF, the employers' federation. Moreover, representatives of these labour market organisations played a major role in the administrative boards of the state responsible for the implementation of the government's social and economic policies.

This system remained largely intact until after the 1988 elections. While other countries were experiencing growing unemployment, cuts in public expenditure, deregulation and privatisation, Sweden seemed to be the exception to the rule (Morris, 1988). Olsson, a consistent commentator on the state of Swedish welfare, felt that the prospects for social welfare were 'rather favourable in Sweden especially as the economy is recovering in the mid-1980s – the national backlash still seems far away' (Olsson, 1988). In his seminal study published in 1990, Esping–Andersen could still point to Sweden as the country which embodied the 'decommodification' of labour more than any other (Esping–Andersen, 1990). When events finally caught up with the country, they did so with great speed.

The Crisis Years

It is now clear, in retrospect, that problems within the Swedish economy had been mounting for some time and that the 1982 devaluation of the kronor had merely delayed its decline. Major Swedish companies had begun to accelerate their investments abroad during the 1980s (Pontusson, 1992). Private sector expansion in output and employment was taking place outside Sweden. The decline in manufacturing employment within the country was particularly severe. Moreover, the Swedish economy was having to adapt to changes in the world outside. The deregulation of financial markets in the 1980s and the subsequent boom in property prices and credit was followed in Sweden as elsewhere by recession. For the Swedes the problem was exacerbated by an overheated economy in which unemployment, by 1989, had fallen below 2 per cent and inflation had, soon after, climbed to 10 per cent.

The Social Democratic government reacted by making the reduction of inflation a major priority, linking the krona with the German mark, and announcing its intention of applying for membership of the European Union. A major tax reform was introduced which reduced the high marginal rates of income tax and replaced them with a greater emphasis on VAT (Södersten, 1990). The government also tried to contain public expenditure and to reduce welfare benefits and services. In these early attempts to adapt to the changing economic climate, the Social Democrats needed the cooperation of the Bourgeois parties in parliament, as their erstwhile Communist allies were unwilling to help in the process of 'social disarmament'.

The perceived failure of the Social Democrats resulted in poor opinion poll ratings. From their usual 45 per cent of public support they plummeted to an all time low of 28 per cent, barely a few points above the Conservatives. In the approach to the election of 1991, the Liberal and Conservative parties called for a system shift in which market forces, choice and competition were to be emphasised (Ny start för Sverige, 1991). When the election finally took place, the result for the parties of the right were ambiguous. The Social Democrats and the small Communist Party together retained 44 per cent of the seats in parliament, but the four established Bourgeois parties (Conservative, Centre, Liberal and Christian Democrat) lacked an overall majority. The balance of power was held by a maverick party, New Democracy, which had gained twenty-five seats on a populist platform which appealed to the growing anti-immigrant sentiments being expressed in Sweden. Because of New Democracy's alleged racialism, the Liberal and Centre parties refused to contemplate the possibility of a five-party coalition. Instead, Carl Bildt, the Conservative leader, became the prime minister of a minority, four-party coalition government.

It soon became clear that any system shift contemplated by the conservatives was going to face problems. In the early months of the government, attempts to reduce public expenditure programmes were frustrated by the inability of the four parties to agree on which programmes to concentrate. Moreover, the leader of the Liberal party, in his role as Minister for Health and Social Affairs, soon began to argue strongly that social programmes had been cut back far enough. Even when the four coalition partners found themselves in agreement, the necessary support from one of the other parliamentary parties was not forthcoming. Only with the currency crisis of September 1992, when Sweden's marginal interest rate rose within a matter of days from 16 per cent to 500 per cent, did a sense of national purpose induce the government and the Social Democrats to agree on a crisis package of costcutting measures to impress the markets that something would be done about Sweden's public sector deficit. Yet, with the country facing its most serious crisis for decades, the measures proved to be inadequate. Critics of the Swedish model blamed the state of public finances while defenders of the system blamed the deregulation of the 1980s and business interests. Whether the fault lay with the public or the private sector, it was clear that political and demographic factors were also contributing to the country's economic problems.

The Public Sector Deficit

In the months that followed, a number of economic studies were published, warning that Sweden's situation was desperate. Eklund, commenting on the government's 1993/4 plan to spend SEK 521 billion while raising only SEK 358 billion in revenue wrote that projected savings of SEK 10 billion a year were quite inadequate (Eklund, 1993). In his view, the continuing deficit was unlikely to go away with the hoped for ending of the recession. Two-thirds of the deficit was structural. Moreover, government consumption and investment expenditure had fallen. The big increase in expenditure was largely due to an increase in transfer expenditure – from 30 per cent of GNP in the late 1980s to 40 per cent in 1993. The deficit was also aggravated by interest payments on the national debt. By the end of 1993 the deficit stood at 14 per cent of GDP and the national debt at 80 per cent of GDP. In the view of one economic commentator, Sweden's 'budget deficit is greater than other countries' and the national debt is rising more steeply than elsewhere' (Schuck, 1994).

Another economist pointed out that this situation had also been aggravated by negative economic growth over the previous three years, an effective devaluation of the krona by 15–20 per cent and unemployment which had, at last, reached European levels (Ståhl, 1993). Unemployment which had been 4 per cent when the government came to power, rose to 6 per cent in the middle of 1992 and 11 per cent a year later. These percentages excluded the approximately 2–3 per cent of the labour force which participated in labour market schemes (*Riksdag & Departement*, 1993a).

For many analysts, the main focus of their appraisal of Sweden's economic problems was public expenditure, and within that the generous level of social insurance benefits. It had already been established that the state earnings related pension (ATP), if it continued on its existing path, would, without economic growth, lead to employers' contributions amounting to over 50 per cent of their payroll by the year 2035 (Ståhlberg, 1991). Equally worrying were the rising costs of sickness, work injury, early retirement and unemployment benefits. Others focused more on the growth in the numbers of those dependent upon the state for both benefits and employment. Södersten, an ex-Social Democratic member of parliament and an economist, showed how the numbers had risen from 2.5 million adults in 1972 to 4.7 million out of a total population of 8.7 million in 1992. The ratio to those employed in the private sector was 0.9 and 2.3 respectively (Södersten, 1992).

The Damage Done by the Private Sector

The defenders of Swedish social democracy sought to cast doubt upon the damage done to the economy by the public sector. Some sought instead to place the blame upon those owners of capital who had made poor investments abroad during the property boom, and the banks who had incurred crippling credit losses – and now expected to be baled out by the public sector (Åmark, 1993). Others sought to blame the deregulation of financial markets which had made interest rates and currency levels much more vulnerable to speculation and called for a restoration of the old system, whereby firms were induced to invest in the long term interests of the country (Bergström, 1993; Wetterberg, 1993). But many also admitted that unemployment had been allowed to fall too far and benefits to rise too much. There was a problem.

Political and Constitutional Obstacles

Part of the problem was the sheer scale of the public sector and the numbers of people who would be affected by its reduction. But more importantly were the political and constitutional obstacles to change. There was general agreement that parliaments with a life of only three years were too constrained by electoral considerations to make tough economic decisions. Others criticised the system of proportional representation for its failure to produce majority governments which could govern effectively without the need for constant parliamentary compromise. Another criticism was that the budgetary process itself was weak in comparison to other countries and was vulnerable to the multiplicity of special interests represented in parliament. Many of these and similar criticisms were expressed by the Lindbeck Commission appointed to examine Sweden's political and economic problems (SOU, 1993, p. 16). The Commission even went so far as to suggest that parliament, because it contained twice as many members as other countries of a similar size, reduce itself by half.

Demographic Change

These economic and political problems also have to be seen in the context of demographic changes. For many years Sweden had had a high proportion – around 15 per cent – of people above the age of 65. In 1990 this had risen to 18 per cent but was due to rise still further to 20 per cent over the next thirty years – a picture not too different from that of other European countries as Table 1.6 showed. A different problem was posed by the fact that the annual numbers of births, which had fallen during the 1970s, rose during the 1980s (Statistiska Centralbyrån, 1985 and 1993). Both of these trends meant that for a few years ahead, the government was faced with growing welfare needs at both ends of the demographic spectrum. Single households had doubled while households containing three or more people had fallen (Swedish, Institute 1992). This also had resource and housing policy implications for government. Lastly, while the number of immigrants had fallen between 1975 and 1983, it had risen in 1990. Part of this increase may have been due to the shortage of labour at the end of the 1980s, but a considerable amount was due to the numbers of refugees granted asylum (SCB, 1993). Not only did these trends have resource implications in a country which had been relatively generous to newcomers in financial terms, but politicians were faced with increasing evidence that the Swedes were becoming less tolerant of outsiders. Not only were examples of racial harassment and violence on the increase but small fascist parties and groups had begun to flex their political muscles.

Welfare Reforms

Social Security

The need to control public expenditure had already been recognised by the Social Democrats before the Bourgeois government came to office in 1991, but neither they nor their successors achieved much success until the crisis of September 1992, when a package of costcutting measures was agreed by the government and the Social Democratic opposition. Sickness benefit, a principal target for reform which had already been reduced a little by the Social Democrats in 1990, was cut still further. In the 1980s sickness benefit had come to 90 per cent of a recipient's income. The 1992 crisis agreement introduced one waiting day for which benefit would not be paid; 65 per cent of income for days two and three; 80 per cent to cover the rest of the first year and 70 per cent thereafter (Vår trygghet, 1993).

Earlier in the year, employers had been made liable for the administration of sick pay for the first fourteen days of sickness. They were also expected to investigate a claimant's need for rehabilitation after eight weeks of sickness (Vår trygghet, 1991). A further major reform of sickness benefit was intended by the government and the main opposition party with the setting up of a commission to examine the possibility of employers' and trade unions taking over the responsibility for the administration of sickness benefit. Another possibility being considered by the commission was that of a private insurance company taking over the task (Midfelt, 1993e). Work injury benfits were brought into line with sickness benefit in May 1993 (Midfelt, 1993b).

Other benefits have also been reduced. The base amount, whereby many Swedish welfare benefits are calculated, and which had been annually upgraded in line with price rises, was, in effect, reduced by 3 per cent between 1989 and 1991, and a further 3 per cent in 1992 (Vår trygghet, 1993). The basic old age pension and the disability pension for a single adult, which had been calculated at 96 per cent of the base amount, were thereby reduced in value. The supplementary pension and pension rates for married couples were similarly affected. The value of these pensions was further eroded in 1993.

Early in 1994, a crossparty parliamentary committee recommended drastic reforms to the old age pension system. Instead of pension increases being linked to rises in prices, they were to be linked to rises in income. Whereas ATP had been based upon only thirty years of contributions, the new system was to be based upon contributions throughout the contributor's working life. Contributions which had previously been paid by employers in the form of a percentage of their payroll, were now to be paid by both employers and employees. Moreover, the employers' percentage contributions were to be reduced over the next few years while those of employees were to rise to 9.25 per cent of pay. These changes were calculated to reduce the pension system's deficit considerably (SOU, 1994a, p. 20). The pension reform had the backing of the Social Democrats in parliament (as did the government proposal to reduce the partial pension) but union leaders were divided, depending upon how they thought it would affect their particular members.

The growing numbers of those claiming disability pensions was also coming under scrutiny. It was becoming obvious to the Social Insurance Board that the growth in claimants from 3 per cent of the labour force in

1970 to 7 per cent in 1993 was not simply a reflection of growing disability. It was suspected that collusion between employers, workers and their doctors was resulting in an abuse of the system. The disability pension was being claimed in preference to unemployment benefit and social assistance. It was being argued towards the end of 1993 that (i) more rehabilitation measures, (ii) bringing disability benefits in line with other social insurance benefits, and (iii) a requirement for more than one doctor's certificate might help reduce the number of claimants (Midfelt, 1993g).

The rising numbers of those on means-tested social assistance was also a source of concern both to central government and the local municipalities who administered the benefit. In 1980, only 4 per cent of the population had been living on social assistance, but by 1992 that figure had risen to 8 per cent. The real costs had more than tripled over the same period (Statistiska meddelanden, 1993 and 1994). Not only were social assistance rates also affected by the reduced value of the base amount, since the National Board for Health and Social Affairs recommended that a single adult's benefit be calculated at 116 per cent of the base amount, but 90 per cent of local authorities were found to be paying at rates below this existence minimum. The variations were as wide as from 46 per cent to 135 per cent of the base amount. As a result, it was recommended by the commission on social services that social assistance be reduced to 100 per cent of the base amount and that all local authorities should be made to respect this figure (Deurell, 1993b).

The number claiming social assistance was expected to rise even further with the increase in unemployment generally and long-term unemployment in particular. Unemployment benefit itself had always been a bit of an anomaly in Sweden in that members of trade unions were part of a voluntary, superior, *income-related* scheme administered by the trade unions themselves, with contributions paid for by the employers. Other unemployed people claimed a *flat rate* benefit administered by the Labour Market Board. Early in 1993, the government proposed that the cost of the earnings related scheme be reduced through the introduction of five waiting days and a replacement rate of 80 per cent of income instead of the previous 90 per cent (Deurell, 1993a; Gauthier, 1993a). This took effect in the summer of 1993. However, in order to reduce the deficit on the unemployment benefit fund, the government proposed that from the beginning of 1994 all employees pay 1 per cent of their income into a new obligatory scheme. From the beginning of 1995, this contribution would be raised to 2 per cent (Nilsson, 1993). Limits were also placed upon the length of time claimants could reregister for unemployment benefit. This would ensure that many claimants would eventually be forced onto social assistance.

Social Services

If social security benefits have deteriorated across the board, the same cannot be said unambiguously about Sweden's social services. On the one hand, municipalities or communes, which have traditionally provided social services, have been prevented from raising their local taxes by governments throughout the 1990s. On the other hand, they have been encouraged to take on extra responsibilities, charge higher fees for their services and to accept alternative ways of organising child care and the care of the elderly. The Social Affairs Minister may have been keen to introduce more choice and competition in service provision, but he has also been determined that Sweden's high welfare standards for the whole population be maintained if not improved.

The Social Democrats had, during the 1980s, moved towards an emphasis upon community care and closed down many institutional homes for both the elderly and the mentally ill. In their last period of office, they introduced a major reform in the care of the elderly by making the communes reponsible for all residential provision for old people. This involved the transfer of many of the services that had previously been provided by the health care authorities, the county councils. The reform of elderly care came into force at the beginning of 1992 after the election of the centreright government. This transition has occurred at the same time as the government has been promoting more private, voluntary and co-operative care.

It is too early to say how the new system is working and perhaps impossible to unravel the combined effects of so many changes. Certainly, less people are being cared for in institutions but the closing down of the latter has sometimes been criticised for being hasty and premature. More housing has been provided for community care and better compensation for carers of elderly relatives, but fees for services have sometimes risen enormously with the poorest complaining the most (Fernow 1992; Midfelt, 1993d, 1993e). Fernow claims that the provision of a range of services (windowwashing, house cleaning, shopping) by housing companies has created an alternative to municipal home help services but that the elderly themselves seem to prefer public provision (Fernow, 1992; Midfelt, 1993f).

While the care of the elderly demonstrated a degree of ambivalence about the general direction of social services under the Bourgeois government, the care of the handicapped seems to have benefited considerably from the influence of the Social Affairs Minister. Not only did the care allowance for parents with handicapped children rise by 30 per cent only months after the election but even bigger changes were afoot (Kjellander, 1991). In 1993, a new law was passed to give more rights to the handicapped and their carers. In particular, the handicapped were to have the right to choose a personal assistant, to be paid for by the municipalities. County councils were given new obligations to rehabilitate and rights to advice, support and various services such as shortstay respite care were also included in the legislation (Midfelt, 1993a). Although the legislation was criticised for again being too hasty in closing down institutions and for not implementing some of the handicap commission's recommendations, it was supported by all parties. The likely cost of these measures over the next four years was estimated to be in the order of SEK 1 billion (Larsson, 1993).

Soon after coming to power the Bourgeois government took steps to make it possible for profit-making child care agencies to be set up. Private and cooperative child care can now receive state grants. Costs to the consumer have however risen with the result that many parents have found their children excluded from day care because fees have not been paid (Johansson, 1993a). Communes are also increasing the size of classes. However, the need for expanded child care provision has been recognised by the government, largely due to the persistence of the Social Affairs Minister. During the 1980s provision had expanded so that only 37 per cent of children under the age of 6 were being looked after by their parents (Swedish Institute, 1990). During the 1990s one solution to increased demand for child care has been to increase the size of groups cared for (*Riksdag & Departement*, 1993b). In 1993, it was decided that all parents, who wanted child care for children between the ages of 1 and 12 years, should have it and that the communes should ensure that it was available (Midfelt, 1993c). At the same time it was decided to introduce a care allowance of SEK 2000 a month for parents who wished to care for children bewtween the ages of 1 and 3 at home (Gauthier, 1993b). This proposal, promoted by the Conservatives and the Christian Democrats, was widely seen as an attempt to encourage women to stay at home (Pilsäter, 1992). In its final form, it was clear that the value of the benefit would be reduced the more hours of subsidised child care the parent used.

As part of the complex of changes in the field of child care, parental leave was also the object of reform. The government intended to reduce the value of parent benefit to 80 per cent of income to bring it into line with other benefits. More significantly, it made one month of the twelve months of leave to which parents were entitled dependent upon the father taking leave from work (Deurell, 1994b).

Health Care

Health care services, which in Sweden are the responsibility of the county councils, expanded considerably during the 1970s and 1980s to the point that they were consuming 10 per cent of GNP and employing 10 per cent of the workforce. While the system had a good reputation internationally, there were clearly suspicions that its cost was not entirely justified. It was felt that there was overemployment of staff, including doctors; that there was too great a reliance on hospitalisation, particularly of the elderly and the mentally ill; that waiting lists were far too long. These criticisms which grew during the 1980s were given added urgency by the country's economic difficulties.

Even before the Bourgeois government's period of office, attempts were made to reduce spending and make the system more efficient. Internal markets based upon pricing mechanisms began to develop. The resulting rationalisation and costcutting have more recently necessitated hospital closures and staff redundancies. The private sector has begun to expand and has already presented problems which demand regulation. While increased competition and a greater reliance on market mechanisms may have resulted in some efficiency improvements, there have been less desirable consequences as well – fewer examinations of patients and referrals to specialists where these are not profitable and excessive intervention where they are (Johansson, 1992; Blomberg, 1993). Health care charges to visit a doctor, for prescriptions and for hospital stay, also, rose considerably between 1989 and 1993 in order to reduce costs drastically and perhaps to discourage overuse or abuse of the system (Vår trygghet, 1988 and 1993).

As with other areas of social policy, a major change occurred within the field of health care, which did not at first sight seem to have much to do with the saving of public money. In the summer of 1993, a decision to introduce *husläkare* (family doctors or general practitioners) into the system seemed to have been taken after months of intense debate. Since this was going to create a need for 4000 doctors, who were either newly trained specialists in general medicine or retrained specialists from other fields, the cost was going to be considerable. The socialist opposition argued that it would damage the preventative work of the existing system of medical centres (*vårdcentral*), while the nonsocialists claimed that not only would patients be able to choose their own doctor but would benefit from the greater continuity of one physician. It seemed a strange innovation none the less at a time of public austerity. The following April New Democracy, with the socialist bloc, voted against *husläkare* but by then more than 70 per cent of the population had already registered with one (Johansson 1994).

More controversially, the government proposed to make the establishment of private practices for specialist doctors and physiotherapists much easier, a measure strongly opposed by the socialist bloc in the Riksdag (Deurell, 1994a).

Education

The 1980s had witnessed a consolidation of Sweden's achievements in education. However, it was felt by some that the emphasis upon equality and democracy in the early 1970s had been abandoned by both the Bourgeois government of the late 1970s and the Social Democrats during the 1980s (Ball and Larsson, 1989). A major change before 1991 was the transfer to communes of the responsibility for the running of local schools. Schools in turn were given greater freedom to manage their resources. Those cuts in expenditure which were made tended to affect the nonessential parts of the system such as adult education, language tuition for immigrant children and nonteaching staff (Gould, 1993a). The age at which children started school was to be reduced from 7 to 6, with the aim of cutting the comparatively expensive costs of child care.

The new Bourgeois government took many of these developments a stage further. A new national curriculum was introduced which de-emphasised practical and social subjects and emphasised the importance of Christian morality. Some communes began to charge pupils at the gymnasium for their, previously free, school dinners and plans were afoot to do the same for the *grundskola*. State grants to higher education institutions became dependent upon research success and student performance. The government took steps early on to encourage the development of independent schools and to give universities more autonomy. The introduction of a system whereby schools received a grant which followed the pupil had encouraged the setting up of many private establishments. By the end of 1993, 212 schools had been started or had been given approval to start by the new administrative board, Skolverket. For each pupil, these independent schools received 85 per cent of the grant that children attending local authority education received (Alfredson, 1993).

But as unemployment grew, any plans the government might have had to reduce expenditure had to be reexamined. Early attempts to reduce the numbers of adults receiving grants for basic education; to stop the expansion of two-year courses in gymnasia into three year courses; and to keep the lid on higher education costs, were all superceded by the recognition that in a time of growing unemployment it was cheaper to provide education places than expensive labour market training and job creation places. One of the last educational measures proposed by the Bourgeois government was to reduce the maximum amount of time for which employees could take study leave and to insist that its purpose be workrelated (SOU, 1994b, p. 41).

Employment Policy

Prior to the 1980s, Sweden's Active Labour Market policy had played a major part in reducing open unemployment when the economy slumped and providing selective measures to increase labour mobility in times of labour shortage (Hedborg and Meidner, 1984). Increasingly, in the last decade, the Labour Market Board has found itself coping with, initially, large numbers of unemployed young people and, more recently, adults as well. Moreover, the numbers of long-term unemployed has steadily climbed since the 1970s. Where the Labour Market Board's reputation in the past had rested on the high quality of its programmes and the relatively high remuneration which those undertaking them received, the arrival of mass unemployment has brought about an incentive to provide cheaper courses at lower rates of benefit. A Work Life Development programme which subsidises the costs to employers of taking on 50 000 unemployed people pays them less than those who were on earlier job creation schemes in the past (Deurell, 1993d). Similarly, the 75 000 young unemployed offered work experience places in 1992 were to receive less than those on previous training schemes (Larsson, 1992). A familiar development was taking place here whereby government deliberately sought to reduce the price of labour, particularly that of young people.

One of the earliest measures of the Bourgeois government had been to abolish the wageearner funds which had been a major feature of social democratic policy in the 1970s. With amendments to the employment protection law and the law on codetermination, the government also reduced the employment rights of individual workers and the rights given to trade unions to be consulted about redundancies (Gauthier, 1993c).

Winners and Losers

Given the recency of Sweden's attempts to control public expenditure, cut welfare benefits and services and tolerate high levels of unemployment, it is difficult to be precise about how the different socioeconomic groups have been affected by them. However, the effects of some of the changes are fairly obvious while others can be estimated.

There is considerable evidence to show that compared with other countries lower socioeconomic groups in Sweden, in the 1960s and 1970s, experienced a high standard of living and low levels of poverty. However, a number of studies have suggested that the trend towards a reduction in class inequalities has been reversed. Some suggest that the reversal began as far back as the early 1970s (Gould, 1993b, p. 170). This is reinforced by recent figures on class access to the theoretical course in gymnasia which lead to university education (Dahlin, 1993). Others, like Vogel, have argued that many socioeconomic differences narrowed from 1975 to 1985 but that since then the gaps have widened (Vogel, 1990). Either way the trend in the 1980s would seem to have been towards inequality rather than the reverse.

It is likely that events since 1989 have reinforced that trend. In particular it is clear that the tax reform of 1990, which increased indirect taxation and reduced direct taxation, and the seventy-five tax changes under the Bourgeois government, have favoured high income earners at the expense of low income earners (Deurell, 1993c; Stenberg, 1994a). Reductions in sickness benefit, work injury and unemployment benefit are likely to hit those groups in society who disproportionately suffer from ill health and unemployment. Not only have the numbers on social assistance increased but the rules governing the benefit have become more strict as the value of the benefit has fallen (Vinterhead, 1991).

Even the elderly, a group for whom it has been said that too much has been done in Sweden, have begun to suffer from the harsh economic climate. Although for some, decreases in the value of their pensions have been compensated by an increase in housing benefit, more pensioners today are dependent upon social assistance. While less elderly people live in institutions, it is also the case that fewer are receiving home help services. Over 250 000 had home helps in the early 1970s. Twenty years on that figure had declined to 150 000 (Jerket, 1994). Moreover, a series of reports in *Dagens Nyheter* and from *Socialstyrelsen* have cast considerable doubt upon the combined effect of reforms of elderly care, health care management and local authority financing. Elderly people are

facing higher fees for services, rehabilitation is not working well and geriatric wards are still overfull (Johansson, 1993b, September/October).
Pensioners with full ATP, however, have seen their disposable incomes rise in the 1990s while young people in the twenties have seen considerable drops in their income (Nilsson, 1994). As a result of the reform of ATP, most of tomorrow's pensioners will on average experience a drop of 12 per cent in their pensions, with immigrants and highly educated women being amongst the chief losers and poorly educated women amongst the few winners (Stenberg, 1994).

Jobs in manufacturing industry declined from 1 000 000 to 800 000 between 1989 and 1992 (Stenberg, 1992). Most of these are likely to have been male blue collar jobs. Consequently, young working-class men are increasingly finding it difficult to enter the labour market. Many white collar workers have also begun to experience redundancy and it is clear that cuts in the public sector are affecting women disproportionately. Women, however, are a powerful force in Swedish society and the formation of a cross-party alliance of women is determined to lessen the impact on them of social disarmament.

Ethnic minorities do not have the same influence and with more of them in low paid jobs, unemployed and in receipt of social assistance, their position is deteriorating. While political leaders continue to speak out and demonstrate against racism, there can be little doubt that resentment about immigrants and refugees is festering in some parts of Swedish society. The political response to this has been to be cautiously sensitive to nationalistic sentiments. According to Marklund, since 1988 refugees have had to claim an alternative benefit to social assistance (Marklund, 1992). More recently, the receipt of assistance has been made conditional upon the attendance by refugees at Swedish classes and work experience programmes (Brink, 1993). This harsher climate is also reflected in the school curriculum where Christian values are to receive greater emphsis than in the past. In the view of one philosopher, this represents a retreat from the 'open and pluralistic character' of Swedish society (Tännsjö, 1993).

In a recent report, *Socialstyrelsen* has stated that social cleavages in Sweden have been growing since the middle of the 1980s. Sweden is no longer the homogeneous society it was. Immigrants, young adults and single parents with children are twice as likely to have problems with money, housing and employment than Swedes, older people and two-parent households (Alfredson, 1994).

The Future

It is difficult to imagine the situation in Sweden improving rapidly in the near future. The budget deficit for 1993/4 was greater than expected and the predicted deficit for 1994/5 was still estimated to be very high. The forecast for economic growth was the lowest in the OECD although exports and industrial production were expected to grow by 8.1 per cent and 7.5 per cent respectively (Axelsson, 1993). The Finance Department still predicted that one in ten Swedish workers would be without a job even by 1998 (Stenberg, 1993). Prime Minister Bildt, opening parliament for his last year of office, said:

> The economic situation is improving gradually. Difficulties are however long from being beaten. A general improvement is still not in sight. On the contrary, economic policy must be directed to a restoration of a social–economic balance. The way back to consistent growth and full employment will be a long one. (Bildt 1993)

The electorate was not prepared, however, to give the centreright parties the task of dealing with this bleak future. The Social Democrats, despite their association with high spending and high taxation, were returned to office in September 1994 with an absolute majority over the four Bourgeois parties and only thirteen seats short of a majority over all the other parties. In part this demonstrated a reluctance on the part of Swedes to further dismantle their welfare state. Surveys had shown that support for publicly financed, publicly provided services remains consistently high. In 1994, only 22 per cent of the population claimed to prefer private medical care compared with 48 per cent three years previously (*Dagens Nyheter*, 1994). In part, the Swedes were returning to the traditional party of government after three years of coalition haggling.

But this was not just a return to the past. The Social Democrats were not intending to expand welfare provision or to proceed towards parliamentary socialism. They had proved through the support they had given to the centreright coalition on many occasions that they accepted the economic realities. In the shadow budget in May 1994, it had been made clear that while unemployment was seen as far too high, keeping inflation low was to be a high priority if they won the election. If jobs were to be created, it would have to be in the private, not the public sector. The tax advantages gained by the rich in recent years would be reversed and even higher taxes imposed, but strict controls would be imposed upon public spending and savings made. The Social Democrats recognised that the current crisis made burdens and sacrifices inevitable but claimed that under them these would be distributed more fairly (Gauthier, 1994).

However, it was also made clear in an interview with the party secretary, Mona Sahlin, that some of the reforms carried out by the bourgeois government would be reversed. The encouragement of private medical practice, of private child care and, through the care allowance, of women to stay at home would cease; as would the financing of schools whereby grants followed pupils. Employees' rights, eroded by legislation, would be restored (Karlsson, 1994).

The party election manifestos of all the major parties indicated an intention to improve Sweden's public finances. The Conservatives committed themselves to savings in all areas but refused to contemplate raising taxes. The Centre party proposed cuts in sickness benefit, parental benefit, child allowances and defence. The Liberals were prepared to advocate increases in taxation as well as to individual social insurance contributions. And with proposals to reduce defence expenditure drastically, they moved closer to the Social Democrats.

As the markets awaited the Social Democrats' manifesto, interest rates rose and the value of the krona fell. They rose again as soon as the manifesto was published. The Social Democrats announced their intention to improve the state's finances by SEK 61 billion, half through tax and employee social insurance contributions and half through expenditure savings. In addition to some expected cuts, one waiting day was to be introduced for parents claiming parental benefit for the care of a sick child; child allowances for large families were to be reduced; and pensions and study assistance were no longer to be protected against inflation.

If there was a common recognition that the economic situation demanded greater public stringency, there had also been a realisation that Sweden's political institutions required improvement for that task to be adequately performed. From September 1994 the lifetime of a Swedish parliament was to be four years. This was to enable future governments to focus their attention on the problems at hand and avoid premature electioneering. The budget process was also to change from 1996. Public income and expenditure proposals were to be placed before the Riksdag at the beginning of the parliamentary year, in September, and would come into force on 1 January the following year (the corresponding dates previously were January and July). The whole process was not only to be much shorter but more disciplined. Additional proposals for expenditure were to be matched by suggested savings (Sjögren, 1994). Both these domestic political changes went some way to meet the criticisms of the Lindbeck Commission mentioned above.

Sweden joined the European Union in 1994. At the time of writing the impact of EU membership on welfare is uncertain. It needs to be said, however, that despite the recent cuts in welfare, Sweden still possesses one of the most comprehensive and generous systems of welfare provision in Europe and the world.

Conclusion

Sweden has been reluctant to face the implications of the increased internationalisation and competitiveness of post-industrial, post-Fordist capitalism. It has at last been forced by circumstances to accept that its welfare state was conceived and developed at a time when national governments had considerably more control over their domestic economies than is now the case. Political and institutional problems have prevented the Swedes from making drastic changes to their welfare system in the past, but there is no doubt that present and future reforms are likely to continue to lead to cuts in benefits and services, or that the system will continue to move in the direction of welfare pluralism. However, the very scale and institutional significance of the Swedish model means that it will be some time before the Swedes descend to the levels of deprivation and inequality seen elsewhere in Europe. What is certainly clear is that the process of decommodification, described so well by Esping-Andersen, has been put into reverse.

Abbreviations

ATP The Swedish state earnings related pension.
LO Federation of manual worker unions
SAF Federation of employers' organisations
SEK The Swedish krona or currency
SOU Public commission

References

Alfredson, L. (1993) '212 fria skolor i höst', *Dagens Nyheter*, 18 August.
Alfredson, L. (1994) 'Allt fler fattiga i Sverige', *Dagens Nyheter*, 18 May.

Åmark, K. (1993) 'Vår tärande privatsektor', *Tiden*, no. 2.

Andersen, B R. (1993) 'The Nordic Welfare State under Pressure: The Danish Experience, *Policy and Politics*, vol. 21, no. 2, pp. 109–20.

Axelsson, O. (1993) 'Svenska tillväxten lägst i OECD', *Dagens Nyheter*, 2 July.

Ball, S. and Larsson, S. (1989) *The Struggle for Democratic Education* (Brighton Falmer:).

Bergström, V. (1993) 'Regeringens vision är att krossa facket', *Tiden*, no. 4.

Bildt, C. (1993) 'Regeringsföklaring', *Riksdag & Departement*, no. 30.

Blomberg, R. (1993) 'Risk för fel ingrepp', *Dagens Nyheter*, 12 January.

Boucher, L. (1982) *Tradition and Change in Swedish Education* (Oxford: Pergamon Press).

Brink, B. (1993) 'Högre krav att flykting lär svenska', *Dagens Nyheter*, 26 October.

Dagens Nyheter (1994) 'Allt färre litar på privat vård', 2 April.

Dahlin, A. (1993) 'Förlust för samhället när arbetarbarn inte studerar', *Riksdag & Departement*, no. 36.

Deurell, M. (1993a) 'Arbetslöshetsersättningen sänks', *Riksdag & Departement*, no. 13.

Deurell, M. (1993b) 'Enhetliga socialbidrag i hela landet', *Riksdag & Departement*, no. 14.

Deurell, M. (1993c) 'Skattereformen gynnar rika mer än fattiga', *Riksdag & Departement*, no. 24.

Deurell, M. (1993d) 'Alla är nöjda med Alu', *Riksdag & Departement*, no. 36.

Deurell, M. (1994a) 'Lättare för privatläkare att etablera sig', *Riksdag & Departement*, no. 1.

Deurell, M. (1994b) 'Pappamånad – praktisk jämställdhet', *Riksdag & Departement*, no. 8.

Deurell, M. (1994c) 'Lättare för privatläkare att etablera sig', *Riksdag & Departement*, no. 1.

Eklund, K. (1993) *Hur farligt är budgetunderskott?* (Stockholm: SNS Förlag).

Ekström, B L. (1993) 'Hur farligt är underskottet', *Dagens Nyheter*, 8 February.

Esping-Andersen, G. (1990) *The Three Worlds of Welfare Capitalism* (Cambridge: Polity Press).

Fernow, N. (1992) 'Swedish Elder Care in Transition', *Current Sweden*, no. 392.

Gauthier, K. (1993a) 'Sänket ersättning till arbetslösa', *Riksdag & Departement*, no. 22/3.

Gauthier, K. (1993b) 'Laglig rätt till dagis från ett års ålder', *Riksdag & Departement*, no. 25.

Gauthier, K. (1993c) 'Arbetsgivare i andra länder har mycket mer att säga om', *Riksdag & Departement*, no. 31.

Gauthier, K. (1994) 'S-märkta punkter för att få upp styrfarten för Sverige', *Riksdag & Departement*, no. 18.

Gould, A. (1983) 'Swedish educational leave in practice', Discussion paper no. 12 (Nottingham: Association for Recurrent Education).

Gould, A. (1993a) *Capitalist Welfare Systems* (Harlow: Longman).

Gould, A. (1993b) 'The Swedish Welfare State in Crisis', in Jones, C. (ed.) *New Perspectives on the Welfare State in Europe* (London: Routledge).

Heclo, H. and Madsen, H. (1986) *Policy and politics in Sweden* (Philadelphia, PA: Temple University Press).

Hedborg, A. and Meidner, R. (1984) *Folkhems modellen* (Stockholm: Rabén & Sjögren).

Jacobssson, C. (1994) 'Här fanns jobben som försvann', *Dagens Nyheter*, 26 February.

Jerket, B. (1994) 'Dyrare vård till färre gamla', *Dagens Nyheter*, 2 January.

Johansson, A. (1992) 'Färre åtgärder på sjukhus', *Dagens Nyheter*, 9 July.

Johansson, A. (1993a) 'Allt fler barn kastas ut', *Dagens Nyheter*, 7 July.

Johansson, A. (1993b) Series of articles on elderly care, *Dagens Nyheter*, September/October.

Johansson, A. (1994) 'Kaotiskt val i flera landsting', *Dagens Nyheter*, 25 March.

Karlsson, B. (1994) 'Beska vallöften från s', *Dagens Nyheter*, 21 February.

Kjellander, C-G. (1991) 'Vårdbidrag höjs med 30 per cent procent', *Dagens Nyheter*, 17 December.

Larsson, G. (1993) 'Handikappreform kostar 1 miljard', *Dagens Nyheter*, 3 December.

Larsson, L. (1992) '75,000 kan få praktikplats', *Dagens Nyheter*, 15 August.

Marklund, S. (1992) 'The Decomposition of Social Policy in Sweden', *Scandinavian Journal of Social Welfare*, vol. 1, no. 1.

Midfelt, R. (1993a) '100,000 handikappade får det bättre med ny lag', *Riksdag & Departement*, no. 17.

Midfelt, R. (1993b) 'Sänkt ersättning för arbetskada', *Riksdag & Departement*, no. 18.

Midfelt, R. (1993c) 'Alla barn får rätt till dagis och fritidsplats', *Riksdag & Departement*, no. 28.

Midfelt, R. (1993d) 'Ädelreformen dyr för sjuka åldringar', *Riksdag & Departement*, no. 30.

Midfelt, R. (1993e) 'Försäkringsbolagen får hand om sjukpenning', *Riksdag & Departement*, no. 31

Midfelt, R. (1993f) 'Ädelreformen har brister men fungerar i stort sett bra', *Riksdag & Departement*, no. 31.

Midfelt, R. (1993g) 'Fler förtidspensionäre än någonsin', *Riksdag & Departement*, no. 40.

Morris, R. (1988) *Testing the Limits of Social Welfare* (Boston, MA: Brandeis University Press).

Nilsson, M. (1993) 'Alla måste betala in till a-kassan', *Riksdag & Departement*, no. 32.

Nilsson, M. (1994) 'Ungdomar – ekonomiska förlorare', *Riksdag & Departement*, no. 15.

Ny start för Sverige, (1991) 'Moderarterna', Stockholm.

Olsson, S.(1988) 'Decentralisation and Privatisation in Sweden', in Morris, R., *Testing the Limits of Social Welfare.*

Pilsäter, K. (1992) 'Kvinnor drivs till spisen', *Dagens Nyheter*, 2 September.

Pontusson, J. (1992) 'At the End of the Third Road: Swedish Social Democracy in Crisis', *Politics and Society*, vol. 20, no. 3.

Riksdag & Departement (1993a) 'Arbetslösheten fortsätter öka', no. 26.

Riksdag & Departement (1993b) 'Växande köer till daghem', no. 25.

Schuck, J. (1994) 'Stortfall efter uppblåst 80-tal', *Dagens Nyheter*, 11 February.

Sjögren, P-A. (1994) 'Riksdagens budgetarbete förändras', *Riksdag & Departement*, no. 8.

Södersten, B. (1990) 'The Swedish Tax Reform', *Current Sweden* no. 375.

Södersten, B. (1992) 'Orgie i verklighetsflykt', *Dagens Nyheter*, 20 December.

SOU (1993) *Nya villkor för ekonomi och politik* (Stockholm: Riksdagen), p. 16.

SOU (1994) 'Reformerat pensionssystem', *Riksdagen & Departement*, no. 8, p. 20.

SOU (1994b) *Ledighetslagstiftningen – en översyn* (Stockholm: Riksdagen), p. 41.

Ståhl, I. (1993) *Suedo-sclerosis* (Stockholm: Timbro).

Ståhlberg, A-C. (1991) 'Lessons from the Swedish Pensions System', in Wilson, D. and Wilson, D. (eds) *The State and Social Welfare* (Harlow: Longman).

Statistiska Centralbyrån (SCB) (1985) *Statistisk årsbok* (Stockholm).

Statistiska Centralbyrån (SCB) (1986) *Statistisk årsbok* (Stockholm).

Statistiska Centralbyrån (SCB) (1993) *Statiskisk årsbok* (Stockholm).

Statiskiska meddelanden (1993) *Socialbidrag under 1992* (Stockholm: SCB).

Statistiska meddelanden (1994) *Socialbidrag under 1993* (Stockholm: SCB).

Stenberg, E. (1992) '40,000 jobb borta nästa år', *Dagens Nyheter'*, 15 October.

Stenberg, E. (1993) 'Många utan jobb trots tillväxt', *Dagens Nyheter*, 24 April.

Stenberg, E. (1994) '"Århundradets reform" vingklippt', *Dagens Nyheter*, 6 February.

Stephens, J. (1979) *The Transition from Capitalism to Socialism* (London: MacMillan).

Swedish Institute (1992) 'Child care in Sweden', Fact sheets on Sweden (Stockholm).

Tännsjö, T. (1993) 'Regeringen utfärdar yrkesförbud', *Dagens Nyheter*, 22 November.

Tomasson, R. (1970) *Sweden: Prototype of Modern Society* (New York: Random House).

Vår trygghet (1988) *Folksam* (Stockholm).

Vår trygghet (1991) *Folksam* (Stockholm).

Vår trygghet (1993) *Folksam* (Stockholm).

Vinterhead, K. (1991) 'Svårare att vara fattig', *Dagens Nyheter*, 10 December.

Vogel, J. (1990) 'Inequality in Sweden', in Persson, I., *Generating Equality in the Welfare State* (Oslo: Norwegian University Press).

Wetterberg, G. (1993) 'Varför gick det som det gick?', *Tiden*, no. 2.

5

The United Kingdom: Radical Departures and Political Consensus

PETER TAYLOR-GOOBY

Public expenditure is at the heart of Britain's present economic difficulties. (Public Expenditure White Paper, 1979, p. 1)

The UK welfare system was established in a series of reforms after the Second World War and evolved through three decades of expansion and modification. As in many countries, the system faced simultaneous pressures from rising demand, economic difficulties and political change by the early 1980s. The UK is unusual in that the same political party has held power from 1979 until the time of writing and has put the reform of welfare high on the political agenda. A consistent political regime enabled government in the UK to pursue a firm policy direction with exceptional vigour.

This chapter will chart the development of the various pressures on social provision and review the impact of policy changes in the 1980s and early 1990s. It will also consider how policy is likely to develop in the closing years of the century, taking politicians' proposals and the pressures of the demographic, economic and social context into account.

First, we must establish a baseline by giving an account of the main features of social welfare provision in Britain at the beginning of the 1980s.

The Social Welfare Services at the Start of the 1980s

Government social services in the UK can be conveniently grouped under five headings: cash benefits, health care, education, housing and the per-

95

sonal social services. In 1980, cash benefits accounted for just over 10 per cent of GDP, the National Health Service and education about 5 per cent each, housing about 3 per cent and personal social services under 1 per cent (Treasury, 1993, table 2.4). Over two-thirds of households received at least one cash benefit, and education and health care services were available to the entire population. Welfare services are the major government activity, accounting for just over two-thirds of public spending and touching the everyday lives of most citizens.

Cash Benefits

The UK scheme is an amalgam of policies with diverse objectives – income maintenance, the relief of poverty and compensation for costs such as those associated with child-rearing. It is administered by central government. There are three main types of cash benefits in the UK – national insurance, means-tested and non-contributory benefits. By 1980, the national insurance system accounted for nearly two-thirds of social security spending, the means-tested system about 15 per cent and the non-contributory system 20 per cent (Barr and Coulter, 1990, p. 287). The biggest slice of national insurance spending is accounted for by the retirement pension. This consists of a flat rate component, available to virtually all households on a contribution test, plus an earnings related component. UK pensions are relatively low, providing the equivalent of less than half take-home pay, against an EU average of 75 per cent (EU, 1994, p. 54).

Legislation in 1975 radically reformed the earnings related component with the intention that state pensions should gradually rise to about half average earnings for those who retired at the end of the century or beyond. In the early 1980s, the process of enhancement of pensions was just starting. In addition, most middle-class people in employment had access to state-subsidised and regulated occupational pension schemes. These supplemented state provision (CSO, 1981, table 5.15). By 1980 they covered about one-third of retired people (Barr and Coulter, 1990, table 7.5).

The other main insurance benefits were unemployment benefit (received by about 750 000 unemployed households) and invalidity and sickness benefits (received by just over a million – CSO, 1982, table 5.6). Entitlement to national insurance unemployment benefit is limited to one year and depends on contribution record. Over half those registered as unemployed were in fact not entitled to the national insurance benefit and were dependent on the assistance benefits. As in most European countries the use of sick and invalidity benefits was beginning to rise in line with the increasing pressures on employment.

The assistance scheme attracts considerable attention because of the discretionary power of officials, the relatively low level of benefits and the stigmatic associations of receipt in the minds of some of those entitled. The main benefits in 1980 were supplementary benefits (last-resort means-tested benefits) and family income supplement (available to low paid workers with children).

The principal non-contributory benefit was child benefit available to mothers in families with children. The benefit rate is equivalent to 8 per cent of GDP per head, slightly behind those for other Northern European EU member states (EU, 1994, p. 49).

The UK benefit system in the early 1980s was a complex mix of relatively low rate insurance benefits with assistance support designed to provide a safety net for the most vulnerable, some private and occupational welfare for the better off and a major non-contributory benefit – child benefit – for all families.

Health Care

State health care in the UK is provided by the National Health Service (NHS) run by central government and financed through general taxation. The service is enormously popular and is often seen as the 'flag-ship of the welfare state'. It provides hospital and GP services almost entirely free at the point of demand for virtually the whole of the population, and subsidised prescription medicines and optical and dental services. By 1980 only 6 per cent of the population were covered by private medical insurance (mostly paid for by employers) which would typically be used to secure swift treatment for specific acute conditions where there were long NHS waiting lists (CSO, 1982, chart 7.38).

Opinion differs over the quality of the services provided by the NHS. On international comparisons the UK ranks at the EU average on crude death rates and on average life expectancy (CSO, 1994, table 1.19). Its infant and perinatal mortality rates rank slightly behind France, Germany, Sweden and Italy (CSO, 1982, table 7.19). However the differences involved are not large. It is agreed that the UK gets its health care cheap. State spending is below that in all other major industrial countries, apart from the US, which has a large private sector (Hills, 1993, figure 38).

The main issues of debate are waiting lists and the influences of medical interests. The average waiting time was seventeen weeks by 1980, with delays of three years in access to non-urgent treatment in some areas (Le Grand *et al.*, 1990, p. 104). Medical professionals had considerable authority within the service particularly in resource allocation between speciality and area. Service users often found it difficult to represent their interests.

The medical emphasis resulted in a low priority being given to preventive medicine. Early detection services such as breast or cervical cancer screening were not routinely established, health education in relation to cigarette smoking, exercise and diet was minimal although there were large immunisation programmes.

The NHS stands in contrast to much of UK public provision in its comprehensiveness, its high public esteem and the evidence that it provides a good standard of care cheaply.

Education

The UK state education system provides mass schooling for the vast majority of the population between the ages of 5 and 16. In 1980, state preschooling was limited, although some children might enter primary school early if places were available. About 30 per cent of children stayed on in school beyond the age of 16 for a further year and 25 per cent entered further education institutions, half of them part time. Less than 20 per cent remained in school for two years after the minimum school leaving age of 16. Universities and polytechnics recruited almost entirely from this group and took less than 10 per cent of the age cohort, focusing mainly on children from middle-class families (Glennerster and Low, 1990, table 3A. 6; table 3.2). The majority of the less academic students were likely to leave at 16 and either enter the labour market (many of them becoming unemployed), or pursue further education courses of lower status than higher education and funded at about two-fifths of the level per head.

The school and further education system contained a delicate balance of power between central government, which set the legislative framework and controlled most of the resources, local government which had considerable discretion over structure and organisation and some influence over spending levels, and professional interests which were decisive in relation to curriculum and examinations. Higher education institutions were formally independent and financed from local and central government.

This dispersion of power led to wide variations in provision between different local authority areas in the amount spent on each pupil, the availability of preschooling and further education and the extent of selection and exclusion on grounds of academic ability. The influential, small but predominantly middle-class private education system mainly provides secondary and particularly 16–18 schooling.

International comparisons indicate that the UK system spends less on each pupil than do many industrial countries and its level of achievement for those of compulsory school age is modest. However, the relatively small group remaining in the system to the age of 18 do extremely well, for example coming top in the International Association for the Evaluation of Educational Achievement study in the early 1980s (IAEEA, 1988, table A.10). This confirms the picture of education in the UK as a mass system with a strong bias towards superior provision for an elite.

Housing

There are three main tenure categories in the UK and government policy provides a distinctive regime of support for each. The most significant is owner-occupation, which accounted for over half of all dwellings by 1980, followed by council-owned rented housing (just under a third) and renting from private landlords (under a sixth – CSO, 1982, table 8.2). A small proportion of homes were rented from non-profit-making housing associations.

Owner-occupation is extremely popular, due in part to the high degree of security involved, and in part to the favourable taxation subsidy system, which allows people to acquire a substantial asset with money borrowed at low interest from specialised non-profit lending institutions. The best housing standards are found in this sector. Over three-quarters of non-manual workers are home owners (CSO, 1994, table 8.24).

Council housing, the principal arm of social housing in the UK, is under the control of local government. About half the annual average cost of a council house was provided in subsidies by local and central government by 1980 (CSO, 1982, chart 8.18). Means-tested rent benefits were available to low income tenants. The system was successful in making subsidised housing of reasonable quality available to low income people, although it also provided for a number of those on middle incomes.

The limited subsidy system for private renting, coupled with rent regulation for much of this sector, made it unattractive to both tenants and landlords. The sector contained disproportionately more low income and unemployed households than either owner-occupation or council housing (CSO, 1982, table 12) and has the lowest level of amenities. Subsidies for this sector consist mainly of means-tested rent benefits for low income tenants.

Access to owner-occupied and privately rented housing is through the market. Local councils have responsibility for rehousing certain categories of homeless people which provides an access route for some of those in the most pressing housing need to the least attractive council housing. Nationally, the number of homes exceeds the number of households, but imbalances in supply in different areas and the inability to pay lead to severe housing stress for low income people especially in big cities.

Personal Social Services for the Elderly

Most elderly people live in the community with little need for support. Those who do need support in the main receive it from family, friends and voluntary workers with some private commercial provision (Webb and Wistow, 1987). Government services fulfil a limited role. The cost of statutory support was estimated at £3.8 billion by 1987, whereas the informal sector provided help worth over six times this amount (Family Policy Studies Centre, 1989).

State support is provided by local government. The emphasis in services has shifted from residential to community care. In 1985, over a quarter of people aged 75 or over received at least one service, but places in state residential homes were available to less than 4 per cent of this group (Evandrou *et al.*, 1990, pp. 252, 261).

This completes our brief review of the main features of social service provision in the UK at the beginning of the 1980s. The chief characteristics of the system overall are a moderate level of spending for the stage of development of the country, a complex interaction between basic universal provision and various mechanisms to facilitate the preservation of social class differentiation (for example, subsidy for private and occupational provision in pensions or housing, the superior standards for a minority in education), and the sharing of power between central and local government and professional groups of service providers. We move on to consider the challenges this system faced over the next decade.

The Environment of Welfare: New Developments in the 1980s

The main factors contributing to welfare debate concerned changes in population structure and family patterns, the rising level of unemployment, continuing economic difficulties and popular expectations of low taxes and good services.

University
of Ulster
LIBRA⌐

Demography

In the UK as elsewhere, demographic change and in particular the rising proportion of elderly people in the population dominated debate throughout the 1980s (OECD, 1988). Like other countries that had passed the 'second demographic transition' to a low birth-rate/low death-rate society, the UK faced the likelihood of a substantial increase in the number of elderly people at the same time that the population of working age was shrinking. The proportion of the population over retirement age was expected to rise from about a quarter in the mid-1980s to a third by the third decade of the next century (Ermisch, 1990, table 5).

Official calculations indicated that the benefits promised by the UK's pay as you go financed state earnings related pension scheme would require substantial increases in contributions in the next century, rising from under 20 per cent of earnings in the mid 1980s to over 30 per cent by the mid-2030s (DHSS, 1986). Since health and social care spending is heavily weighted towards older people, demographic change implies substantial increases in spending on this group – according to one estimate an increase of 70 per cent on the 1980 level by 2041 (Hills, 1993, figure 40).

It is possible to question whether demographic shifts are as disastrous as the determination of government to reduce spending on these grounds implies. A reduction in the proportion of younger people will lead to savings in education and unemployment benefits, health in old age may improve (Fries, 1980, p. 130), a fall in unemployment and a continuation of the trend for women to enter employment will mean that more people have occupational pensions (Falkingham, 1989, p. 276), and extra resources from economic growth may resolve the problem by the time it arrives. Over the period from the late 1951 to 1991, the number of retirement pensioners increased from 6.5 to 10 million and the level of benefits more than doubled in real terms (CSO, 1994, table 1.5). This was not viewed as a crisis since economic growth over the period provided the additional resources. In any case, the UK is favourably placed in its demographic structure. It faces a smaller increase in the proportion of elderly people than Japan, the USA and Northern and Western European countries (Ermisch, 1990, p. 48).

Whatever the accuracy of these comments, demographic pressures were the prime justification for a wholesale restructuring of pension policy which had the effect of cutting back the state earnings related scheme and encouraging people to take private pensions. It was also influential in reform of the health service and of personal social services for elderly people.

Some aspects of demographic change acquire more relevance when considered in the context of social change. First, the increase in the proportion of elderly people needing care coincides with a shift of younger women (who have traditionally provided the bulk of informal care) into paid employment. Either men will have to do more care work or the government and the private sector will have to fill the gap.

Second, the proportion of families headed by a single parent rose from 2.5 per cent in 1961 to 6 per cent by 1981 and over 20 per cent by 1992 (CSO, 1994, table 2.6; Table 1.7). Nine out of ten one-parent households are female headed, and the majority are dependent on state benefits. Whether one parenthood is an issue in itself is highly contestable. Concern has been expressed about benefit costs, the socialisation of children without fathers and about the poverty of many members of this group. Government policy is designed to cut benefit spending by enforcing stringent maintenance liabilities on absent parents.

Demographic change in general does not appear to provoke insuperable problems for policy, although the impact of change was affected by social context. The pressures on welfare can best be understood by considering other aspects of the social context which generate social needs and affect the ability to meet them.

Unemployment and Labour Market Change

The second distinctive feature of the policy environment of the 1980s was the very high level of unemployment. Unemployment in the UK peaked at over 13 per cent in 1983 (by the OECD definition) and remained close to the average for the decade of 10 per cent up to 1990. This was the highest level in any of the seven major industrialised nations (OECD, 1990, p. 130). Unemployment was particularly high among unskilled manual workers, young people and older workers, as in most countries, but rather lower among women than among men. In addition to high rates of unemployment, the proportion of part-time, low-wage and insecure jobs increased in line with government policy to develop a more flexible labour market by reducing regulation and trade union rights.

High unemployment in the 1980s placed increased pressure on the benefit system and reduced the revenue from income tax. Government policy officially placed greater priority on the control of inflation than on the reduction in unemployment, although a large number of schemes existed to encourage job training particularly among younger people. The impact of the high levels of unemployment was to limit the scope for manoeuvre in policy-making by throwing greater emphasis on the desirability of cost containment and to generate bitter party controversy over the priority that should be accorded to this issue. Labour market policy was the main factor that lay behind the British government's decision not to accede to the Social Chapter as contained in the Maastricht Treaty, and to press for a Europe based on free market principles rather than on social dialogue and on the closer integration of employment policies and benefit systems.

Change in the Economic Context of Policy

Apart from a short burst of growth in 1988 that was not sustained, the UK economy has continued to grow at a relatively slow pace compared with other industrialised countries. Growth rates again rose in 1994 and it is not clear at the time of writing whether this can be sustained. At 2.3 per cent the average growth rate over the 1980s was lower than in all seven major industrial countries, with the exception of France where it averaged 2.2 per cent (OECD, 1990, p. 181). The manufacturing sector continued to decline and the balance of payments did not improve. The level of public indebtedness as measured by the net public debt remained high compared with other Northern European countries at 41 per cent of GDP (France, Germany and Denmark all stand below 35 per cent – Table 1.10).

The government pursued cuts in direct taxation, reducing the standard rate of income tax from 33 to 25 per cent and the highest rate from 85 to 40 per cent. At the same time indirect taxes were increased, so that the tax burden was shifted to lower income groups. Official calculations indicate that overall tax bills do not fall until a family's income exceeds one and a half times average earnings (Hansard, Written Answers, 1990, vol. 176, cols 699–708).

The impact of the failure to resolve the country's long-standing economic difficulties, combined with the cuts in direct taxation and the fact that welfare spending was limited but not cut back in total, was that the government was forced to increase borrowing. This resulted in fiscal instability and withdrawal from the European Monetary System in the exchange crisis of 1992. Since the government placed great store by sound money in accordance with loosely monetarist principles, the effect was to redouble efforts to transfer state services to the private sector and to contain spending.

Shifts in Public Expectations

The evidence of opinion surveys and of the salience of welfare issues in election debates indicates strong public support for the main services and a high level of concern at the impact of reform particularly on the NHS and education. At the same time, tax cuts are highly popular and there is an undercurrent of suspicion of welfare cheats and of unnecessary state bureaucracy (Taylor-Gooby, 1991, pp. 112–19). The structure of opinion makes it difficult for government to carry out a direct frontal attack on the main areas of welfare spending, but suggests that there are possibilities for undermining support for welfare by focusing attention on the least attractive areas. It also indicates that tax cuts are desired if they can be dissociated from levels of service.

Over the period since 1980, the structure of need has changed as a result of high unemployment and an increase in the number of one-parent families. Further shifts are anticipated in future years as a result of population ageing. Continuing economic difficulties, coupled with government determination to reduce tax further, mean that state spending must be cut wherever possible.

The Response of the Government: New Policies in the 1980s

Britain was governed by the Conservative party for the period from 1979 to the time of writing in 1995. The party had very substantial majorities for much of that period and a charismatic leader from 1979 to 1989 who was able to set the terms of political debate. Circumstances were thus as favourable as they can be in a modern liberal democracy for the achievement of radical policy reform and for the maintenance of a consistent direction in policy. The response to the economic and social pressures outlined above in Britain has been more thoroughgoing than in most European countries, although demographic pressures are arguably less severe.

Policy developments in the 1980s and early 1990s pursued four main themes – containing the level of spending; expanding the role of the private sector; allied to this an extension of the use of markets; and a greater centralisation of power over the welfare system and over other aspects of national life. In this section we will review these changes and their impact on various social groups.

Containing Spending

The emphasis on spending constraint has been one of the most consistent policy themes. It is justified by three considerations: first, at the theoretical level the government pursued a monetarist economic policy that defined state spending as detrimental to economic growth because it pre-empts resources that might otherwise be used in the private sector of the economy, which is seen as the centre of 'wealth-creation'. Second, at the level of pragmatic politics, the popularity of the Conservative party was linked to tax reductions for the groups which contained its strongest supporters. In general, in British political debate consideration of taxation is divorced from consideration of the level of state provision, so that the undoubted popularity of the big-spending state services did not undermine this policy. Third, at the ideological level, the government allied itself to notions of individualism which justified tax and welfare spending cuts on the grounds that they left more money in people's pockets and thereby extended freedom of choice over 'what they do for themselves, their families and others less fortunate', as the 1987 election manifesto puts it (Conservative Party, 1987, p. 27).

In practice the government has pursued a large number of policies which have not substantially cut government spending across the board, but have contained the tendency for spending to increase as a result of the pressures detailed above and have reallocated resources between service areas. It is possible that some of the new policies may have opened the door to more substantial cuts in the future. The chief changes are in the areas of the reform of pensions and other cash benefits, and in the subsidy arrangements for social housing.

In 1982, responsibility for sick pay provision for the first six weeks of sickness was transferred to employers. Initially, the cost of occupational sick pay was subsidised by government, but the subsidy has been subsequently reduced. Government spending on sick pay fell from £1.2 billion in 1980 to £700 million by 1983 (Barr and Coulter, 1990, p. 333). In the same year, the indexation of cash benefits to wages was removed. Benefits are now linked to price increases only, and fall in relative value as real living standards rise. By 1988 this amounted to the equivalent of a 15 per cent cut (Ermisch, 1990, p. 47).

In 1987, the state earnings related pension was also cut back and incentives for individuals to 'opt out' of this component of pension provision and choose private personal pensions to top-up their basic state pension were introduced. The reforms weakened the indexation of the state earnings related pension, cut back the element of redistribution contained in it and halved the component of a spouse's pension that a surviving partner would be entitled to inherit. The object was to reduce public spending on the scheme by 50 per cent in comparison to what it would have been by the year 2000.

The stick of state pension cuts was reinforced by the carrot of tax subsidises and, for a limited period, contribution subsidies for those who transferred to private pensions. The result was a substantial shift, so that by 1993 4.95 million people had contracted out of the state earnings related pension scheme (DSS, 1993, p. 15). The reforms also included a package of deregulation measures for private schemes, which stimulated provision by cutting back the requirements for benefit indexation. The changes in pension policy achieved considerable savings in public spending. They also proof pension spending in the UK against the effect of shifts in population structure, since the private schemes are actuarially funded whereas the state scheme is pay-as-you-go financed. However, the pensions paid by actuarially funded schemes cannot be guaranteed against poor performance of investments so that future pension levels for many people are uncertain. The fact that the remaining state basic pension will be substantially lower in relation to earnings by the early years of the next century will minimise the impact of demographic change on government pension liabilities. In other European countries, most of which have pay-as-you-go schemes and face more thoroughgoing demographic shifts, the impact of population ageing on pension spending will be far more significant.

Alongside the pension reforms of the late 1980s, the main assistance benefits, Supplementary Benefit and Family Income Supplement were replaced by Income Support and Family Income Supplement. These benefits were calculated according to different principles, so that the system was able to discriminate more finely between the needs of different groups.

There is considerable debate about the impact of the changes on benefit levels. Official calculations suggested that only 12 per cent of claimers were worse off. However, other calculations estimate that up to 48 per cent are penalised and point out that the effect of these losses is exacerbated by the tax changes which have increased the liability of those on lower incomes (Barr and Coulter, 1990, p. 306; Johnson, 1990, p. 44). These changes have weakened the redistributive effect of the cash benefit system, in the face of the changes making for greater inequality over the 1980s. Between 1979 and 1991–2, all groups except the poorest tenth of the population experienced a real rise in incomes. In the case of the poorest group, incomes after housing costs actually fell by about 17 per cent (DSS, 1994). While the reasons for this shift involve a number of interrelated factors, the rise in poverty among unemployed people and other groups on benefits played an important role (Hills, 1995, pp. 61–2).

Further social security reforms in 1995 replaced insurance unemployment benefit, available for up to a year, with a 'Job-seeker's allowance' limited to six months and with the requirement that the recipient must show evidence of the continued pursuit of employment in order to receive the benefit.

In the area of housing, the object of government policy was to reduce the capital subsidies for local authority social housing. New building has been cut back radically, so that only 4000 homes were built by local authorities in the 1992, compared with 100 000 in 1980 (CSO, 1994, table 8.1). In addition, authorities are required to raise rents to market levels and to keep their housing revenue account in balance on an annual basis. The means-tested benefits to help low income tenants pay rent have become a charge on the local housing account so that better-off local government tenants are the first source of support for the poorest tenants. The result is that public spending on housing fell from 3 to less than 1 per cent of GDP between 1980 and 1993 (Treasury, 1993, table 2.4).

These changes allied with other social changes have increased housing pressure. The numbers presenting themselves as homeless to local authorities rose from 240 000 to 325 000 between 1986 and 1992 (CSO, 1994, table 8.14). One outcome has been the proposal that the obligation on local authorities to provide housing to homeless families should be removed.

Other changes designed to contain spending include treating benefits as income for tax purposes, keeping child benefit increases below the level of inflation, and in other social service areas, encouraging payment for state services such as home support services for the elderly, the sharp increases in prescription dental and optical charges in the NHS, the phasing out of maintenance grants to university students and the ending of the school meals subsidy.

These changes have enabled government to contain the impact of the pressures on state welfare expenditure spending and to enable further reductions in spending commitments in the future, although the high levels of unemployment have made it impossible to resist some increase in spending on benefits (see Table 5.1). They must be seen in the context of the transfer of some functions from the state to the market, to which we now turn.

Privatisation

The expansion of the private sector has helped to make possible the containment of demands for increased government spending discussed above.

TABLE 5.1   *Trends in public spending, 1978–79 to 1992–93; general government expenditure as a percentage of GDP*

	1978–79	1983–84	1988–89	1992–93
Employment and training	0.6	0.9	0.7	0.6
Housing	2.7	1.5	0.7	1.0
Education	5.4	5.2	4.6	5.4
Health	4.6	5.1	4.8	5.8
Personal social services	0.8	0.9	0.9	1.0
Cash benefits	10.0	12.1	10.5	13.2

Source: HM Treasury (1993), table 2.4.

It is also driven by the assumption that private provision is both more responsive to consumer demands and more efficient in the use of resources than are administratively organised services. Throughout the 1980s and continuing into the 1990s, a stream of privatisations have returned state-owned industries to the private sector wherever practicable, in the process generating once-off revenue for government. Thus water, gas, telecommunications, electricity, the national grid, airlines, airports, state-owned car and bus manufacturers, docks, ordnance factories and many other undertakings have been privatised through transfer of ownership by the sale of shares. At the time of writing, the selling of the remaining state-owned shares in denationalised power companies and the privatisation of the mail service and the railways are under consideration. In the welfare sector, privatisation has moved at a slower pace, and has typically involved the participation of private undertakings in the provision of state regulated services rather than a simple transfer of ownership from public to private.

The principal welfare privatisations are two – the vast extension of the scope of private pensions through the reforms outlined above and the selling off of council housing. Through legislation initially passed in 1980 and strengthened in 1984 and 1986 tenants of local authority housing were entitled to buy their dwellings at a substantially discounted price. Discounts of up to 70 per cent of valuation were available to longstanding tenants. Under these favourable terms, a considerable proportion of council housing and especially the more attractive three- or four-bedroomed houses were sold off. An additional scheme for the transfer of council housing away from public ownership, set up in 1988, permits the transfer of whole estates (unless a majority of tenants vote against the transfer) to the ownership of private landlords or non-profit-making independent housing associations. The housing association route has proved attractive in many authorities and has led to a considerable number of transfers. A total100 000 houses had been transferred by 1991 and negotiations covering a further 2 million are in train (Forrest, 1993, p. 46). Between 1980 and 1992, the proportion of housing owned by councils fell from 32 to 21 per cent (CSO, 1994, table 8.2).

There are a large number of minor extensions of the private sector in welfare policy. Many policies encourage the development of the private sector by weakening state alternatives. Examples of minor privatisations are schemes to extend tax subsidies for private medical insurance premia to those over 65, or the creation of a subsidy scheme for the purchase of private school places. Examples of privatisation by omission include the expansion of private drug dispensing following sharp restrictions on NHS dispensing, and the withdrawal of many dentists from the NHS in protest at rates of pay.

Welfare privatisations have gone furthest in those areas where spending constraints have been most vigorously pursued. They are associated with the extension of market principles into the state sector, to which we now turn.

Market Forces

Privatisation frequently results in the use of markets, although market choice is limited in cases like the transfer of housing estates to housing associations, where the range of willing estate managers between whom the tenants can choose in their ballot is often in practice limited to one. Policies which expand the use of market forces in welfare state services are often seen as paving the way to privatisation.

The trend to the use of markets as an administrative tool gathered force after 1987, especially in the highly popular services which had proved most resistant to privatisation – the NHS and education. The NHS was a highly centralised bureaucracy. Concern at the impact of spending constraint on NHS standards was particularly marked at the 1987 election, when such prestigious figures as the Presidents of the Royal Colleges of Physicians, Surgeons and Obstetricians entered public debate. The response of government was sweeping reform embodied in the 1990 NHS and Community Care Act. This legislation swept away the bureaucratic allocation of resources and substituted a market system. Budgets for patient care were to be held by individual family doctors or (where doctors were not willing to take on the role) by District Health Authorities. Services were to be purchased from the NHS's directly managed hospitals, clinics or facilities, from the new independently managed NHS 'Trust' hospitals, or from the private or voluntary sector.

For the most part this system runs as a market internal to the NHS. An analogous market system is to be set up in relation to social care services for vulnerable groups such as elderly people. Here local authority social workers act primarily as case managers, assessing and monitoring service recipients and allocating appropriate packages of services according to need. The services are purchased by the local authority from its own directly employed staff or from private or voluntary agencies. The service-users may be charged at different rates according to local policy and in some cases the authority may simply advise recipients to make their own arrangements with private care agencies.

These reforms set up a market in which choice is limited by government policy, and in which prices are also set. The education reforms follow a similar system. At the beginning of the 1980s, schools were managed by local government according to a framework of law laid down by central government, but with a considerable amount of local discretion. By 1988, the government had introduced a system of open enrolment, which made it much more difficult for schools to refuse to take particular pupils or for local government to plan the system by directing pupils to particular schools. Finance was allocated in proportion to the number of children a school recruited. Thus schools had strong incentives to compete for pupils and the least attractive ran the risk of entering a spiral of decline. The education market was strengthened by provision for schools to opt out of local government control entirely. In 1993, a new central government agency was set up to manage such schools, completely bypassing local government in some parts of the country.

Market reforms within the state sector are controversial. It is too early to judge whether the results show gains in efficiency and in responsiveness to the wishes of consumers (Le Grand and Bartlett, 1993, pp. 13–19). Most commentators agree that the changes strengthen both incentives and opportunities for service providers to pick and chose between consumers, with the likely outcome that the opportunities for the most attractive pupils and patients to secure access to the best facilities will be enhanced. Correspondingly, there is a tendency for consumers to differentiate between service providers.

Centralisation

Social welfare in the UK in the early 1980s was provided through a plural system of administration, which had grown up largely as a result of historical accident. Central government set the framework of law and inspection, and directly managed the NHS and the cash benefit systems. Local government managed most of education and social housing and personal social services, although these services were financed largely through taxes levied by central government. Professional staff with a high level of unionisation had a strong influence on the direction of the health and education service which made these areas highly resistant to change.

The reforms of the 1980s and early 1990s drew much of the power into the hands of central government, while placing considerable emphasis on the role of the citizen as a consumer. Thus central government through a series of measures effectively took control of local government's independent tax-levying powers, and removed much of its influence on education and social housing. The larger metropolitan authorities and the biggest English authority, the Greater London Council, were abolished in 1986. The extension of the market system weakened professional independence in the NHS and education, while the imposition of a detailed National Curriculum and compulsory diet of examinations in the latter area and the establishment of a restricted list of drugs in the former, together with new monetary controls tightened central control. A series of trade union reforms which ended the 'closed shop', curtailed the right to strike and made most forms of picketing, sympathetic industrial action and occupation of premises in pursuance of a trade dispute illegal, further weakened unions in the state welfare sector as elsewhere in the economy.

The UK's constitution, with its reliance on 'first past the post' voting and lack of a tradition of centre-party politics, is often seen as encouraging the development of strong central government. The changes in welfare go hand in hand with changes in trade union law, in the weakening of the independence of universities, in the conflict between state and church, and in the restrictions on media independence. The result has been a centralisation of power in the hands of government which facilitates further reform in welfare as in other areas.

The Effect of the Policy Changes

In general, the policy changes have had a fivefold impact. They have enhanced the role of means-tested assistance and private benefits, and reduced the role of national insurance benefits for old age, unemployment and sickness; cut state spending commitments, particularly in the area of pensions and cut back spending levels on social housing; shifted the organisation of the health education and personal social services in the direction of more pluralism in the detail of administration and more centralisation in control; and weakened the power of professional groups and trade unions in the welfare sector. Taken together these changes add up to a stricter delineation rather than a rolling back of the welfare state. They set the stage for a real reduction in government welfare activity in the future.

The impact on different groups in society can be considered along two dimensions: inequality and consumerism. Social changes in relation to the structure of employment, rising levels of unemployment and shifts in the patterns of family life have enhanced inequalities between the best and the worst-off groups (Table 5.2). The restrictions on the level of the basic national insurance pension, the weakening of the redistributive element in the state earnings related scheme and the substitution of private schemes, which were funded on a non-redistributive basis, reduce the capacity of policy to limit inequalities in old age; the constraints on benefits for unemployed people in the face of a shift in the tax burden in the direction of lower income groups means that the system is less well fitted to cope with poverty among younger people at a time of high long-term unemployment.

Inequality is also a theme in relation to the housing reforms, where the access of the weakest groups in the housing market to social housing has been limited by the cutbacks in subsidy and by the reduction in the available stock through the system of selling off. In relation to the internal market in the health, education and personal social services, it seems that providers will seek to cater for the most attractive consumers unless there are mechanisms which encourage them not to do so.

TABLE 5.2   *Income changes between 1979 and 1991*

	Percentage change in real income 1979–91/92
Bottom 10% of individuals	−17
11–20	0
21–30	+ 6
31–40	+16
41–50	+23
51–60	+29
61–70	+33
71–80	+39
81–90	+46
Top 10% of individuals	+62

Source: DSS (1994): income after housing costs for equivalent households. From 'Households below average incomes 1979–1991/2'.

In the NHS, the healthiest patients and those who do not make too many demands on their doctors are the most attractive. A recent report by the Association of Community Health Councils (ACHC, 1994) indicates that over 30 000 patients were removed by doctors from their lists in 1993–94 – more than twice the number before the reforms were introduced. In education, middle-class children who in general perform better in examinations and require less disciplinary resources are more attractive. There is already evidence that such children find it easier to secure a wider range of choice in the new educational market-place, and that the most demanding children, and especially those categorised as having special needs, are finding access to schooling more difficult to obtain (Taylor-Gooby and Lawson, 1993, p. 115).

Thus welfare reforms tend to make the new UK system more responsive to the structure of class inequality. In relation to gender inequality the pattern is more mixed. Social security changes bear most heavily on women, since they tend to be lower paid than men and are more likely to have interrupted patterns of lifetime earnings, so that they are less well able to gain good pensions from actuarially funded private schemes and are penalised by the weakening of the redistributive element in state schemes. The particular group of women who make up about 90 per cent of lone parents, most of them dependent on benefits, is affected severely by benefit cutbacks. However, gender and class inequality cut across each other. There is some evidence that middle-class women are relatively advantaged in the new education system, and are beginning to outstrip middle-class men in A-level performance and in entrance to higher education (CSO, 1994, table 3.18). The changes may well continue the process of assimilating gender and social class inequalities.

The reforms imply greater emphasis on consumer choice in areas like health care and education. As argued above, this may enhance the cultural and fiscal advantages of middle-class people. At the same time, it represents a response to public concern at the inflexibility of bureaucratic systems and may allow the development of more user control over services in the future. In the next section we consider the options for the development of welfare policy in the UK over the next few years.

Looking to the Millennium: Welfare under Altered Circumstances?

Policy over the past decade and a half has been directed by the assumptions of the party of government. That party is now suffering a substantial decline in popularity. A change of government at the general election due by 1997 appears possible. A review of the policy proposals of the opposition parties (Labour and the small Liberal Democrat centre party) indicates that electoral reverse might not alter the broad direction of policy. The following account is based on the analysis of 1992 election manifestos and other policy documents contained in George and Miller, 1994, chapters 2 and 10.

The main parties share agreement on the basic framework of public policy. At the economic level both are committed to a private enterprise economy, the prioritising of the reduction of inflation over unemployment, participation in the Single European Market and the view that any marked increase in direct taxation would be politically unacceptable. There are differences of detail. The Labour and centre parties would pursue a more active labour market policy involving a substantial training programme and a minimum wage, and would assent to the Social Chapter of the Maastricht Treaty. Both would undertake modest tax increases and would shift tax burdens towards the better off. However, no party is talking about a return to the nationalisation and industrial subsidy policies, to the trade union legislation and to the levels of direct taxation that existed in the 1970s. The landscape of public policy has shifted.

In relation to specific policies there are clearer differences. Opposition parties would spend more on national insurance benefits, the NHS, personal social services, further education, pre-schooling and social housing than the present government has been willing to do. However, they are extremely cautious about delineating proposed spending increases precisely, fearful that concern about the tax implications will deter voters. All parties accept the importance of the role to be played by the private sector in housing and pensions, with some difference of degree. All agree that the distinction between insurance and assistance benefits should remain (although the centre party is exploring a negative income tax scheme). There is also substantial agreement on the administrative changes which have created the managed internal market in the NHS, schooling and personal social services, although opposition parties would suggest a stronger role for local government. The debate on the pattern of social service provision is about emphasis and about fine-tuning of the level of spending rather than about the broad outlines of the system.

No parties are suggesting policy reforms that seem capable of restoring levels of welfare provision in the face of the challenges of the 1980s and 1990s. These concern rising unemployment, greater social inequality, continued industrial decline and, in the longer term, the needs of an ageing population. The Conservative government has retrenched state welfare and opened the way towards the establishing of a residual regime. The alternatives on offer would limit the pace of contraction and provide better standards for the most vulnerable groups, but they would do little to halt the increase in social inequality, or to prevent the more privileged groups from gaining access to superior standards of housing, pensions, education and probably health care which are publicly subsidised. In this sense the UK has passed a watershed. The prospects for a return to welfare citizenship are bleak.

References

Association of Community Health Councils (ACHC) (1994) Press release on research on GP fund-holding, *The Guardian* 11 July.

Barr, N. and Coulter, F. (1990) 'Social Security: Solution or Problem?', in Hills, J. (ed.), *The State of Welfare* (Oxford: Clarendon Press).

Bennington, J. and Taylor, M. (1993) 'Changes and Challenges Facing the UK Welfare State in the Europe of the 1990s', *Policy and Politics*, vol. 21, no. 2, pp. 121–34.

Cecchini, P. (1988) *The European Challenge 1992: The Benefits of a Single Market* (Aldershot: Wildwood House).

Central Statistical Office (CSO) (1970–94, annual) *Social Trends*, nos 1–24 (London: HMSO).

Conservative Party (1987) *The Next Moves Forward* (Election Manifesto) Conservative Control Office, London.

Dean, H. and Taylor-Gooby, P. (1992) *Dependency Culture – the Explosion of a Myth* (Hemel Hempstead: Harvester Wheatsheaf).

Department of Health and Social Security (DHSS) (1986) *Report by the Government Actuary on the Financial Effects of the 1986 Social Security Bill on the National Insurance Fund*, cmnd 9711 (London: HMSO).

Department of Social Security (DSS) (1993) *The Government's Expenditure Plans 1992–93 to 1994–95*, cm 1914 (London: HMSO).

Department of Social Security (DSS) (1994) *Households below Average Income, 1979–1991/92* (London: HMSO).

Ermisch, J. (1990) *Fewer Babies, Longer Lives* (York: Joseph Rowntree Foundation).

Esping-Andersen, G. (1990) *The Three Worlds of Welfare Capitalism* (Oxford: Polity Press).

European Community (EU) (1993) *Employment in Europe* (Luxembourg: Commission of the European Communities).

European Community (EU) (1994) *Social Protection in Europe* (Luxembourg: Commission of the European Communities).

Evandrou, M., Falkingham, J., Hills, J. and Le Grand, J. (1992) 'The Distribution of Welfare Benefits in Kind', Discussion Paper WSP68, STICERD (London: London School of Economics).

Evandrou, M., Falkingham, J. and Glennerster, H. (1990) 'The Personal Social Services', in Hills, J. (ed.) *The State of Welfare* (Oxford: Clarendon Press).

Falkingham, J. (1989) 'Dependency and Ageing in Britain', *Journal of Social Policy*, vol. 18, no. 2, pp. 211–34.

Family Policy Studies Centre (FPSC) (1989) *Family Policy Bulletin*, no. 6 (London: FPSC).

Forrest, R. (1993) 'Contracting Housing Provision: Competition and Privatization in the Housing Sector', in Taylor-Gooby, P. and Lawson, R. (eds) *Markets and Managers* Milton Keynes: Open University Press).

Fries, F. (1980) 'Ageing, Natural Death and the Compression of Morbidity', *New England Medical Journal*, vol. 303, no. 3, p. 130.

George, V. and Miller, S. (eds) *Social Policy towards 2000* (London: Routledge).

Glennerster, H. and Low, W. (1990) 'Education and the Welfare State: Does It Add Up?', in Hills, J. (ed.), *The State of Welfare* (Oxford: Clarendon Press).

Hansard, (1990), *House of Commons Proceedings*, House of Commons, London.

Hills, J. (1993) *The Future of Welfare: A Guide to the Debate* (York: Joseph Rowntree Foundation).

Hills, J. (1995) *Joseph Rowntree Foundation Inquiry into Income and Wealth*, vol. 2 (York: Joseph Rowntree Foundation).

International Association for the Evaluation of Educational Achievement (IAEEA) (1988) *Learning Mathematics and Science* (Slough: NFER).

Johnson, N. (1990) *Reconstructing the Welfare State* (Hemel Hempstead: Harvester Wheatsheaf).

Le Grand, J. and Bartlett, W. (eds) (1993) *Quasi-Markets and Social Policy* (London: Macmillan).

Le Grand, J. Winter, D. and Woolley, F. (1990) 'The National Health Service – Safe in Whose Hands?', in Hills, J. (ed.) *The State of Welfare* (Oxford: Clarendon Press).

Office of Health Economics (1987) *Compendium of Health Service Statistics* (London: OHE).

Organisation for Economic Cooperation and Development (OECD) (1988) *Ageing Populations* (Paris: OECD).

Organisation for Economic Cooperation and Development (OECD) (1990) 'Economic Outlook', no. 47 (Paris: OECD).

Taylor-Gooby, P. (1991) *Social Change, Social Welfare and Social Science*, (Hemel Hempstead: Harvester Wheatsheaf).

Taylor-Gooby, P. and Lawson, R. (eds) (1993) *Markets and Managers* (Milton Keynes: Open University Press).

HM Treasury (1993) *Public Expenditure Analyses to 1995/96*, cm 2219 (London: HMSO).

Webb, A. and Wistow, G. (1987) *Social Work, Social Care and Social Planning* (London: Longman).

6

Italy: Right Turn for the Welfare State?

MAURO NIERO

> Every citizen unable to work and without the necessary means of subsistence has the right to maintenance and social assistance. It is the right of workers to have the means adequate to their necessities of livelihood foreseen and provided for in the case of injury, sickness, disablement, old age and involuntary unemployment. (Italian Constitution, 1948)

Article 38 above of the Italian Constitution of 1948 (Moss and Rogers, 1980, p. 161) reflected the welfare philosophy of the past rather than the new and more positive role of the state in welfare envisaged by such reports as those of Beveridge in the UK, Laroque in France, and so on. It talked about 'maintenance' for those 'unable to work' rather than national unity and social rights for all. For this reason, even though social expenditure in the 1960s and early 1970s as a proportion of GDP was high by OECD standards (see Table 1.2), the philosophy and the method of provision of welfare were dated. It was not until the late 1970s that Italy adopted a universalist approach in the area of health and also extended its social security system to most groups in society. Interestingly enough, this climax in the development of social policy in Italy was reached at a time when the welfare state was already under attack in many other West European countries.

It was not long, however, before debates on the crisis of the welfare state surfaced in Italy, too. Questions were raised about the muddling through of its decision-making process (Donolo and Fichera, 1981); the patchwork of its underlying philosophies (Ardigo, 1976); the overwhelm-

117

ing dominance of the public sector and the lack of public participation (Donati, 1978); its legislative overregulation (Ascoli and Dente, 1985; Dente, 1985); and the nature of the political market with its aberrations of patronage, clientelism and corruption (Rusconi, 1984; Ferrera, 1985; Pizzorno 1992).

Although several proposals for a more modern welfare state emerged from this debate, they were left practically unattended. Instead, governments of the 1980s introduced a number of restrictive reforms designed to keep inflation and public expenditure under control without altering the guiding principles of the welfare state. The insufficiency of these measures as well as the lack of an overall strategy led to the radical policy changes of the early 1990s (Saraceno and Negri, 1994). This could be seen as a new watershed in Italian welfare state policy, the nature of which is still unclear and confused. It is taking place at a time when the Italian political scene is changing radically with the rise of a new right government.

While the 1980s and the early 1990s will be the focus of the central sections of this chapter, the last section will try to outline some possible future developments during the remaining years of this decade. This is always a difficult task but particularly so today with the current political turmoil and the extremely fluid political situation in Italy.

The Social Services at the Beginning of the 1980s

As already mentioned, the late 1970s witnessed a wide expansion of welfare provision. Beginning with health care, the National Health Service introduced in 1978 has to be seen as the first universalist welfare state scheme ever introduced in Italy (Ferrera, 1993). It was also the most symbolic example of decentralised policy. It instituted regulations at the regional level while local authorities (*Comuni*), through local health units, provided services to the local population. The local health authorities (USL) were responsible for the management of hospitals; for medicine provision; for general practice through ageements with GPs; for specialist consultations; laboratory tests; preventive services such as hygiene, environment, work medicine; for psychiatric services since psychiatric hospitals were suppressed in 1978; and for family planning services.

Despite the fact that all these services were generally devised as universal and free, user charges were introduced and inequalities in service standards soon became apparent. At least three reasons explain this state of affairs. First, there was the very mechanism of funding that was used for the new service. The National Health Fund was composed mostly by contributions while general taxation was used to top up any imbalances in the fund. Second, the lack of an overall National Health Plan (foreseen but never actualised) proved to the advantage of the most affluent and best organised regions and towns. Third, there was the creeping adoption of user charges for such services as laboratory tests and medicines. This took place very early in the life of the NHS, in an effort to contain costs. They became part of the service, they were made means tested and refined several times during the 1980s (Niero, 1993).

Social Security Benefits

In social security, the benefit system was expanded and centralised while the provision of personal social services was decentralised. Although using different adjectives, the literature on the Italian social security system seems to agree upon classifying it as occupational (Alber, 1983; Ferrera, 1985; Esping-Andersen 1990).

As in other such systems, its structure was very fragmented due to the struggle waged by the various parties over many decades. Nevertheless, in the Italian case fragmentation proved to be particularly accentuated and it went on increasing during the 1970s (Regonini, 1990).

The INPS (the National Institute of Social Insurance), which managed up to 85 per cent of the pension system, was (and is) divided into four main funds (employees, self-employed farmers, self employed tradesmen and salesmen) and into more than forty other minor funds. Funds for civil servants were managed by the Treasury. As in many other countries, public employees were treated more favourably than private employees both as regards the formula of calculating pensions and the minimum contribution years necessary for qualification. Substantial differences also existed between the main funds administered by the INPS, especially between the self-employed and employees. Dissimilarities affected the levels of coverage, the contribution conditions and, in the case of retirement pensions, the age of retirement (Sarpellon, 1982).

Unemployment benefit was calculated at 20 per cent of the previous earnings for a maximum of 180 days per year. In special cases, the unemployed were assisted by a fund named *Cassa integrazione guadagni* (fund for the integration of earnings, INPS). This provided the temporary unemployed with benefits of 80 per cent or more of the previous earnings. Another measure connected with unemployment was the *prepensionamento* ('premature retirement'), namely the provision of pensions to industrial workers who were made redundant three years prior to the retirement age. These two kinds of provision had to be authorised by the government and they were seen as tools of labour flexibility in support of an active industrial policy.

The compulsory period of maternity leave for women was two months before and three months after the birth of the child at 80 per cent of the mother's previous wages plus six months of optional leave at 30 per cent of wages. Moreover, the job had to be kept open for the mother for a period of one year after the birth of the child. There were also provisions enabling the husband to take post-natal leave in the place of his wife. As in other benefits, there were significant differences between the provisions of the various funds (Ferrera, 1985; Regonini, 1985; Rossi 1990).

Assistance benefits in cash were provided by various levels of the institutional framework. Most of them, however, were supplied by the state level or the INPS (Artoni and Rangi-Ortigosa, 1989; Niero, 1992). This latter's main non-contributory provisions are: non-contributory retirement pensions; *integrazioni al minimo*, providing a minimum pension to those who had incomplete contributory situations; family allowances (*assegni familiari*), always provided by INPS. The state, however, provided war pensions directly, non-contributory invalidity pensions, and pensions for the blind, the deaf and the dumb.

Local Authority Assistance

The above network of social security benefits was complemented by a range of assistance benefits provided by local authority institutions. They were means tested and discretionary for low income people in need, irrespective of whether they were already in receipt of a pension for invalidity or old age or were receiving a wage. As expected, a homogeneous rationale for these local authority assistance benefits was not devised with the result that different minima were adopted in the various areas. Unlike many European countries which provide a uniform national assistance benefit, Italy relies on a multiplicity of varying local authority schemes.

In addition to assistance benefits, local authorities were responsible for the provision of personal social services through funds channelled from the state to the regions. These services included means-tested contributions for residential care for the elderly, the handicapped and children; for community and home services for the handicapped, the elderly and the family; for laundry, hot meals, and so on. Finally, local authorities were authorised to provide precompulsory education such as crèches and kindergartens, and accessory services for schools such as transportation and cafeterias.

In the course of the 1980s, services for young people such as day centres, information bureaux, delinuency prevention, etc. were also added in several areas. However, all these local authority services were very unevenly distributed. In the course of the 1980s all regions had laws for cash benefits and home care but it is unclear how many municipalities really implemented them (Artoni and Rangi-Oxtigosa, 1989).

A couple of observations need to be added to this brief discussion of local authority services. First, in several regions an attempt was made to integrate health and social assistance with varying degrees of success. Second, voluntary and cooperative social service associations (especially social assistance) oppeared at the beginning of the decade and grew in importance in the following ten years, partly as a result of legislation to deal with youth unemployment.

Education

Moving now to education, compulsory schooling was raised to the age of 14 years in 1962. Compulsory education was mostly managed by the state (as it is now) and was completely free, except for the purchase of books which is the financial responsibility of families in the three years of middle school, that is ages 10–13 years. As mentioned above, precompulsory education (0–3 years) was provided through crèches and kindergartens (3–5 years) managed by the local authorities. Vocational training (age 14–16) was managed by the regions while high school (age 14–18) was (and is) managed by the state. High schools have always been divided into diffcrent kinds: classical, scientific, commercial, industrial and other minor branches.

University education is generally managed by the state and the curriculum usually lasts for four years, except for medicine which is six years and for engineering, architecture and psychology which are five years. Money provisions for low income students (*presalario*) have been devised over the years. The *presalario* has decreased in importance in recent years (Capparucci and Frey, 1988), while its rationale is being revised in the light of the new policy affecting the autonomy of universities in the 1990s.

Housing

Social policy for housing has consisted of several measures. At the beginning of the 1980s, housing for low income families managed by the

Communi and the ICAP (Institute for Public Housing) was one of the lowest in Europe (Sarpelion, 1982). A policy of fair rents (*equo canone*) was introduced in 1978 attempting to regulate the market level. In one sense, the scheme proved successful for it protected tenants against high rents. On the other hand, however, the scheme led to the decline of the privately rented sector as many landlords found it more profitable to sell their houses or flats. This in turn created a strong demand for owner occupation with the result that house prices rose enormously, thus creating a serious problem for those in search of a house. A policy for the '*sfrattati*' was then initiated by the *Communi* which provided assistance for tenants who received notice to quit and who had no other solution at their disposal.

Although the problem of totally homeless persons has been highlighted only recently (Commissione di Indagine, 1992, section 4.2, in CENCIS, 1992), some of its characteristics are clearly related to the inadequacies of policies for such groups as psychiatric patients, alcoholics, and ex-prisoners. These groups together accounted for 35per cent of the homeless in researches carried in the mid-1980s (see Berzano, 1987). Moreover, their average age seemed to be worryingly increasing in the course of the 80s. Despite this information, only some local authorities and voluntary organisations in areas where the problem is most acute have introduced relevent housing programmes in the 1990s.

Economic, Demographic and Social Changes during the 1980s

As in many other European countries, the great worries of the 1980s can be summarised under three headings: inflation, increase of public expenditure and the ageing of population.

Population and the Position of Women

Beginning with the issue of population ageing, the average rate of fertility today is 1.2 children per woman – the lowest rate ever recorded and also one of the lowest rates among EU countries. Fertility rates have implications for the proportion of elderly persons in the community and ISTAT's demographic forecasts are very gloomy. According to its most optimistic hypothesis (fertility increasing), the population over 65 will be as much as 133 per cent of the population under 14 by 2038. If fertility remained constant, the corresponding rate would be 280 per cent and the Italian population would fall from 57.5 million (1988) to 46.6 million by 2038. While the first hypothesis looks too optimistic, a third hypothesis put out by ISTAT has been neglected here because of its excessive gloominess (ISTAT, 1989b). The second hypothesis appears to be the most realistic.

The reasons for this trend in fertility are similar to those in all other European countries: the increase in women's participation in higher education; the growing employment rates for women and their aspiration for even higher rates; and the cultural change concerning women's role. Starting from the 1980s female participation in post-compulsory education (14–18) was 2 per cent higher than that of males, while for university education the rates for men and women became equal by the end of the 1980s (De Sandre, 1991). Meanwhile, women's employment rate, although much lower than in Northern Europe, increased from 31.5 of those in employment in 1981 to 34.5 per cent of the employed in 1990. Women's aspiration for employment is very strong and still partly hidden. This is testified by the fact that during the 1980s, the employment rates of girls aged 14 to 24 years reached the same rates as those of boys in Northern Italy, although in the South the difference was still significant (CENSIS, 1992). The proportion of men aged 15–64 in employment declined by 5.9 per cent during the 1980s while the corresponding employment ratio for women increased by 2.4 per cent during the same period (OECD, 1994, table 16, p. 115).

Finally, these increases in the employment and education rates of women have to be located in the more liberal moral attitudes that followed the social movements of the late 1960s. They made possible more liberal family and sexual lifestyles and contributed to the introduction of various pieces of relevant legislation. Thus divorce was introduced in 1970; the advertisement of contraception was allowed in 1971; family planning ser vices in 1975; and abortion was made legal in 1978.

Family changes have also been quite substantial during this period. The average family size declined from 3.6 in 1960 to 3 in 1988. The extended family, which was the general pattern of life, showed the most remarkable decline all over the whole country during the 1980s, including Southern Italy (ISTAT, 1989c). This inevitably led to an increase in the number of people living alone from 10.6 per cent of all families in 1960 to as much as 16.3 per cent in 1988. This rise particularly affected women of the older age groups for obvious demographic reasons. In 1988, one woman in two was living alone after the age of 75, while the corresponding proportion for men was only 1 in 8 (De Sandre, 1991).

In contrast to the situation in the Northern European countries, the proportion of one parent families is low and does not seem to be increasing at the moment. This group of families amounts to 9.2 per cent of all families with two or more members and only as much as 2.5 per cent had children under 18 (Rossi-Sciumi and Scabini, 1991). This may well be due to the lower divorce rates of Italy compared to those of Northern Europe. Similarly, the rate of cohabiting couples is much lower than in northern countries. A study made on 1984 data showed that cohabiting couples were only 1.2 per cent of all couples with children (De Sandre, 1991). Moreover, the trend was flat and it seemed to be a generational peculiarity. These couples came mainly from among the immediate post-war generation – those born between 1944 and 1953.

Employment

Turning now to levels of employment, Italy has witnessed a similar trend to other European countries, that is a rise in unemployment rates from 5.4 per cent of the labour force in the mid-1970s to as much as 12 per cent in 1987 (Conti and Cossutta, 1986; OECD, 1987; Valli, 1988). The typical unemployed person can be said to be mostly young, female and southern Italian. Thus, although in 1991 the general unemployment rate was 11 per cent (European average was 9 per cent), the unemployment rate of people under 25 was 30 per cent compared to the EU average of 15 per cent (Pugliese, 1993).

As expected, there is no agreement on the causes of and solutions to unemployment (Maruani *et al.*, 1990). Traditionally, trade unions supported policies aimed rather at protecting the employed than helping the unemployed or fostering youth employment. This is reflected by the dubious popularity of measures such as the *contratti di formazione-lavoro* (law 285, 1977) that introduced part-time work for youth with less social security charges for companies. It showed a decline after an apparent initial success. Instead, the 1970s witnessed the increasing use of the *Cassa integrazione guadagni* which was seen as the most relevant measure against unemployment. Nevertheless, its success as a tool for labour market flexibility was very questionable (Garonna, 1988). This problem was treated more seriously in 1984 by a law (no. 863) which introduced limited time and part-time contracts besides the contracts of solidarity ('working less by working all' in companies in crisis). The same law improved the *contratti di formazione-lavoro*.

The outcome of all these changes was not as substantial as was expected. The use of contracts of solidarity has been very modest in the 1980s accounting for only 500 out of a total of 220 000 workers from 1984 to 1986

(Gasparini, 1988). Part-time contracts did not prove a significant solution either, since they amounted to only 5.3 per cent of all contracts (Eurostat, 1987). Instead a solid increase of jobs created by the new regulations on the *contratti di formazione-lavoro* took place. The success of this formula culminated in 1989 with 529 297 newly employed youth (Gasparini, 1988; CENSIS, 1992) but it has been declining in more recent years.

Immigration was another issue that had implications for social policy developments during the 1980s. During this decade, Italy changed from a labour exporter into a labour importer (EEC, 1991) thus experiencing prolems of racial and cultural conflict that were totally unknown before. As elsewhere, immigrants suffer more from unemployment, low wages and other forms of discrimination in the labour market. In addition, there are several other problems which are created by illegal immigrants whose exact numbers are unknown (Natale, 1990).

Public Expenditure

Public expenditure as a percentage of GDP roce from 28.9% in 1960 to 53.1% in 1990. Expenditure on social security and on paying the interest for the public debt show the sharpest increase. The rise in social security expenditure is the result of both demographic and economic factors associ ated with the rise in unemployment. The rise in the public debt was the result of the low taxation policies pursued by governments in the late 1960s and 1970s. The reasons for these policies have been discussed in both the international literature (Ferrera, 1985a; Wilensky and Luebbert, 1985) and in the national literature (Romani,1980; Franco, 1993). They enabled governments to meet public demands for more services without raising taxes and thus avoiding public tax revolts experienced in other countries. It was, however, a policy that could not continue indefinitely and taxes had eventually to be raised. They now account for 42 per cent of GDP compared with 30 per cent in 1980. Despite this and other fiscal measures, inflation and interests rates rose pushing up the size of the public debt which is now seen as the most serious concern for any government (Salvemini, 1992).

The Impact of Social Policy Changes during the 1980s and the Early 1990s

After the major policy reforms of the late 1970s, the 1980s witnessed minor policy changes only, leaving the more important reforms for the early 1990s. Nevertheless, these minor changes had implications for the nature of the welfare state and it is these that we examine in this section.

Health Care

Despite the introduction of user charges in the NHS, costs continued to rise because of the price of drugs. During the 1980s, pharmaceutical companies increased the price of medicines thus neutralising the impact of user charges (Niero, 1993). This problem seems to have been overcome only recently by a new system of user charges. Hospital expenditure, too, showed a significant increase during the 1970s and the 1980s as a percentage of GDP. Calculations made by Franco (1993) showed that this increase could be attributed mainly to the salaries and wages of the hospital personnel. At the same time, the reduction in both the number of hospitalisations per person and the decrease in the average length of stay per hospitalisation helped to offset some of the high personnel costs.

Despite the fact that the NHS was seen as available and largely free to everyone at the point of consumption, general research highlighted inequalities in access brought about by organisational as well as cultural attitudes towards health services. The use of community health services (GPs, specialists' consultations, and so on) was higher in northern regions; similarly, people living in small and peripheral Comuni showed a higher use of hospitals irrespective of region (ISTAT, 1985). Also, those with low income and the elderly were more likely to be in hospital than other population groups.

During the 1980s, health standards rose, morbidity and mortality rates declined but health inequalities persisted. It is, of course, very difficult to know how much of all this is due to improvements in medical services or to the adoption of healthier lifestyles. Research carried out during the 1980s showed (ISTAT, 1990) that a non-educated person had a double risk of dying (between the age of 14 and 54) than a graduate. Other research, however, showed that mortality from the so-called welfare illnesses of cancer and cardiovascular diseases was lower in deprived regions (Geddes, 1990). Within the same areas health differentials were shown to be always in favour of the educated and the white collar groups. Child mortality has decreased considerably in the last decade (1979–80 = 14.8; 1988–90 = 8.8), and differentials between southern and northern regions have also narrowed.

Since its institution, the NHS has been stigmatised for its lack of quality and the Eurobarometer showed that the Italians were the least satisfied with their NHS among European citizens (Eurobarometer, 1993). It is for this reason that the controversial reform of the NHS in 1992 took place with total public indifference.

According to this law, the local health units and the hospitals will be separated from the Local Health Authorities of which they are now part. They will be transformed into independent enterprises, responsible for their administrative and financial affairs. Health enterprises cannot go into debt except in very narrow circumstances regulated by law; regions provide a share of the national health fund to each enterprise which cannot be refunded *ex-post* and they are obliged to balance their accounts, and so on. In exchange private rooms are provided for patients who are prepared to pay; doctors employed by the hospitals are allowed to practise private medicine in the same hospitals and a percentage of their fees from private consultations is paid to the hospital administration. Different insurance schemes will be promoted by the regions starting from 1995, for example by the institution of voluntary mutual organisations, which would allow their members access to particular conditions or services. Internal market rules are likely to be adopted within the agreements with GPs which are designed to turn them into fundholders.

Universalism in health care services will be decidedly jeopardised by this law. It foresees the creation of a sort of dual regime in health provision and a strong development of the private health sector. Moreover, though introduced as a measure to contain and reduce public expenditure on health services, several authors have concluded that its impact on expenditure is very questionable (Granaglia, 1993; Prezioso, 1994).

Pensions

The Italian pension system of the 1980s appears as undoubtedly very generous by European standards. Kangas and Palme (1989) showed that the replacement rate for the pension of a worker in manufacturing was around 70 per cent of earnings in 1980 compared with 53 per cent for a German worker and 40 per cent for a worker in Britain. Franco (1993) shows that the increase in social security expenditure during the 1980s was due especially to the high number and level of retirement and invalidity pensions for workers, while the cost of other kinds of provision, such as unemployment allowances and family allowances, decreased or showed very modest increases during the decade.

The indexation of pensions to wage rises and the calculation of pensions as a proportion of wages, rather than on the contributions record, pushed expenditure upwards in the course of the 1970s and increased it further in the first years of the 1980s. The high level of inflation was another contributory factor for this.

A revision of the indexation system (as an anti-inflation measure) in 1984 seemed provisionally to have kept expenditure under control, although very soon afterwards other measures such as the increase in minimun pensions pushed expenditure in the opposite direction. Tight controls on contributory invalidity pensioners were introduced in 1993 in order to reduce potential fraud in the system. Contributory invalidity pensions that were connected with clientelistic practices (Ferrera, 1985; Dente, 1990) were used as sorts of social minima in Southern Italy. Though the cost of contributory invalidity pensions has recently declined, a shift of these pensions to non-contributory invalidity pensions is more than likely, since these latter increased heavily in importance during the decade.

Family allowances also saw several changes. Having been revised in 1982 and in 1988, they are now provided according to family size and household income. Benefits for the unemployed and for job creation were also changed during the 1980s. At the beginning of the decade, the law on *prepensionamento* was revised. Its use was made simpler, and more than 350 000 *prepensionamenti* took place in this decade compared with only 1000 in the 1970s under the previous law. The coverage of the *Cassa integrazione guadagni* decreased by covering no more than 55 per cent of the previous earnings compared to 85 per cent or more, previously.

Data provided by Ascoli (in Paci, 1993) show several types of inequalities in the pension sytem. Inequalities between workers of private and public sectors have already been referred to. Class inequalities were obvious by the fact that at the end of the 1980s one-quarter of the pensions in the private sector was not beyond the minimum level. Regional inequalities are shown by the fact that the average level of pensions in the South was much lower than in the North, due to the different average years of contribution and the relevant use of *integrazioni al minimo*. In 1986, the level of the INPS pensions in northern regions was 3 per cent over the national average while in Southern Italy the level of pensions was as much as 10 per cent below this threshold. Gender inequalities were also much in evidence. While only 10 per cent of men's pensions was provided as *integrazioni al minino*, the corresponding figure for women was 36 per cent whose average pension is 26 per cent less than the men's average.

The pension system has been thoroughly revised by the legislation of 1992. The reform aims to decrease the impact of the overall pension system on public expenditure and to reduce the fragmentation of pension schemes by gradually adopting similar treatment for schemes of all employees. Nevertheless, the minimum age for retirement will be raised progressively to 60 for women and 65 for men by 2001; pensions will be calculated for all on average earnings of the last ten years; for those who started their working career after 1992, pensions will be calculated on the average earnings of their working life. In addition, indexation will be made on prices instead of wages, as it is now. Finally, supplementary voluntary pensions will be encouraged.

Education

No significant institutional reforms were introduced in the field of education during the 1980s, although experiments of new educational solutions are ongoing in the high school and there is wide agreement on increasing compulsory education to the age of 16 years. Despite the reduction in the number of children and young people, education expenditure showed an increase of 0.6 per cent in GDP by the end of the decade. Franco's data (1993) show that this is due to two factors in particular. The first is the increasing rate of participation in precompulsory and post-compulsory education. The rate of precompulsory education has increased from 47 per cent in 1960 to as much as 85 per cent in 1990; the participation rate in high school curricula has increased from 20 per cent in 1960 to as much as 68 per cent in 1990; and in the university sector, the figure went up from 4.5 per cent in 1960 to as much as 21 per cent in 1990.

The second pressure causing expenditure increase has been the teacher–student ratio. Despite the decline in demographic pressures, this ratio remained pretty constant during the decade: 10.4 per cent in 1980 and 10.9 per cent in 1990 for the overall educational system (OECD, 1985). During the same period, however, the average teacher's salary decreased considerably as a proportion of GDP. It is, therefore, the number of teachers that appears to be of serious concern. In precompulsory education in 1988 each teacher had 15 pupils (France, 34; Germany, 19); an elementary teacher had 14 (France, 19; Germany, 18); and in high school the corresponding figure is 9 (France, 13; Germany, 14) (Unesco, 1990).

Turning now to other issues, youth unemployment has grown from about 19 per cent (1980) to over 25 per cent in 1990. It reached 30 per cent in 1987 and has increased consistently in the last period of crisis. This shows the weakness of the measures on youth unemployment adopted in the 1980s, as we saw in one of the previous sections. The promise of effective interventions against youth unemployment has been one of the linchpins of the electoral campaign of the right in the recent elections.

Poverty

The extent of poverty increased during the 1980s. Using the EU poverty line, the problem increased, as Table 9.4 shows, from 12.0 per cent of households in 1980 to 22.0 per cent in 1988. Using the International Standard of Poverty Line, poverty showed a yearly increase of about 0.5 per cent from 13 per cent in 1983 to 15.3 per cent in 1988. Moreover, its distribution was very uneven in the various Italian regions. In Northern and Central Italy the rate was 9 per cent in 1988, while in Southern Italy it was 26.4 per cent, with a maximum of 35 per cent in Calabria. In the case of the elderly, 'among those aged 66–75 the poverty rate (as measured by those with disposable incomes below 50 per cent of the average) is 34.1 per cent in the south and 14.9 per cent in the north, while for those aged 75 and over the figures are 41.5 per cent and 22.6 per cent respectively' (Walker, Alber and Gullermard, 1993, p. 36). Research has also corroborated the usual correlation between certain structural variables and the extent of poverty: age and gender in Northern Italy, while family size and unemployment were the crucial variables in the South (Presidenza, 1985; Commissione 1992; Sarpellon, 1992).

The Future of the Welfare State in Italy

The general election in the spring of 1994 not only radically changed the entire political scene but it created an extremely uncertain political situation, which makes forecasts of future developments very hazardous. All that can be attempted, therefore, is a rough sketch of the likely broad welfare developments in the remaining years of this decade.

There are two contrasting ideal party political positions in Italian welfare debates. On one hand, the Forza Italia (Berlusconi's party) envisages a residual welfare state where most of the current welfare provisions (including pensions) become the responsibility of the market, the state confining itself to providing means-tested services for the poor. Opposing this view is the position of the PDS (the ex-communist party) which argues for a universalist welfare state that guarantees minimum welfare services to all as a matter of citizenship, and where the market provides additional benefits over and above the state minima to those who want them and can afford them. These polar political positions will influence but will not determine the future development of the welfare state in Italy. To begin with, the positions of the other political parties on welfare do not belong to either of these two polar positions even though they veer towards one or the other. Since coalition governments are the most likely scenario for the immediate future, the views of the other parties will influence the nature of the welfare state. Moreover, there are several structural factors which will play their part in determining the type of compromise in welfare that will emerge in the future, whichever coalition government is in power.

First, there is the increasing number of actors in the provision of social welfare including the expanding role of the market. The rise in the number of these actors has been under way since the 1980s with the development of the voluntary and non-profit sectors. The importance of these agencies is likely to increase in the future, fostered by recent laws regulating voluntary associations and social cooperatives. But in the second half of the 1990s this group of actors will expand further with the arrival of private profit-making agencies in the sector of pensions (regulated by the decrees 503/1992 and 585/1993) and in the area of health (decree 502/1992). Interestingly enough, the need for a greater role of the market in welfare provision has been supported by parties with opposing ideologies albeit for different reasons.

Second, the administrative sructure of delivering state services is much in question. The inadequacy of the current regional system of administration and the need for decentralisation has been expressed in several ways by different political parties. Federalism, therefore, became one of the leading issues in the recent electoral debate supported in different versions by the various parties. The Northern League supports a very radical version of federalism while the PDS espouses a different type that empowers the autonomy of the current regions. This is reinforced by a law on local authority autonomy approved in 1992 (law 142), the implementation of which is under way, aimed at giving the Comuni a wider decision-making and financial autonomy. Real decentralisation of decision-making will inevitably reduce the power of the central government and will blunt its policy direction.

Third, radical change towards either universalism or residualism will be resisted by the cultural tradition in welfare which in Italy has been strongly occupational. This tradition has meant a reliance on insurance based services and it has reflected the balance of power between employers and trade unions. As Ferrera (1993) points out, various attempts in the recent past to introduce universalist pensions schemes have failed because of this tradition.

We also referred earlier to the problems that the universalist health care system has encountered in being accepted. Similarly, the recent strong public and trade union reaction to Berlusconi's attempt radically to change the pension system is a reflection of the influence of cultural factors on social policy. The same is also likely to be the case with future attempts to shift the welfare system radically towards either universalism or residualism.

Fourth, the reforms of 1992 had more severe implications for both social security and health than many people realised at the time. These reforms had been accepted by several of the parties and their gradual implementation will proceed whichever coalition government is in power during the next five years or so.

Fifth, the Italian welfare state is based on a series of ideological and sectional compromises which are very difficult to disentangle. Attempts, therefore, to reformulate it drastically so that it reflects one ideology and ignores the interests of whole sections of the population are bound to fail. Incrementalism has been the overarching principle in the development of the welfare state so far and it will continue to be the same in the future.

Sixth, whichever coalition government is in power will have to face up to the difficult task of reforming the taxation system so that it becomes more efficient at both the national and local level. The size of the public debt is such that reductions in taxation are not possible. By the same token, it is difficult to see how any government can hope to deal with the public debt and increase welfare expenditure at the same time.

Finally, there is the influence of the EU directives on social protection. So far these have been more advisory than regulatory but this may well change in the future.

All the above suggest strongly that though the welfare state in Italy is likely to become less generous in the immediate future, it will continue to be based on the same principles and any changes will be gradual and incremental. This is not to deny the importance of politics but rather to put the significance of party politics within the broader cultural, economic and social climate of the country.

References

Alber, J. (1983) 'Alcune cause e conseguenze della espansione della spesa per la sicurezza sociale in Europa occidentale: 1949–1977', *Stato e Mercato*, no. 7, April, pp. 90–131.

Ardigr, A. (1976) 'Introduzione alla sociologia del Welfare-State e alle sue trasformazioni', in La Rosa, M. and Minardi, R. (eds), *I servizi sociali tra partecipazione e programmazione* (Milan: Angeli).

Artoni, R. and Rangi-Ortigosa, E. (1989) *La spesa pubblica per l'assistenza in Italia*, (Milan: Angeli).

Ascoli, U. and Dente, B. (1985) 'Recenti tendenze del Welfare State in italia', *Stato e Mercato*, no. 14, August.

Berzano, L. (1987) 'Uomini senza territorio', *Sisifo*, no. 11.

CENSIS (1992) *Rapporto sulla situazione sociale del paese* (Rome: Commissione d'indagine sulla povertà e l'emarginazione, 1992); *Secondo rapporto sulla povert' in italia* (Milan: Angeli).

Conti, V. and Cossutta, D. (1986) 'Il problema dell'occupazione: diequilibrio strutturale e transitorio', in 'Ente per gli studi monetari, bancari e finanziari 'Luigi Einaudi'" (ed.), *Oltre la crisi* (Rome: Il Mulino).

Capparucci, M. and Frey, L. (1988) 'L'efficienza della spesa universitaria, collana di Quaderni di economia del lavoro', no. 33 (Milan: Angeli).

Dente, B. (1985) *Governare la frammentazione* (Bologna: Il Mulino).

Dente, B. (1990) (ed.) *Le politiche pubbliche in Italia* (Bologna: Il Mulino).

De Sandre, P. (1991) 'Contributo delle generazioni ai cambiamenti recenti nei comportamenti e nelle forme familiari', in Donati, P. (ed.), *Secondo rapporto sulla famiglia in Italia, CISF* (Milan: Edizioni Paoline).

Donati, P. (1978) *Pubblico e privato: fine di un'alternativa?* (Bologna: Cappelli).

Donolo, C. and Fichera, F. (1981) (eds) *Il governo debole: forme e limiti della razionalità politica* (Bari: De Donato).

EEC (1991) *Demographic Statistics* (Brussels-Luxembourg: Commission of the European Communities).

Esping-Andersen, G. (1990) *The Three Worlds of Welfare Capitalism* (New York: Polity Press).

Eurostat (1987) 'Enquete sur les forces de travail. Population et conditions sociales', theme 3, sirie 5 (Luxembourg: Office for Official Publications of the European Communities).

Eurobarometer (1993) *Attitudes towards Social Protection* (Luxembourg).

Eurostat (1992) *Statistiche della comunità* (Brussels: CEE).

Ferrera, M. (1985) *Il Welfare-State in Italia* (Bologna: Il Mulino).

Ferrera, M. (1993) *Modelli di solidarietà* (Bologna: Il Mulino).

Franco, D. (1993), *L'espansione della spesa pubblica in Italia* (1960–1990) (Bologna: Il Mulino).

Garonna, G. (1988) 'Le poltiche sul tempo di lavoro e il sistema delle relazioni industriali in italia', in Valli, V. (ed.), *Tempo di Lavoro e occupazione; il caso italiano* (Rome: NIS).

Gasparini, G. (1988) 'Il dibattito sul tempo di lavoro in sociologia', in Valli, V. (ed.), *Tempo di Lavoro e occupazione*, pp. 39–66.

134   *Italy*

44

44

Geddes, M. (ed.) (1990) *La salute degli italiani. Rapporto 1990* (Florence: La nuova Italia).

Granaglia, E. (1993) 'I rischi delle mutue', *Prospettive sociali e sanitarie*, no. 4.

Graziano, L. (1979) 'Clientelismo', in Farneti, P. (ed.), *Politica e società* (Florence: La Nuova Italia).

ISTAT (1985) *Indagine sulle strutture e i comportamenti familiari* (Rome).

ISTAT (1988) 'I conti delle amministrazioni pubbliche e della protezione sociale (anni 1980–86)', *Collana d'informazione*, no. 12.

ISTAT (1989a) 'I conti delle amministrazioni pubbliche e della protezione sociale (anni 1980–87)', *Collana d'informazione*, no. 8.

ISTAT (1989b) 'Previsioni della popolazione residente per sesso, età e regione', base 1.1.1988, tomo1, *Note e relazioni*, no. 4.

ISTAT (1989c), 'Caratteristiche strutturali delle famiglie nel 1983 e nel 1988', *Notiziario*, no. 13.

ISTAT (1990) 'La mortalità differenziale secondo alcuni fattori socio-economici', *Note e relazioni*, no. 2.

ISTAT (1991) 'I conti delle amministrazioni pubbliche e della protezione sociale (anni 1984–89)', *Collana d'informazione*, no. 6.

ISTAT (1992) 'I conti delle amministrazioni pubbliche e della protezione sociale (anni 1985–90)', *Collana d'informazione*, no. 16.

ISTAT (1993) 'I conti delle amministrazioni pubbliche e della protezione sociale (anni 1986–91)', *Collana d'informazione*, no. 13.

Kangas, O. and Palme, J. (1989) *Public and Private Pensions* (Stockholm: Institut for Social Forskning).

LABOS (1992) *Regioni e politiche socio-assistenziali* (Rome: TER).

Maruani, M., Reynaud, E. and Romani, C. (eds) (1990) 'La flessibilità del lavoro in Italia", *Quaderni di Economia del lavoro*, nos 41–2.

Ministero del Bilancio (from 1983 to 1990) *Relazione sulla situazione economica del Paese* (Rome: Zecca di Stato).

Moss, D. and Rogers, E. (1980) 'Poverty and Inequality in Italy', in George, V. and Lawson, R. *Poverty and Inequality in Common Market Countries* (London: Routledge & Kegan Paul).

Natale, M. (1990) 'L'immigrazione straniera in Italia', *Polis*, no. 2.

Niero, M. (1992) 'Italian Welfare State: A Long and Winding Road', paper prepared for the conference on Comparative Studies of Welfare State Development: Qualitative and Quantitative Dimensions, Research Committee 19 ISA, 3–6 September, Bremen.

Niero, M. (1993) 'Health Policy, Drugs and Quality of Life Measurement', *British Journal of Medical Economics*, vol. 6C, pp. 63–74.

OECD (1985) *Education in Modern Societies* (Paris: OECD).

OECD (1987) *Employment Outlook* (Paris: OECD).

OECD (1991) *Historical Statistics* (Paris: OECD).

OECD (1994) *New Orientations for Social Policy*, (Paris: OECD).

Paci, M.(ed.) (1993) *Le dimensioni della diseguaglianza* (Bologna: Il Mulino).

Pizzorno, A. (1992) 'Lo scambio occulto', *Stato e Mercato*, no. 34, April.

Presidenza del Consiglio dei Ministri (1985) *La povertà in Italia* (Rome: Istituto Poligrafico e Zecca dello Stato).

Prezioso, A. (1994) 'Salute, risorse e solidarietà', *Prospettive sociali e sanitarie*, no. 1.

Pugliese C. (1993) *Sociologia della disoccupazione* (Bologna: Il Mulino).

Regonini, G. (1985) 'Effetti non previsti del "patto previdenziale"', *Stato e Mercato*, no. 14, August.

Regonini, G. (1990) 'La politica delle pensioni', in Dente, B. (ed.), *Le politiche pubbliche in Italia* (Bologna: Il Mulino).

Romani, F. (1980) 'Crisi dello stato democratico? Alcune riflessioni sulle finanze pubbliche italiane negli anni settanta', *Note Economiche*.

Rossi, F.P. (1990) *La previdenza sociale* (Padua: CEDAM).

Rossi Sciumi, G. and Scabini, E. (1991) 'Le famiglie monogenitoriali in Italia', in Donati P., *Secondo rapporto sulla famiglia in Italia* (Rome: CISF, Edizioni Paoline).

Rusconi, G.E. (1984) *Scambio, minaccia, decisione* (Bologna: Il Mulino).

Salvemini, M.T. (1992) *Le politiche del debito pubblico* (Bari: Laterza).

Saraceno, C. and Negri, N. (1994) 'The Changing Italian Welfare State', *Journal of European Social Policy*, vol. 4, no. 1, pp. 19–34.

Sarpellon, G. (1982) *La povertà in Italia*, 2 vols (Milan: Angeli).

SVIMEZ (1986) *La questione meridionale nel quarantennale della Svimez*, Coll. Documenti Svimez, no. 26 (Rome).

UNESCO (1990) *Statistical Yearbook* (Paris: UNESCO).

Valli, V. (1988) (ed.) *Tempo di lavoro e occupazione; il caso italiano* (Rome: NIS).

Walker, A., Alber, J. and Guillermard, A-M. (1993) *Older People in Europe: Social and Economic Policies* (Brussels: EU).

Wilensky, H.L., Luebbert, G.M. *et al.* (1985) *Comparative Social Policy: Theories, Methods, Findings* (Berkeley: The Regents of the University of California).

7

Greece: What Future for the Welfare State?

PETER STATHOPOULOS

> To secure gentle treatment of the poor is not an easy thing, for the ruling class is not always humane. (Aristotle p. 13)

With the fall of the military junta in 1974, democracy was restored to Greece with the general elections that brought the New Democracy conservative party to power. During its six years in office, the government paid little attention to the social services with the exception of education which is not seen as a social service in Greece. The elections of 1981 brought the Panhellenic Socialist Party (PASOK) to power and for most of the period covered by this book, 1980–95, Greece has been ruled by socialist party governments. It is during these years that the social services were expanded and reformed and state expenditure on social welfare rose substantially. As Tables 1.2 and 1.5 have shown, public expenditure grew from 17.4 per cent of GDP in 1960 to 33.1 per cent in 1980 and a high 53.3 per cent in 1990. The corresponding figures for social expenditure were 7.1 per cent, 11.1 per cent and 20.9 per cent, respectively.

This rise in public and social expenditure must be seen in the light of the very high rates of economic growth during the early part of this period and the low rates of growth during the latter years. Unlike Northern European countries where the welfare state expanded during the years of high economic growth, the Greek welfare state expanded during the lean economic circumstances of the 1980s. It is a pattern of growth that is not too dissimilar to that of Spain.

Despite this recent growth in social expenditure, all the social services have their roots in the past and the influence of history, the church and charitable organisations is still very strong. As in other countries, the nature of the contemporary Greek welfare state is the outcome of a complex web of historical, social, economic and political factors, some of which go back beyond the creation of the modern Greek state in 1830 (Costandellos, 1968; Woodhouse, 1986).

Unfortunately, space does not allow a discussion of these factors and we begin our account with a description of the services as they existed at the beginning of the 1980s when PASOK assumed power with the declared intention of radically improving the social welfare services of the country.

Social Services at the Beginning of the 1980s

Health Care

The health care services consisted of the public hospitals, the rural clinics in the remote areas and the private clinics. The public hospitals provided services on a differential fee scale. Those who could pay or who were covered with good medical insurance were admitted to class A wards with one or two beds and with high quality services. Those covered by low quality medical insurance were admitted to class C wards with twelve or more beds and low quality facilities. Those who were not covered by any medical insurance scheme had to undergo a means test to determine eligibility for free treatment. Apart from the cumbersome and humiliating nature of such means tests, they were also subject to political patronage and nepotism. As far as mental patients are concerned, they were looked after in mental institutions.

Doctors could practise at the public hospitals, private medical clinics in which they were shareholders and also maintain their own offices for private practice. The geographical distribution of all types of medical services was very uneven with heavy concentration in the major cities and scarcity in the small towns, the remote rural areas and the islands. In short, the quality of health care was generally low, the services were uncoordinated, unevenly distributed and ineffective in meeting the needs of the general population.

Social Security

Social security provision was fragmented, lacking coordination and differential in the quality of benefits. A vast number of insurance funds, organised among trades and other occupations, were the backbone of the social security system. The Social Security Foundation (IKA) covered 47 per cent of the population, leaving whole population groups such as farmers, divorced women, etc. without any insurance cover. For most of the insured, the funds provided low level pensions and inadequate medical coverage. A small minority of upper-class professionals, such as senior military personnel, professors, judges, and so on, enjoyed high benefits as they received protection from more than one fund. Inevitably expenditure as a proportion of GNP was low and not surprisingly it rose fast during the 1980s, as mentioned above and elsewhere (Solomos, 1991, p. 8).

Education

During the seven years of military rule, the educational system was used as a blatant tool of propaganda and as a means to advance the nationalistic ideology of the ruling junta. The curriculum was structured with heavy emphasis on classical education, classical Greek and Latin. The New Democracy embarked on a serious reorganisation of the educational system in 1976–7. First, it introduced the modern version of Greek (*demotiki*) as the official language of government and of schools. The teaching of classical Greek and Latin was drastically reduced apart from a few schools which specialised in classical studies.

Second, it made education compulsory from age 6 to 15. As it will be pointed out later, however, the legislation was not enforced to the full as no provisions were made to provide the services necessary for its enforcement. Third, the government established the technical and vocational high schools which were to prepare pupils for a job. Their aim was to link education to the labour market and to divert pupils from seeking admission to universities. Fourth, in order to strengthen the capability of the educational system to provide skilled personnel, the government upgraded the post-secondary Technical Colleges.

No significant changes were introduced to the function or administration of universities. As before, the centre of power was vested in the Chair. Full professors had absolute authority to run their departments in a fully autonomous manner, with the result that the curriculum was not responsive to the changing needs of the Greek economy and society.

Housing

Housing conditions were very low during this period. In 1971, only 36 per cent of urban dwellings and a mere 6 per cent of rural dwellings had a bath or shower. The rural migration to the cities during the 1960s and 1970s resulted in unauthorised housing construction around Athens. Whole areas were built without any town planning with the result that the quality of housing was poor and no provision was made for parks, schools, churches and recreational facilities.

The state made little provision for public housing to meet the needs of low income groups. What publicly supported housing existed was built in low income areas, was of low quality and was so segregated that it created a ghetto environment. Government housing assistance took the form either of subsidised mortgages for home buyers or the donation of dwelling units to low income families, to large families, to elderly impoverished couples, and so on. There was no legislation for rent subsidies or for making housing as well as the city accessible to handicapped persons.

Personal Social Services

It is true to say that up to the end of the 1970s, personal social services had been seen as a form of unproductive government activity and were thus grossly neglected. They were treated as a residual form of service for those categories of the population who could not look after themselves. Almost all forms of such services were based in institutions: residential facilities for abandoned, deserted or neglected children and young persons; institutional provisions for the blind, the deaf and so on; and residential homes for the elderly who had no relatives to care for them. Moreover, a high proportion of the personal social services were provided by private non-statutory bodies. In 1980, 33 per cent of the existing 1053 social welfare agencies were in the private sector. As we shall see later, the 1980s witnessed a growth of the statutory and a reduction of the private sector in this area (Kremalis *et al.*, 1990, p. 46).

In brief, the personal social services at the beginning of the 1980s were for the most part based in institutions, were geared to specific categories of deprived people, and were poorly coordinated and inadequately funded.

Economic, Demographic and Family Changes in the 1980s

Since the early 1980s, the country's economy has been experiencing severe difficulties in a number of ways that were common to most European countries. As mentioned earlier, growth rates have been very low while inflation rates have been very high. Table 1.3 has shown that the annual average growth of real GDP during the period 1980–93 was a mere 1.5 per cent, while inflation during the same period grew by an annual average of 18.5 per cent. To put all this in a comparative context, the growth rate was the second lowest – after Sweden – among the countries covered by this book while the inflation rate was the highest. Inevitably this meant that the country had both to borrow and to raise its tax revenues in order to finance its public services. As Table 1.9 has shown, general taxes in 1981 amounted to 26.9 per cent of GNP while in 1991 the figure rose to 36.7 per cent. In order to service its national debt, the country had to pay an increasing proportion of its national wealth – 2.2 per cent of its GDP was used to pay the debt interest in 1979 while the corresponding figure for 1990 rose to 11.2 per cent.

Despite increased borrowing and higher taxes, the general government financial balances were in the red for every single year for the whole period 1980–94 by very considerable sums. The lowest figure was 2.9 per cent in 1980 and the highest 18.1 per cent of GDP in 1990 (OECD, 1993, table A.25, p. 150). In order to reduce the public deficit, the 1995 budget estimates an overall increase of 13.5 per cent for both direct and indirect taxation will be necessary (*Kathimerini*, 27 November 94).

Unemployment, too, rose during this period. As Table 1.3 showed, the annual average rate of unemployment for the period 1980–93 was 7.5 per cent. It started, however, from a low 2.8 per cent in 1980 and grew steadily to 10.0 per cent in 1993. What is more, the official statistics underestimate the extent of the problem in a variety of ways, the most glaring of which being the omission of young people who never entered the labour force. Those who have never been able to find a job are not officially counted as unemployed! As in other industrial countries, the proportion of those in part-time employment has increased and, similarly, the majority of them are women – 65 per cent.

The New Democracy government tried to deal with the fiscal problems of the country in a variety of ways, including attempts to reduce public expenditure as well as policies designed to privatise public sector companies such as electricity, telephones and shipyards, but without any success because of trade union and left-wing party resistance. It also 'failed utterly in its attempts to bring under control the galloping public deficit which was (and remains) the most critical problem' (Mavrogordatos, 1994, p. 316). Another glaring fiscal problem in Greece has been the massive avoidance of taxes. Attempts to make the collection of taxes more efficient and thus reduce the vast sums of unpaid taxes have proved equally unsuccessful.

On the positive side, tourism has expanded considerably over this period, creating many jobs in various branches of the economy and bringing much needed foreign currency. Also, considerable net subsidies from the EU have been used to improve the country's infrastructure and to develop human resources. In 1993, the EU funding was 993 billion drachmas and for the period 1994–9 it is expected that Greece will receive 1 trillion drachmas in EU subsidies, in order to complete all major projects so as to integrate itself fully in the Union.

Demographic and family changes in Greece have been, on the whole, very similar to those of other EU countries. There has been a decline in the birth rate and it is unlikely that this trend will reverse itself in the near future. The proportion of live births outside marriage rose from 1.2 per cent in 1960 to 2.4 per cent in 1991, but even so it was, and still is, by far the lowest figure in EU countries. As Table 9.3 shows, fertility rates declined from 2.32 in 1965 to 1.41 in 1992, one of the lowest in the EU group of countries, and obviously below population replacement level. On the other hand, infant mortality rates have declined from 17.9 per 1000 live births in 1980 to 9.7 in 1990 (*Kathimerini*, 27 November 1994). Similarly, general mortality rates have declined while life expectancy has risen – 74.5 years for men and 79.5 for women.

The proportion of the elderly has grown and this will continue in the future. Table 1.6 shows that the proportion of people aged 65 or over rose from 8.1 per cent in 1960 to 13.7 per cent in 1990 and is expected to reach 19.9 per cent in the year 2020. The corresponding figures for those aged 75 or over are 3.0, 6.0 and 9.2 per cent respectively, one of the highest estimated figures in EU countries. Life expectancy at age 60 is 21.2 years for women and 18.2 for men while the corresponding figures for age 80 are 7.6 and 6.7 years respectively. All these figures are very similar to those of the other EU countries despite the country's lower material standards (Walker, Alber and Guillemard, 1993, table 4.1, p. 101).

Marriage rates have declined and divorce rates have increased though neither of these trends is as pronounced as it is in northern European countries. Thus during the thirty year period 1960–90, the number of divorces increased by three and a half times but the divorce rate was still one of the lowest in EU countries. There is, however, some evidence that in recent years divorce rates are rising sharply. Thus, according to the National Census data, there were 9.7 divorces for every 100 marriages in 1991 but for 1992 the corresponding figure was 13.0.

The proportion of lone parent families is, as Table 1.7 has shown, low and it is not generally seen as a major social issue. Though there are several government programmes designed to assist lone parent families, it is difficult to consider these schemes as being of sufficiently good standard, and this year unmarried mothers organised themselves into a pressure group to campaign for better provisions.

Poverty data are very patchy but Table 9.4 showns that the proportion of households in poverty as defined by the EU declined from 20.5 per cent in 1980 to 17.4 in 1985, only to rise to 21.0 per cent in 1988. Bearing in mind the adverse economic situation of the past few years and the restrictive social protection policies pursued by the New Democracy government, it is more than likely that this figure will be higher today. In the absence of data, it is difficult to know which population groups are most vulnerable to poverty, but the retired group is one of them because of the very low pensions among ex-farmers whose pensions have 'an average value of one-sixth of the minimum wage. In all, people aged 65 and over make up one-third of the population in poverty. The actual poverty rate among those aged 65–74 is 26 per cent and for those aged 75 and over it is 42 per cent' (Walker, Alber and Guillemard, 1993, p. 37).

As in other industrial countries women are more likely to be in poverty than men because of the usual demographic, labour market and family reasons. The Achilles' heel of the Greek social security system in combating poverty has been the absence of a national and enforceable state minimum income guarantee scheme. So long as this absence persists, poverty on a large scale will also continue.

The Development of the Social Services in the 1980s

In this section, we shall discuss the development of the main social services – health, social security, personal social services, housing and education – from the beginning of the 1980s to the mid-1990s. The socialist party that came to power in 1981 with an overwhelming majority had promised to bring 'social change here and now', thus raising public expectations on both the speed and the nature of social policy developments. We will now describe briefly the changes in the structure, the extent of benefits and the effectiveness of each service in meeting the needs of the population during this period. The general conclusion is that though PASOK's grand vision achieved some results, it fell very short of its initial ambition.

Health Care

One of the first pieces of legislation introduced by the socialist government of 1981 sought to replace the then fragmented and inadequate mixture of private and public health care provision with a National Health System. The new state service tried to develop a comprehensive network of services throughout the country, free to all users at the point of consumption. Moreover, it attempted to regulate and control the expansion of private medical care. Thus doctors could not be employed by the NHS and engage in private practice at the same time. It was a bold attempt to elevate the importance of the state health sector and it met with some success. Between 1981 and 1988 'the number of doctors in hospitals increased by 60% and the number of nurses by 88%, while salaries were increased to make employment in the public sector attractive' (EU, 1993a, p. 104).

As the service became free, it inevitably encouraged demand which it subsequently found difficult to meet satisfactorily. The large hospitals in Athens and Thessaloniki became overcrowded to the point that almost all space in the corridors was occupied by patients. As a result, patients and their relatives were bribing the staff to secure treatment to which in theory they were entitled anyway. The private sector has expanded mainly in the form of diagnostic services employing high level technology and providing expensive hotel services. These conditions prevail to the present day.

The conservative government (1990–3) attempted to change the situation by increasing competition between the state and the private sector, by introducing private practices within the state sector and by the introduction of nominal hospital outpatient fees in order to reduce demand. Since the return of the socialist government in October 1993, efforts have been made to improve the quality of service, to raise efficiency and to eliminate bribery. There is no evidence, however, to show whether these efforts have met with any success. The current government also abolished the outpatient charges introduced by the previous government. Patients still have to pay '10% of the cost of certain drugs and 25% of all others, except those for chronic or mental illnesses and AIDS cases' (Abel-Smith and Mossialos, 1994, p. 107).

At present, it is true to say that a large segment of the population does not have much confidence in either the government health care system or the private health sector as evidenced by the large number of middle- and upper-class patients who are seeking medical treatment abroad, mainly in the UK, and prepared to pay large sums of their own money for it. Indeed, the number of these patients has increased from 523 in 1988 to 812 in 1990 and 2273 in 1992 (*Nea*, 19 March 94), and with this the amount of money spent as well.

Progress in mental health care has been equally slow despite the progressive ideas embodied in the reform of 1981. Large mental institutions were to be phased out, to be replaced by community mental health clinics and small short-stay wards in general hospitals for those in need of hospitalisation. It took the publicity for the appalling conditions prevailing in the Leros mental institution, huge sums of EU money, as well as very close monitoring from EU officials before patients began to leave state mental institutions. Some community health centres have been established in different cities but there is a shortage of trained personnel to deal with the difficult tasks of community care and the pace of change is very slow.

Public expenditure on health has risen from a mere 2.16 per cent of GDP in 1970 to 3.36 per cent in 1980 and 4.14 per cent in 1990. Despite this rise, however, the sum spent on health in Greece as a proportion of GDP is, along with Portugal's, the lowest among all EU countries. The same is true when one looks at total expenditure, that is public and private expenditure (OECD, 1994, table 2, pp. 70–2). Even if one adds to all this the expenditure of those seeking medical treatment abroad, the overall conclusion must be that the country does not spend enough on its health services. It goes without saying that in situations of scarcity and the existence of private medical services, inequalities of access to medical treatment are inevitable in terms of class and of urban versus rural residence.

Social Security

The PASOK government of the early 1980s acted on three fronts in the area of social security. First, it increased the amount of the monthly pensions of a large section of the population who were receiving, by any standards, starvation payments. Second, it introduced minimal pensions for retired farmers who had not paid insurance contributions and also covered them for medical treatment. Third, it provided social insurance coverage for whole categories of repatriated Greek nationals form Egypt, Turkey, the Soviet Union and elsewhere. On the whole, it is correct to say that no major reforms of social security have been introduced during this period, despite the very substantial rise of expenditure and the multitude of minor administrative changes that inevitably accompany any social security system in any country.

Social security and health in Greece are the responsibility of approximately 330 funds under the jurisdiction of the Ministry of Health and Social Security, with the exception of unemployment benefit and family allowances which are under the jurisdiction of the Ministry of Labour. It is a complex, inefficient and costly form of administration. It reflects the unplanned historical process that gave rise to it, as well as the influence of political criteria 'such as party political affiliations and clientelistic relationships' (Petmesidou, 1991, p. 43). Most private employees belong to the main Social Security Fund (IKA); most public employees to their own fund; and the third largest fund (OGA) covers the farmers and fishermen as well as all those who upon their seventieth birthday have no other coverage. The remaining funds have been set up by employees of specific trades – banks, lawyers, bakers, and so on.

The whole system is financed largely through earnings related contributions by employees and employers. More specifically, employees pay earnings related contributions with the exception of civil servants who pay no contributions; farmers pay little in contributions but they also get little in pensions; and the self-employed pay fixed contributions and qualify for fixed pensions. Increasingly, the system is made viable through government subsidies that vary enormously from one fund to another but with those representing professional groups getting the most. For example, 'financial support for IKA hardly reaches 0.5 per cent of total revenue, while financial support to the Fund of Engineers, Architects and Surveyors amounts to 55 per cent of its revenue and to that of Lawyers to 54 per cent' (Petmesidou, 1991, p. 38). It is not only that funds representing professional groups receive more government subsidies, but they also provide higher benefits, better medical services and other supplementary services than either IKA or OGA can provide.

Since 1980, all governments have tried unsuccessfully to reduce the number of funds and the government is considering this issue again today. There is now greater appreciation from both the main political parties of the need for action to deal with both the administrative structure and the pensions fiscal issue perhaps along the lines recommended by the IMF report in 1992. Administrative streamlining, however, is bound to be resisted by the various professional groupings which do comparatively well out of the existing system, if it means levelling down.

Expenditure on social security has risen from about 9 per cent of GDP in 1980 to about 17 per cent in 1991, reflecting both the rise in the number of beneficiaries and the real increase in the level of some of the benefits. Table 7.1 shows that expenditure on retirement pensions dominates the social security budget to a far greater extent than in other countries within the EU, while expenditure on unemployment is far below the EU average.

All benefits are earnings related and until recently they were increased every year to take account of the rise in prices. There is no national assistance scheme for those who do not qualify for an insurance benefit or whose insurance benefit entitlement period comes to an end. The only exception is the non-contributory pension for those over the age of 70 retiring from work who did not pay contributions to qualify for the earnings related state retirement pension.

The replacement ratios for retirement pensions are very generous by EU standards. According to EU statistics, a single person who was on average industrial earnings while at work and who met the maximum necessary contribution conditions will receive a retirement pension equivalent to 'as much as 107% of average earnings in Greece, 97% in Spain, 94% in Portugal and 89% in Italy' while in the UK, the Netherlands and Ireland it is less than 50 per cent of these earnings (EU, 1993a, p. 55). These are theoretical ratios and they do not, of course, reflect the differences of satisfying the maximum contribution conditions in the various countries or, of course, the varying level of their wages.

TABLE 7.1   *Division of social security benefits by function, 1991 (percentages)*

	Greece	EU 12
Sickness benefit	10.3	25.4
Invalidity, disability	11.7	8.9
Occupational accidents/diseases	0.1	2.1
Old age	56.9	37.4
Survivors	11.4	8.3
Maternity	1.0	0.3
Family	1.4	6.4
Vocational/resettlement	0.0	1.3
Unemployment	1.8	5.6
Housing benefit	0.9	1.8
Miscellaneous	5.2	1.8
Total	100.0	100.0

Source: EU (1993a), table 2, p. 45.

It is logical for low wage economies to have high replacement ratios for otherwise the absolute level of pensions will be extremely low even by national standards. Thus Greece, Spain and Portugal with high replacement ratios end up by providing pensions which in money terms are low by European standards. They amounted to only 52.5 per cent, 61.1 per cent and 36.8 per cent respectively, of the EU average in 1992 (EU, 1994, table 1, p. 4). The simple fact is that the low-waged economies are inevitably the low-pension welfare states.

Despite, or because of, the high esteem in which the family has always been held in Greek society, family benefits account for only a tiny proportion of the social security budget and an even lower proportion of the country's GDP. This applies to the three other Mediterranean EU member countries – Spain, Portugal and Italy – where 'the amount of benefits that households receive to meet the cost of bringing up children and caring for other members of the family is far below the European Union average' (EU, 1994, p. 7). It seems that the tradition of the family looking after its own members is too strong still to permit government intervention on a generous level.

Education

Education in Greece is compulsory and free for the ages 6 to 15 years. It is provided by the central government which appoints the teachers and sets the school curricula. Local authorities have not been liable for education although recently they have been given the responsibility of looking after the maintenance of school buildings. Children aged 3 to 6 years may register for nursery schooling if there are places for them. Schooling after the age of 15 is a parental responsibility and it can take place in technical and vocational schools, in general secondary schools that prepare young people for entry examinations to higher education establishments, or in schools that combine the vocational with the academic.

Universities and Technological Educational Institutions (TEI) are the responsibility of the central government and entry to them is very competitive. There are usually 120 000 candidates every year for approximately 40 000 places. Many students study abroad so that in the academic year 1991–2 20 000 Greek students were registered in EU universities comprising almost 10 per cent of the Greek student population, compared to an EU average of 1.3 per cent (*Kathimerini*, 30 October 94).

There has always been a high preoccupation with access to university education because of the widespread and historically valid reason that such education was the avenue to secure, professional and well-paid jobs. Although this is no longer as true, students and parents alike still hold on very strongly to this belief. In Tsoukalas's words education is still considered as 'the safest basis for social upgrading' (Tsoukalas, 1986, p. 269). During the 1980s, there was a large increase in the number of university students though this has steadied during the last five years. Of particular concern is the high drop-out rate from Technological Educational Institutions, particularly from some departments such as nursing.

Class inequalities in higher education exist in the same way that they do in other countries (Chrysakis, 1991). Gender inequalities, however, have declined substantially so that today women may outnumber men in the tertiary sector of education. In the mid-1980s, according to EU statistics, 49 per cent of all students in higher education were women – the fifth highest rate in EU countries (EU, 1991, table 3.7, p. 34). In 1988, according to a Greek study, '35 per cent of women aged 19–24 compared to 34 per cent of men aged 19–24 were attending or had attended tertiary education' (Karantinos *et al.*, 1992). Thus, one of the initial aims of PASOK governments to reduce inequalities in education has been partially achieved – in relation to gender but not to class or region.

Traditionally, continuing education has taken place outside the universities and the Technological Educational Institutions and has been of the vocational kind. It is only in the last few years that this type of education has expanded with EU funds and has been directed mainly towards the young unemployed. Its purpose is to train or retrain them in marketable skills and thus reduce the very high rates of youth unemployment – 20.5 per cent of males aged 14–24 are unemployed and the corresponding proportion among females of the same age group is 42 per cent (National Statistical Service, 1994).

Expenditure on state education has increased only slightly over recent years – from 12.7 per cent of all public expenditure in 1975 to 13.5 per cent in 1984 (Petmesidou, 1991, p. 34). Despite a rise in the early 1980s, it amounted to only 3.4 per cent of GDP in 1985 – the third lowest among EU countries (EU, 1991, p. 36). To this must be added the expenditure incurred by the large number of Greek students in overseas universities, but it is doubtful whether this will make any significant difference to the country's ranking within the EU group of countries.

Although there is general recognition of the need for an overall reform of the country's educational system at all levels, governments of both the main parties have refrained partly because of fear of opposition from various quarters and partly because there is no political consensus on what form such a reform should take. The New Democracy attempt in 1992, for example, to promote the establishment of private universities failed because of opposition from students and from PASOK.

Housing

Home ownership has always been greatly valued in Greece. Families will do all they can to buy a plot of land and build their own house, often over a number of years depending on their finances. The state owns no housing stock but assists people with their housing expenses in a variety of ways. First, it provides low interest mortgage loans for public employees, military personnel and for workers who cannot meet their housing needs because market interests rates can be very high. The government subsidy varies with the family status, number of children and family income. About 15 000 families receive such subsidies annually (*Kathimerini*, 27 November 1994).

Second, through its own construction agency, the government has developed low cost housing for families, mostly those on welfare benefits, who cannot buy their own housing despite the above mentioned interest subsidies. The quality of this housing has traditionally been low though it has shown some improvement in recent years. In the past, such housing was concentrated in certain areas but this practice has now been abandoned to avoid the further creation of ghettos with all the stigma attached to them. The allocation of this type of housing is done on a lottery basis with the result that those families that win may find that they have to move away from their neighbourhood, with all the social dislocation that this entails.

Third, the government has recently instituted a measure of subsidisation of rents for the elderly and for families on low incomes, and it was estimated that in 1995 more than 40 000 families would benefit from this programme.

Finally, there is a statutory rent control system for small apartments to prevent steep increases in rent and evictions. Over recent years, however, the trend has been to relax such controls in order eventually to allow the housing market a free hand.

Like many other European countries, Greece experienced a great deal of devastation during the last world war. What perhaps is unique to Greece is the high rates of rural migrations to the towns during the post-war era and the unplanned growth of the towns, with the result that Athens today suffers from excessive pollution, traffic congestion and lack of green or recreational spaces. In Greater Athens, for example, only 4 per cent of households live in dwellings larger than 120 square metres (Maloutas, 1990).

Personal Social Services for the Elderly

During the past forty years, Greece has changed from a rural to an urban society so that today half its population lives in the two metropolitan areas of Athens and Thessaloniki. Inevitably this change has had significant implications for family structures and family networks. The rural exodus to the towns has meant that most villages are inhabited predominantly by older people. Nevertheless, several recent studies have concluded that the Greek family remains a closely knit unit functioning within a broad network of relatives that support one another in a variety of reciprocal ways (Teperoglou, 1990). Contact between grandparents and their children's families is high and, for at least one third of them, the contact is on a daily basis (Moussourou, 1985).

The available evidence suggests that only 1 per cent of the Greek elderly are in institutions, 7 per cent are dependent and 25 per cent are housebound. Government and other day care services reach at best only 10 per cent of the elderly so that the majority of them live independent lives or are assisted by their families. During the past decade, the central and local governments have created a number of community care centres (KAPI) for the elderly in urban areas which provide social, recreational and limited medical services. They are of good standard but in short supply. In addition to the state KAPI, there are the day care facilities provided by the church but these vary considerably in standard.

The situation is more acute in remote villages and on some of the islands where there are no KAPI, very few residential facilities and very limited medical services, despite the fact that most of the residents are over the age of 65. Bearing in mind the very small size of many villages, it is unlikely that any KAPI will ever appear in these places. Though family and community bonds are very strong in these rural areas, it has to be remembered that many elderly have no children living near them because they emigrated to the towns.

In summary, services for the elderly are limited especially in terms of community based services for the frail elderly who need multiple social and medical care. There are only 278 KAPI in the whole country serving an estimated 6 per cent of the elderly population (Karantinos et al., 1992). The situation is likely to become worse in the future as the numbers of the very elderly rise unless the government improves existing provisions quite considerably, which is unlikely because of economic constraints.

There were no major government reforms in the area of the personal social services during the 1980s though changes inevitably took place. The introduction of KAPI and the limited growth of professional social work are two such examples of change. The personal social services have traditionally been financed and delivered by the central government. Under the new legislation of 1994, however, they will be extensively decentralised to become the administrative responsibility of the fifty-two prefectures of the country. The central government will retain responsibility for strategic planning, financing, the establishment of eligibility criteria and evaluation programmes. Admirable though the ideas behind this legislation may be, there are serious doubts about the actual implementation of the legislation because of the current government resolve to reduce public expenditure in a variety of ways, including the restriction on hiring new public employees.

Prospects for the Remaining Years of this Decade

During the 1993 general election, PASOK 'reassured the electorate that neither a devaluation of the drachma nor new taxes would be required' to deal with the country's fiscal problems. Instead, 'it promised economic recovery through a vague corporatist "social contract"' (Mavrogordatos, 1994, p. 316). When returned to power, however, it was forced to adopt much more stringent measures. On the economic front, the government is pursuing several restrictive policies some of which it rejected while in opposition. In order to reduce unemployment, raise productivity and increase economic growth the government is implementing both labour deregulation policies and active labour investment policies. The first set of policies include more flexible working hours, lower social security benefits for new workers and easier lay off and rehiring policies. The second set of policies include training and retraining programmes for workers mostly funded by EU initiatives, as well as the implementation of large-scale projects in transportation and communication.

In an effort to reduce public expenditure and raise much needed revenues, the PASOK government has been forced to move ahead reluctantly with privatisation of public companies including utilities. PASOK had been extremely critical of the efforts of the New Democracy government towards privatisation and had pledged that once in power it would halt such measures! Ideology has had to give way to practical considerations in the face of the strong demand for social services and the weak state of the economy to finance them.

The government is also making a serious effort to curtail public deficit, reduce public debt and lower interest rates in order to boost investment and gradually satisfy the Maastricht convergence objectives by 1999. These austerity programmes have been pursued in different ways and to different degrees for a whole decade now and they have become very unpopular. Public employees' real income has declined by 40 per cent while the economy has not shown any substantive signs of recovery. There are pressures on the government to relax these policies and to begin hiring party members and sympathisers in order to counteract the mounting public disappointment with PASOK. This is politically important to countries like Greece, Spain and Italy with their high proportion of public employees and their clientelistic system of public appointments and welfare benefit provision.

The demographic trends discussed earlier will continue in the future. The new factor in all this is the influx of legal and illegal immigrants form a variety of countries which threatens to intensify social tensions as Greek workers blame migrants for the high unemployment and the low wages. Although racism is not a major problem at present, this may well change if uncontrolled immigration continues.

The expansion and improvement of social policies are and will continue to be limited by sheer economic necessity. If anything, we are likely to witness containment rather than expansion of social provision in the future. There is growing recognition among political parties, for example, that the retirement age should be lifted to 65 for both men and women and that retirement pensions should become less generous. Standards in education and health will continue to lag behind public aspirations with the result that middle and upper income groups will use the private sector at home and abroad.

The future of social services in Greece depends not only on the economic situation of the country but on the level of EU subsidies. It is estimated that Greece will receive at least 50 billion drachmas in subsidies till the end of this decade in order to develop the infrastructure of its statutory and voluntary personal social services. Another added factor affecting the development of social policy, which is particular to Greece among the countries covered in this book, is the country's political relationships with Turkey, Albania and the former Yugoslavian republic of Macedonia. In the current politically volatile situation, governments are forced to maintain high levels of defence expenditures irrespective of their party political orientation.

Most Greeks today feel disappointed with the current political parties. They believe that things could not be different whichever party is in power. There is a pervasive sense of impotence particularly in view of the growing public belief that major decisions affecting life in Greece are taken not in Athens but in Brussels. All this may be objectively exaggerated but it is none the less real, especially in view of the constantly rising public expectations for higher standards of living and better services (Stathopoulos and Amera, 1992).

In conclusion, if the current economic difficulties continue, as they appear to, the major political parties will be forced to pursue similar social policies. If the evidence from the 1980s suggested that party politics matter in welfare developments, the evidence from the recessionary 1990s suggests the opposite.

References

Abel-Smith, B. and Mossialos, E. (1994) 'Cost Containment and Health Care Reform: A Study of the European Union', *Health Policy*, vol. 28, no. 2, pp. 89–132.

Aristotle (1905) *The Politics*, transl. Jowett, B. (Oxford: Oxford University Press).

Chrysakis, M. (1991) 'Trends of Inequality in Access to Upper Tertiary Educational Institutions', *Greek Review of Social Research* (Athens) (in Greek).

EU (1991) *A Social Portrait of Europe* (Brussels: Commission of the European Communities).

EU (1993a) *Social Protection in Europe* (Brussels: Commission of the European Communities).

EU (1993b) *Digest of Statistics on Social Protection*, Eurostat, vol. 4, *Family*, (Brussels: Commission of the European Communities).

EU (1994) *Population and Social Conditions*, Eurostat, vol. 5 (Brussels: Commission of the European Communities).

Costandellos, D. (1968) *The Byzantine Philanthropy and Social Welfare* (New Jersey, USA: Rutgers University).

Kanellopoulos, K. (1984) *The Elderly in Greece* (Athens: KEPE) (in Greek).

Karantinos, D., Ioannidou, Ch. and Cavounidis, J. (1992a) *Social Services and Social Policy to Combat Social Exclusion* (Athens: Ministry of Labour) (in Greek).

Karantinos, D., Cavounidis, J., Ioannou, Ch., Koniordos, M. and Tinios, P. (1992b) *EC Observatory on National Policies to Combat Social Exclusion: Consolidated Report: Greece* (Athens: National Centre for Social Research) (in English)

King, J. (1990) 'An Olympic Struggle: Social Work Training in European Community Countries', *Community Care*, October, pp. 20–3.

Kremalis, K., and Stathopoulos, P. (1990) 'Social Welfare', (Athens) (in Greek) no publisher.

Maloutas, T. (1990) *Housing and Family in Athens* (Athens: EKKE) (in Greek).

Mavrogordatos, G. (1994) 'Greece', *European Journal of Political Research*, vol. 26, nos 3/4, December, pp. 313–19.

Moussourou, L. (1985) *Family and Child in Athens* (Athens: ESTIA) (in Greek).

National Statistical Service of Greece (1994) *Study of the Labour Force* (Athens: NSSG) (in Greek).

OECD (1993) 'Economic Outlook', no. 54, December (Paris: OECD).

OECD (1994) *New Orientations in Social Policy* (Paris: OECD).

Petmesidou, M. (1991) 'Statism, Social Policy and the Middle Classes in Greece', *Journal of European Social Policy*, vol. 1, no. 1, pp. 31–48.

Solomos, G. (1991) *Social Insurance* (Athens: Nea Synora) (in Greek).

Stathopoulos, P. (1991) 'Community Development', in Hill, M. (ed.), *Social Work and the European Community* (London: Kingsley Publishers).

Stathopoulos, P. and Amera, A. (1992) 'Family Care of the Elderly in Greece', in Kosberg, J. (ed.), *Family Care of the Elderly: Social and Cultural Changes* (London: Sage).

Teperoglou, A. (1990) *Evaluation of the Contribution of Centres of Open Protection of the Aged* (Athens: National Centre of Social Research) (in Greek).

Tsaliki, P. (1991) *The Greek Economy: Sources of Growth in the Postwar Era* (New York: Praeger).

Tsoukalas, K. (1986) *State, Society, Employment in Post World War Greece* (Athens: Themelio) (in Greek).

Walker, A., Alber, J. and Guillermard, A-M. (eds) (1993) *Older People in Europe: Social and Economic Policies* (Brussels: Commission of the European Communities).

Woodhouse, C.M. (1986) *Modern Greece: A Short History* (London: Faber and Faber).

Newspapers

Elephtheria, Daily
Kathimerini, Daily
Nea, Daily
Vima, Weekly

8

Spain: Growth to Diversity

ELISABET ALMEDA and SEBASTIÀ SARASA

> We have a mixed system, midway between the Bismarck and the
> Beveridge models, which is far from the development of the so-called
> 'welfare state', in most European countries. (Jordi Estivill, 1993,
> p. 255)

By the end of the dictatorship of General Franco in 1975, Spain had developed a 'despotic–corporatist' welfare regime. Social spending was relatively low by European standards and services were financed and administered through social insurance and mainly available to workers and their dependents rather than to citizens, as of right. The insurance scheme covered some three-quarters of the population. There were strict divisions between the rights available to different groups in the occupational hierarchy. The Catholic Church exerted a strong influence and policies were designed to support the patriarchal family. The concern of government was to secure the support of key population groups and of the Catholic Church, while permitting the development of capital and retaining the allegiance of the armed forces (Moreno and Sarasa, 1993; Rodríguez Cabrero, 1993).

Social expenditure grew rapidly during the 1970s in order to ensure the legitimacy of the new democratic order – indeed spending increased faster at that time than in any subsequent decade. The Socialist (PSOE) Party that came to power in 1982, and has remained in government since, inherited the modified Francoist regime. Its policies have expanded the coverage of social insurance, established a universal health service and extended secular education. In recent years, the desire to retrench social policy commitments in the face of economic pressures has come into conflict with the need to retain working class electoral support. In this

155

chapter, we discuss the development of social policy in Spain since 1982 in the context of demographic and economic change. We also consider likely developments in the future.

Social Welfare Services in the Early 1980s

In order to set the scene for the subsequent development of policy, we will set out the main features of the social welfare system as it existed in the early 1980s. The principal areas of provision were cash benefits, health care, social housing and education. Social care services were limited.

The state social security system provided earnings related contributory benefits for retirement, disability, sickness and widowhood. In addition, insurance-based unemployment benefits were available to some groups for periods of entitlement depending on the length of contribution record. The schemes were organised entirely through central government and regional and local administrations played no part in them. The pension scheme was financed through employers' and employees' contributions and received virtually no subsidy from direct taxation.

Different groups of workers received different benefits. A general insurance regime applied to most industrial and service sector workers, while special regimes covered twenty categories, ranging from agricultural workers and civil servants to the armed forces and professional groups. Social insurance rights thus reflected occupational status, following the Bismarckian model.

By the end of the 1970s, contributions to the general regime provided nearly 90 per cent of total contribution income, although the regime covered only two-thirds of social security contributors. Sarasa and Moreno (1993) demonstrate that workers affiliated to the general regime were subsidising the welfare benefits and services of the generally more affluent groups affiliated to the special regimes. The imbalance between contributions and benefits was further aggravated by the incorporation of other social groups such as the Catholic clergy, international civil servants, insurance agents and footballers on favourable terms, an indication of the importance of 'clientelist' social relations in Mediterranean welfare regimes. Expenditure of contributory pensions and unemployment benefits grew rapidly in the 1980s.

The Socialist government added a non-contributory assistance scheme in 1984 under the Law for the Social Integration of Disabled Persons. This consisted of subsidies and financial aid awarded by the National Social

Aid Fund (FAS) for disabled persons. Entitlement depended on the discretionary decisions of social workers employed by the charity Caritas, the local administrations or specific voluntary bodies. The groups least likely to fulfil the contribution conditions for insurance unemployment benefit were women with insecure employment contracts or without previous work experience, young people, or long-term unemployed people.

The Francoist regime had previously repealed the family policy reforms of the Second Republic (1931–9) in relation to divorce, paternal authority, contraception and abortion, and had embarked on an extensive ideological crusade in favour of the strengthening and protection of the 'traditional family'. The concern with support for patriarchy had led to a system of financial aid to married couples, benefits for wives who did not work outside the home, maternity benefits, child benefits and 'birth awards' which rewarded large families. A 'family salary' was also available, which paid benefits in relation to the financial pressures on a family. The emphasis on child benefits and the family salary reflected the assumption that married women were subordinate to paternal authority and should not work outside the home. In the case of some working-class families, the benefits received through these schemes might exceed their earnings. There were also family tax reliefs (Meil, 1992).

The recession of 1973 and the social and political modernisation of post-Francoist Spanish society led to cutbacks in family benefits. Since that time, there has been a tendency to identify pro-natalist and paternalist family policy with the patriarchal values of the Franco regime. Family allowance, maternity and single parent benefits are now among the lowest in the EU, and the emphasis of family policy is on tax allowances (EU, 1993, pp. 57–61).

Health care in Spain was provided through four systems: social insurance, private, occupational and charitable. Private services were run on commercial lines and constituted a parallel health care system. Charitable provision was locally administered, of variable quality and stigmatic.

The social insurance system provided hospital and front-line medical services and subsidised prescriptions. In practice, the majority of social insurance financed hospital care was provided through private hospitals, over half by hospitals run by the Catholic Church (Rodriguez Cabrero, 1993, section 3.2; de Miguel and Guillén, 1990). The special regimes for civil servants of the central and local administrations, the armed forces and non-industrial workers operated alongside the general regime of the Department of Social Security. As a result, the health system was mixed but uncoordinated, with an overlapping of functions. Planning was difficult and there was substantial inequality in the services available in different regions and localities and to various social groups. A national Ministry of Health was created in 1977. Until 1982 it concentrated its efforts more towards rationalisation and the transfer of services to the recently created Autonomous Communities than towards a formal reform strategy for the system as a whole. In 1982, the National Health Institute (INSALUD) was set up to take over the services previously run by the Department of Social Security. This provided services financed principally by workers' and employers' contributions, and covered 86 per cent of the population. About a third of hospital beds were publicly provided, the remainder belonging to private hospitals, although the public sector covered the hospital costs of about four-fifths of hospitalised patients. The remaining 20 per cent were financed equally by private health insurance and through direct fees (de Miguel and Guillén, 1990).

Social care provision for elderly people was limited. Some nine out of ten Spaniards of retirement age or above live with their own or their children's families. However, substantial numbers of elderly people on low incomes live alone, in most cases widows who are more concentrated in rural areas which have lost population as a result of the successive country-to-city migrations of the 1960s (Flaquer, 1990). Only 5 per cent are in retirement homes (Castells and Pérez, 1992, p. 86). The development of community health care in the 1980s was piecemeal, being the responsibility of the Autonomous Communities who each produced their own legislation at different times. Home care services were practically non-existent, so that responsibility for those in need of care and support devolved on to families and to a lesser extent to a poorly established series of residential institutions.

The housing policies pursued under Francoism encouraged home ownership through mortgage subsidy. Some social housing was also constructed. Such policies benefited the middle class and had little redistributive impact. Rents had been frozen during the transition to democracy, which severely reduced the profitability of urban landlordism, and prevented the development of a rented property market. In 1981, less than one-fifth of properties were rented.

The educational system at the end of the 1970s combined public and private provision and displayed marked inequalities. Almost half the non-university students were registered at private centres, which were mainly financed through public funds. In spite of the fact that the primary school programme (*Enseñanza General Básica*) was free and in theory compulsory until the age of 14, many children did not continue their education beyond the age of 12 due to shortage of places. The expansion of the system extended the effective age-range of compulsory schooling to 5–14 by 1987 (Rivière and Rueda, 1993). The class inequalities of the system are illustrated by the fact that working-class students made up only a quarter of 19-year-old university students, while they constituted over half of the total population in that age group (CIDE, 1992).

Changes in the Economic and Socio-demographic Environment

In this section we consider the changes in the economy, population structure, the labour market and public opinion that have influenced the recent development of social policy in Spain.

The Economic Context of Social Policy

The Spanish economy suffered badly in the recession of the 1970s. It was characterised by state-protected corporatism which favoured the defence of established national interest groups against competition from external corporations. It was mostly dependent on foreign raw materials, energy and foodstuffs, while relying on an industrial base in which twice as many individual sectors were in recession as was the average for an OECD country (Fuentes Quintana, 1993). The political weakness of the regime led the government to place a higher priority on maintaining levels of consumer spending in its response to the recession than on strong measures to adapt the economic system to the new international situation. These policies produced an inflation rate of over 25 per cent (the highest in Europe) at the time of the first democratic general elections in 1977, together with a major deficit in the balance of payments on current accounts (5 billion dollars) and a foreign debt of 12 billion dollars (Fuentes Quintana, 1993).

An attempt to secure the agreement of all political parties on economic regulation in the Moncloa Pacts of 1977 proved ineffective. On winning the election in 1982, the Socialist Party abandoned its electoral programme, which had been based on the social democratic orthodoxy of nationalisation and the use of public spending to regulate the level of demand in the economy. The failure of the French Socialist government to achieve stable growth through such methods, combined with the financial costs of maintaining the unproductive industries which had developed at the expense of the public sector during the protectionism of the Franco era and the evident difficulties of the Scandinavian model, strengthened the position of the market-oriented 'social liberals' in the Socialist government.

The fact that the Socialist Party had secured an absolute parliamentary majority permitted the development of the Mid-Term Economic Programme from 1983 to 1986. It had four basic aims: to reduce the level of inflation to EU levels, to improve profitability, to make the economic system more flexible and liberal, and to restructure industry to adapt to the new recession. The policies pursued included a restrictive monetary policy, the promotion of exports (including a currency devaluation in 1982 and the adoption of a free-floating exchange rate), and the moderation of the growth of salaries and other incomes. In this period Spain recovered the relative advantage in labour costs which had diminished as wages rose during the democratic transition. By 1985 total labour costs were 43 per cent below the average for industrialised countries. Social security entitlement rules for pensions and unemployment benefits were tightened in early 1985, nationalisation policies were cut back and an unsuccessful attempt was made to reduce the public deficit.

As a result of this plan, and of the international recovery from 1983 onwards which improved the export situation, the inflation rate fell, the balance of payments went into the black and growth and profitability increased. These policies also led to a sharp increase in unemployment. The job losses resulting from the restructuring of industry coincided with a rising trend in the number of people and particularly of women seeking employment.

The world economic recovery, together with a fall of nearly 50 per cent in the price of oil and raw materials, and a decline of the value of the dollar against the peseta of 32 per cent between 1985 and 1988, stimulated an increase in foreign trade. A policy of fiscal incentives for investment, allowing firms to write off the capital costs of new equipment, was introduced towards the end of 1985. Spain's entry into the EU in 1986 generated a major injection of foreign capital. The balance of payments improved still further. As a consequence, more than one and a half million jobs were created, and the unemployment rate dropped for the first time since 1969. Investments expanded rapidly as a result of the growth in internal demand, corporate gains, the control of inflation and investment incentives. This increase peaked in 1989 and then declined as a result of falling corporate profits and rising interest rates.

The public deficit was substantially reduced during the same period. Government revenues improved as a result of the decline in demand for unemployment benefits and business subsidies resulting from the economic recovery, the new measures to combat fiscal fraud and the pension reforms of 1985. The deficit fell from 6.9 per cent of GDP in 1985 to 2.8 per cent in 1989, although there was an increase to 4.9 per cent in 1991. The privatisation of public corporations helped to reduce the public deficit and also ended the traditional Spanish policy of nationalising private losses.

Demographic Changes

At the end of 1991, the Spanish population was estimated at just under 39 million, an annual growth rate of only 0.2 per cent since 1981. This is the lowest demographic increase for the country this century (Council of Europe, 1993). The principal explanation is the continuing decline in fertility rates since the 1970s. The fertility rate in Spain fell from 2.8 in 1970, to below 2.1 in the 1980s, which is the level necessary to ensure generational replacement. From this point on, the decline continued steadily until it reached a rate of 1.23 in 1992, the lowest in Europe (Eurostat, 1992; Table 9.3).

The decline in fertility, combined with a falling mortality rate and the virtually insignificant migration rate (less than 1 per cent of the Spanish population in 1988 were resident foreigners), have led to a rapid rise in the average age. The proportion of the population aged 65 or over grew from 10.9 per cent of the total in 1980 to 13.2 per cent by 1990 and is projected to increase to 18.3 per cent by 2020 (Table 1.6; OECD, 1988, table 6).

Women are tending to marry and give birth to their first child later and marriage rates are falling as a result of unemployment, the difficulty of finding work and the rising cost of living in urban areas (Delgado, 1994). The changes, which are parallelled in other southern European countries, are most marked among those born between 1950 and 1960. This generation has been the first to experience the growing incorporation of women in formal education and in the labour market.

In Northern European countries, the drop in the marriage rate and the later age of marriage are compensated by major increases in cohabitation. In Spain, such relationships account for just over 1 per cent of the total population in 1991. The proportion of children whose mothers are unmarried is very low in Spain, which may indicate that even cohabiting couples tend not to have children.

Divorce in Spain is a phenomenon of the 1980s. The divorce rates, like the cohabitation rates, are substantially below the European average (barely 0.6 divorces per 1000 against 1.7 – see Table 9.3). There is every indication that the rates will rise in the next few years (Castells and Alonso, 1992).

Although the families of the divorced and single mothers represent a very small percentage of Spanish families, there are numerous studies which show that single parent families are increasing in Spain since the 1970s and will continue to do so in the future. Statistics are sparse, but the 1991 Census indicates that four-fifths of single parent families are female-headed, and that single parent families with children under 15 represent just over 5 per cent of nuclear family households with young children (see also Table 1.7).

The Spanish single parent family owes its origin more to widowhood than to divorce or single parenthood (Almeda and Flaquer, 1993). According to a CIS (Sociological Research Council) survey of 1985, widowed mothers represented 61 per cent of all single mothers, followed by the group of separated or divorced mothers (27 per cent), and finally by unmarried mothers (12 per cent). In France and Great Britain, by contrast, families headed by widowed mothers represent only 20 and only 8 per cent respectively. Divorced and separated mothers in these two countries account for approximately two-thirds of the total, and single mothers represent almost a quarter in France and nearly a third in Britain (Roll, 1992).

Labour Market and Unemployment

Between 1981 and 1990 the number of people seeking work grew from little more than 13 to 15 million. The Spanish economy has been unable to absorb this growth. The size of the group in work fell from 1977 to 1985, when the unemployment rate reached nearly 22 per cent. From this year on a period of strong economic recovery began, which brought the unemployment figures down to 16 per cent by 1990. The recovery affected the social structure unevenly. Since more women joined the labour market over this period the female unemployment rate remained almost exactly steady (25.2 per cent in 1985 and 24.1 per cent in 1990). Male unemployment dropped from 20.3 per cent in 1985 to 11.9 per cent in 1990. This occurred in spite of the fact that the service sector which has traditionally tended to employ a greater proportion of women, generated the largest number of jobs. Between 1981 and 1989, employment generated by industry grew at an average annual rate of 0.2 per cent, while the total employment growth was over 5 per cent each year and the agricultural sector shed nearly a quarter of its workforce (Sarasa and Moreno, 1993).

The new jobs differ from those previously available. New legislation in the early 1980s facilitated the hiring of workers on temporary contracts. More than a third of the labour force are now in temporary jobs (Fernández *et al.*, 1991). This figure is much higher than the European average. The growth of temporary work is associated with greater divisions between different groups of workers in earnings, working conditions and social security rights. It affects women, young people and underqualified or undereducated people disproportionately, particularly those who work in construction, agriculture, commerce, the hotel trade and social services (Castillo and Toharia, 1993).

Public Opinion with Respect to Social Expenditure

Successive opinion polls on attitudes to social expenditure indicate that, in general, the Spanish population strongly supported an increase in spending on social welfare services in the early 1980s. They were also prepared to pay more taxes, if necessary, to cover the costs. The declared willingness to pay more tax weakened somewhat by the end of the decade, although it did not fall to the level of the period of democratic transition (Alvira and García, 1988). Dissatisfaction with social provision is now rising (see Table 10.3). According to the 1992 Eurobarometer survey, 48 per cent of Spaniards believe that social security is too costly, and that public contributions should be reduced even if this involves a reduction in services. Only 36 per cent of those interviewed think that services should be improved at the cost of an increase in taxation.

Social Policies in the 1980s

The first Socialist government directed public resources more energetically towards industrial restructuring than towards improving social services. This approach was initially supported by the trade union UGT (Unión General de Trabajadores), allied to the Socialist Party, and received more coldly by the CCOO (Comisiones Obreras), a union traditionally associated with communist parties. The policy was still actively pursued during the period of economic recovery which began in 1986, but the loss of affiliated members of UGT to the benefit of CCOO caused a change in UGT strategy. This brought about the general strike of 1988 and the breakdown of the neo-corporatist practices which had characterised the period of political transition of the early 1980s.

Economic prosperity and trade union pressure from 1986 onwards led the government to favour social spending. The Ministry of Social Affairs was created in 1988, unemployment benefit was increased, pensions were improved and basic education at primary and secondary levels was made universal. To these social reforms we should add the Health Law of 1986 which committed the government to the creation of a universal National Health Service. However, the increasing instability of employment, the inability to achieve any substantial reduction in the unemployment rate, the successive attempts to make the labour market more flexible and the absence of a redistributive housing policy have increased the pressure on social welfare services.

Policy on Pensions and Cash Benefits

The 1980s and 1990s have been a period of expansion in cash benefits. Public spending on social provision grew at a more rapid rate from 1983 to 1985 than at any time since the 1970s, especially in the areas of health care, education and housing. The general strike of 14 December 1988, in which wage earners demanded greater equality in the distribution of social spending, led to increases in pensions and unemployment benefits (Rodríguez Cabrero, 1993). The number of pensioners rose by 1.7 million between 1980 and 1992, mainly as a result of the rapid increase in the number of disability pensions (especially in the early 1980s) as well as demographic factors. The greater part of the expansion of disability pensions appears to have resulted from fraud and from the 'clientelist' relations between employers and prospective claimants, a process comparable to that identified by Ferrera in Italy (1994). An additional pressure on spending was provided by the social security reforms which integrated hitherto unprotected or weakly protected groups, such as home helps, maritime workers, writers, artists and small traders, into a special regime.

Further changes to the cash benefit system increased minimum pension levels and restructured entitlements according to the age and dependents of the beneficiary (Ramírez de Arellano, 1993). Entitlement conditions were tightened and an upper limit to state pensions set in 1984. The net effect of these changes was to increase spending on social insurance benefits.

The Spanish pensions system was universalised in 1990, with the creation of a new category of means-tested 'non-contributory benefits'. These benefits extended the coverage of retirement and disability pensions to include all citizens considered to be in need who did not receive social security benefits or whose benefits were below the threshold of the contributory scheme. These non-contributory benefits subsumed and repealed the old assistance subsidies of the National Social Aid Fund and the financial benefits for disabled persons, which had already been considerably improved (Jiménez, *et al.*, 1993).

In relation to unemployment benefits, the formula calculating the size of benefit has been improved and the range of coverage increased. As a result of legislation in 1984, entitlement to the contributory benefit has been extended to two years and new forms of aid have been established, particularly for older unemployed persons. Those over 55 (lowered in 1989 to 52) may claim unemployment benefit until they reach retirement age (Jiménez *et al.*, 1993).

After the application of the 1984 law, and the simultaneous granting of an agricultural subsidy in some Autonomous Communities, coverage of unemployment benefit has expanded from about a quarter of all unemployed persons to just over half in 1991 (Anuario el Mundo, 1993). Over the same period, the cost of unemployment benefits has grown from around 400 to 1600 billion pesetas (equivalent to 2 to 7.5 billion pounds) although the unemployment rate has fallen from about 21 to 16 per cent. On the other hand, the salary substitution rate of contributory unemployment benefits varied from 100 per cent for those who earnings were equivalent to the minimum wage to 34 per cent for those on the highest salaries covered (Jiménez *et al.*, 1993).

Legislation in 1985 and 1990 confined family benefits only to those on very low incomes. All other family benefits have been replaced by tax deductions (Meil, 1992; Iglesias de Ussel and Meil, 1994).

Educational Policy

One of the Socialist Party's first measures after the 1982 election victory was to guarantee the academic freedom of teachers – a radical step in a country where Catholicism remains influential – and to increase the participation of the school community in the running of educational centres. The Right to Education Organic Law (LODE) proposal in which these measures were included, as well as others aimed at increasing control over public grants to private institutions, provoked a powerful reaction by the Catholic Church and the school managers. This led to the strongest conservative social reaction against the government of the 1980s (see Giner and Sarasa, 1992).

Over this period, the public provision of educational services expanded rapidly at the expense of church education. At the same time, school enrolment increased and considerable efforts were made to improve equality of opportunity. The number of pupils in secular state schools has increased. The proportion of secondary pupils enrolled in Catholic schools fell from 21 per cent in 1983 to 18 per cent by 1989, a decline attributable more to trends established from the early 1970s than to the policies of the Socialist government (Labrador, 1985). Where higher education is concerned, the Catholic Church has had to create its own confessional universities since it was unable to retain its influence over the public system.

Regarding access to education, there have been notable improvements in the enrolment rate for 4-year-olds, and for children over 13. However, the rates for children under 4 are still very low, and just over a third of 16 year olds are not attending school, despite the legal obligation to do so. Spending on university scholarships increased by nearly six times between 1982 and there is thought to be a high level of fraud by self-employed workers (Moltó and Oroval, 1990). As part of the scheme to improve access to education there are grants for compensatory education, adult education and ethnic minority education (gypsies and immigrants), as well as schemes to prevent children from leaving school prematurely in urban areas (Rivière and Rueda, 1993).

The education system has certainly expanded overall. It is still too early to judge the effect of these policies on social inequality. Some studies suggest that there has been little territorial redistribution of educational resources (Rivière and Rueda, 1993), and that inequalities may even have deepened. Women are overrepresented in subject areas with lower social prestige which have poorer employment prospects and which ultimately lead to less well-paid jobs (Archanco, 1993).

Housing Policy

During the second half of the 1980s, Spain experienced a housing boom which increased the price of property on average by 72 per cent between 1985 and 1990. The increase was much greater in the big cities, and was more than double the rate of increase in family incomes (Naredo, 1993). The proportion of family income committed to mortgage repayments rose from about a third to just over a half between 1985 and 1992. A number of factors have contributed to the rise in house prices, including a shift in savings from the industrial sector towards property speculation, the escalation of legal fees, the use of house purchase as a means of laundering illegal incomes, and anti-inflationist policies which have kept mortgage interests above those of the majority of European countries (Leal and Cortés, 1993). Housing policy has focused on interest relief and building subsidies rather than the construction of social housing (Bandrés, 1993, p.143). The gap between average family incomes and house prices makes some three-quarters of the population eligible for mortgage interest subsidies, so that these benefits are not targeted on those with low incomes. In practice, the policy operates more to support the property market than to redistribute access to housing.

Legislation in the mid-1980s weakened rent controls. The result has been a narrowing of access to housing which has affected young people in particular and those who did not acquire a house before the price boom. The most severe effect has been on foreign immigrants, a third of whom live in overcrowded conditions, although nationally the overall number of homes (12 million) exceeds the number of households (11.8 million).

Housing problems have led to a postponement of the average age of marriage amongst young people and have reinforced the traditional tendency for the extended family to occupy the same dwelling – a strategy to reinforce the social capital of the most disadvantaged families in urban areas, rather than as a hangover from rural household patterns (Requena, 1993).

Health Policy

At the time of the first Socialist electoral victory, the Spanish health system was faced with a choice between the development of a universal national health service on the British model or the improvement of the existing Bismarckian social insurance system. The trade unions, left-wing parties and consumer organisations supported the first approach, whereas medical associations, private institutions and conservative political parties favoured the latter (Rodríguez Cabrero, 1993; Ayala, 1994). The Socialist Party's electoral programme included a universal national service.

The 1986 General Health Law committed the government to establishing a universal National Health Service which guaranteed the right to health care for all Spaniards and all foreigner citizens resident on Spanish soil. Coverage, which was already very high in 1980 (83.1 per cent of all citizens and residents), was almost total by 1991 (99.79 per cent).

Access to health benefits is now in practice universal. Despite the new legislation there has been little progress in the unification of the various existing health services, so that the public system continues to buy most of its hospital services from the private and charitable sector, occupational systems remain for particular privileged groups of employees and private health insurance covers about 8 per cent of the population (Freire, 1993). The expansion in coverage has not been accompanied by a corresponding increase in resources, so that the quality of health services has fallen. Average waiting times for surgery has increased sharply. This deterioration is reflected in high levels of dissatisfaction with the public health system (Rodríguez Cabrero, 1993). Nevertheless, average life expectancy for both women and men has continued to increase from 75.6 to 77 years over the 1980s (Ministry of Social Affairs, 1992). The infant mortality rate (11 per 1000) is amongst the most favourable in developed countries (de Miguel and Guillén, 1990).

Personal Social Services for the Elderly

Since the early 1980s the local and autonomous authorities promoted the development of community centres in Spain's large urban areas which soon overtook the 'social centre' system established by the Catholic Church since the 1960s. This trend was reinforced when the Ministry for Social Affairs was established in 1988.

Older people, particularly women, make up the majority of households in poverty. Their homes are often of poor standard. At the same time, there is a substantial shortfall in residential provision, which covers only 2 per cent of those over 65 years of age, against a European Union guideline of 5 per cent (Castells and Pérez, 1992). There has been recent discussion of a building programme, but no clear policy lead from the Ministries of Health or Social Affairs. The scarcity and dispersion of data for the Autonomous Communities make it impossible to establish a reliable picture of the situation.

Decentralisation and Privatisation

Administrative decentralisation has been more important than privatisation in Spain. The socialist government laid particular stress on moving responsibility closer to the community. Progress at the level of regional government has been rapid. In 1979, 90 per cent of the public budget was run by the central administration. By 1990 this had fallen to less than 60 per cent, with about a quarter run by Autonomous Communities and a sixth by the local administrations.

By 1991 over half of health spending was managed by the Autonomous Communities, while the volume of spending in the hands of commercial and non-profit-making private insurance has declined (Rodríguez *et al.*, 1993). There has been a move towards the creation of internal quasi-markets in health services, especially in Catalonia, through the separation of the roles of the purchaser and provider.

Educational responsibilities have shifted towards the Autonomous Communities in a similar manner, and the involvement of the private sector in this field has also decreased. However, the fact that the growth in volume of state education has not been accompanied by a proportionate increase in resources may indicate a relative reduction in quality. Conversely, public subsidies to private schools have grown, although the number of students at such schools has fallen (Bandrés, 1993, p. 142).

Social services are, according to the Spanish Constitution, 'the exclusive responsibility' of the Autonomous Communities, although the national Ministry for Social Affairs has the role of coordinating policy in this area. The constitutional position, however, has allowed the Autonomous Communities to move towards the provision of 'minimum family incomes', requiring proof of need, in spite of the explicit opposition of the Ministry. These benefits provide last resort means-tested incomes to people of working age ineligible for social insurance or the national disability benefits in the regions where they have been established.

The creation of the Autonomous Communities has restricted decentralisation to the regional level. Regional governments have monopolised power at the expense of local administrations, without bringing services closer to citizens. Despite conflict between regions with competing interests, there has been a gradual movement in the direction of greater territorial equality. The Autonomous Communities which have benefited most from this are Andalusia, Galicia, Estremadura, La Mancha and Murcia in the south and east of the country (Alcaide, 1993). Three-quarters of this reduction is estimated to be produced by social benefits (Bandrés, 1993).

Conclusion – the Impact of Change and Options for the Future

Over the whole decade social spending in Spain grew more rapidly than the EU average, from 17 to 19 per cent of GDP between 1980 and 1990 (see Table 1.5). Universal pensions and health care systems have been established, education and unemployment benefits have expanded, a system of social assistance covering the whole country is in process of being created and social care provision is developing from a very low base. However, despite these successes, the social welfare system has encountered a number of problems, so that the increased levels of spending have not realised to the full the benefits that might have been anticipated when the PSOE first came to power.

Three factors are of particular importance in weakening the impact of increased welfare spending. These factors have affected social protection across Europe, but are of especial significance in the Spanish context. First, persistent long-term unemployment is undoubtedly the most significant problem of recent years. Spain's levels of unemployment are the highest in the EU (Table 1.3). Levels fell somewhat towards the end of the 1980s but are rising to substantially above 20 per cent in the recession of the early 1990s. High unemployment has resulted from the impact of international competition – Spanish industry is increasingly open to competition from cheaper labour in less developed countries – the increase in the number of people seeking jobs and the immediate recessionary pressures. The massive expansion of unemployment benefit spending (at an annual growth rate of over 9 per cent by the late 1980s) has not succeeded in achieving coverage of more than two-thirds of all unemployed people.

The second factor concerns the increasing flexibility of labour markets. Legislation since 1990 has weakened employment protection and further deregulation was one of the key issues in the 1993 general election (del Castillo and Lopez Nieto, 1994, p. 426). As a result about a third of the workforce and over half of those employed under 25 are on temporary contracts, with diminished social security rights. This results in strong demands for assistance benefits. The third factor is simply the ageing of the population, which produces demands for health and social care and pensions (see Table 1.6).

As a result of these factors, increased public expenditure has improved standards of provision, but has had a limited effect on social inequality. Social spending in the 1980s grew more slowly than in the 1970s (Rodríguez Cabrero, 1993, Table 1; Sarasa and Moreno, 1993). The ageing of the population has been the most important cause of the growth in social spending, so that expansion has barely been able to keep pace with demand rather than provide improved coverage for groups which were previously unprotected (Bandrés, 1989).

In addition, the redistributive effects of public spending have only succeeded in matching the growth of inequalities resulting from persistent uncmployment, unstable employment and the appearance of new forms of poverty. The redistributive impact of total public expenditure grew by 24 per cent during the 1980s but most of this redistribution resulted from the growing inequality of incomes (Gimeno, 1993; Lasheras *et al.*, 1993). The net reduction in inequality is much less than that which occurred during the previous decade of the democratic transition (Alcaide, 1993). Improvements in pensions have had little effect on the risk of becoming poor for old people. Similarly, despite the increase in coverage of benefits during the decade, the proportion of unemployed households who fall below the poverty line has remained stable at around 30 per cent, a much higher figure than elsewhere in Europe. Lastly, the risk of poverty has increased substantially for households where the main breadwinner is a woman aged under 30. Although such households make up no more than 1 per cent of Spanish homes, the proportion considered poor has grown from 10.8 per cent in 1980 to 16.2 per cent in 1990 (Ayala *et al.*, 1993, Ayala, 1994). Poverty in Spain, as elsewhere in Europe, is increasingly affecting women.

Developments over the next few years are likely to put further strain on the social welfare system. The impact of progress towards a Single European Market is as yet uncertain. However, the emphasis in the Maastricht Treaty on fiscal prudence and the high priority given to containing inflation seem likely to restrain state spending on welfare at the same time as intra-European competition intensifies pressures for further deregulation of the labour market. The 1993 general election confirmed a long-term trend to a weakening of support for the PSOE, whose share of the vote has declined from 48 per cent in 1982 to 38 per cent, forcing it for the first time to seek partnership with a smaller party to enable it to form a government. The choice of the CiU – the liberal-leaning Catalonian nationalist party – as coalition partner, rather than the Eurocommunist-inspired IU, is revealing, indicating the commitment of the Socialist Party to the market-centred policies of recent years.

The choice of the CiU also gives evidence of a growing problem in Spanish internal politics – the pressure for a greater measure of independence from the centre on the part of some of the historical nationalities and communities which make up the country. While Basque or Catalonian secession is difficult to envisage, the strength with which localism and regionalism is pursued reduces the authority of central government to direct internal policies in areas such as social welfare, education and labour market regulation and threatens its capacity to gather revenues. At the same time, persistent corruption scandals involving prominent government figures threaten to undermine the political legitimacy of the centre (del Castillo and Lopez Nieto, 1994, p. 427).

In this context the future direction of Spanish social policy is difficult to predict. One indication that the present dilemmas are not a new departure in Spanish affairs comes from an examination of history. Rodríguez Cabrero (1993) points out that neither working nor ruling class has succeeded in establishing a commanding position of hegemonic power in the country this century. Government has been pursued through corporatist compromises. Francoism represented such an accommodation between the traditional landed classes and the church, in an uneasy relationship with developing industrial capital. The transition to democracy occurred as the pressures resulting from the developing industrial system destabilised the alliance. Under democracy, corporatism was initially expressed through the Moncloa Pacts of 1977–8, agreed between all parliamentary parties. These were extended up to 1986 in agreements between government, the employers' association and the main unions. The alliance forged between the new progressive middle classes and the working class which underlay the Socialist Party election victory of 1982 started to disintegrate from the mid-1980s onwards. The government was drawn into conflict with trade unions over issues such as labour market deregulation, the level of pensions and other benefits and job creation schemes. These conflicts led to general strikes in 1988, 1992 and 1994.

It is possible to envisage three directions which the Spanish welfare system might pursue, corresponding roughly to the political left, centre and right. The left perspective, shared by the United Left (Izquierda Unida), the left wing of the Socialist Party (Partido Socialista Obrero Español) and the unions, envisages the development of a universalist welfare system, with a strong emphasis on the integration of excluded groups. The centre reformist groups (the regional parties based in the most economically advanced part of the country bordering on France – the Catalonian Convergencia I Unio, the Basque Nationalist Partido Nacionalista Vasco – and the 'liberal social democrats' on the right of the PSOE) are concerned to manage the constraints imposed by EU membership, the Maastricht Treaty and the fiscal crisis without making drastic cuts in social benefits. They wish to postpone the further extension of social rights until the competitiveness of the economy is restored. The right-wing Popular Party (Partido Popular), which has now emerged as the largest opposition party with 35 per cent of the vote, and the employers' association, the CEOE, regard social programmes as an economic burden and favour privatisation of services and the reduction of state spending.

However, the main political parties (PSOE, PP, IU, CiU) signed the 'Toledo Pact' in February 1995, which commits them to sustaining the existing social security system. Compulsory social insurance will remain the mainstay of welfare policy, supported by non-contributory means-tested assistance financed from general taxation. A second voluntary tier of private funded pensions will also be permitted, under the legislation originally passed in 1989.

The main unions (the UGT and the CCOO) have endorsed the Toledo Pact, but organisations representing finance capital have expressed misgivings and would prefer a much greater role for private pensions. Although the Popular Party initially sided with finance capital it has now ratified the Pact, so that social insurance welfare seems likely to remain as the basis of the Spanish welfare system.

The PSOE government, electorally weak, in coalition with a centrist party and divided between welfare universalists on its left wing and modernising liberal social democrats on its right, is unable to give clear leadership in this context. It is hard to see further developments in universal provision in Spain in the immediate future. The real choice is between a consolidation of the current system, with the concessions to the market of a further deregulation of employment and a shift towards assistance benefits, or a move in the direction of privatisation and retrenchment, which might result from the PP gaining greater influence in government, especially if it bows to finance capital and withdraws from the Toledo Pact. In any event, the shift towards greater regional autonomy in the provision and management of welfare and other services is unlikely to be halted.

References

Alcaide, J. (1993) 'La distribución de la renta', in García Delgado, J.L., *España, economía* (Madrid: Espasa-Calpe).

Almeda, E. and Flaquer, L. (1993) 'La monoparentalidad en España: Claves para un análisis sociológico', working paper 93/1, Institut d'Estudis Socials Avançats (Barcelona: Universitat Pompeu Fabra).

Alvira, F. and García, J. (1988) 'El gasto público y la sociedad española', *Papeles de Economía Española* no. 37, pp. 56–77.

Anuario el Mundo (1993) *Anuario Estadísticas Laborales (1992)* (Madrid: Ministerio de Trabajo).

Archanco, M.T. (1993) 'La desigualdad social en el sistema educativo formal', in *I Simposio sobre igualdad y distribución de la renta y la riqueza* (Madrid:

Fundación Argentaria), special vol. on *Información estadística sobre desigualdad social*, pp. 103–26.

Ayala, L. (1994) 'Social Needs, Inequality and the Welfare State in Spain: Trends and Prospects', *Journal of European Social Policy*, vol. 4, no. 3, pp. 159–79.

Ayala, L., Martínez, R. and Ruiz-Huerta, J. (1993) 'La distribución de la renta en España en los años ochenta. Una perspectiva comparada', in *I Simposio sobre igualdad y distribución de la renta y la riqueza* (Madrid: Fundación Argentaria), vol. 2, pp. 101–136.

Bandrés, E. (1989) 'Evolución demográfica y gastos sociales', in *Economistas*, no. 39, pp. 26–34.

Bandrés, E. (1993) 'La eficacia redistributiva de los gastos sociales: una aplicación al caso español, 1980–1990', in *I Simposio sobre igualdad y distribución de la renta y la riqueza* (Madrid: Fundación Argentaria), vol. 7, pp. 123–72.

Boletin Estadísticas Laborales (1992) (Madrid: Ministerio de Trabajo).

Castells, M. and Alonso, C. (1992) *España, fin de siglo* (Madrid: Alianza Editorial).

Castells, M. and Pérez, L. (1992) *Análisis de las políticas de vejez en España en el contexto europeo* (Madrid: Instituto Nacional de Servicios Sociales).

Castillo P. del and Lopez Nieto L. (1994) 'Spain – the 1993 Election', *European Journal of Political Research*, vol. 26, pp. 423–9.

Castillo, S. and Toharia, L. (1993) 'Las desigualdades en el trabajo', in *I Simposio sobre igualdad y distribución de la renta y la riqueza* (Madrid: Fundación Argentaria), vol. 4, pp. 7–88.

CIDE (1992) *Las desigualdades sociales en España* (Madrid: Ministry of Education and Science).

CIS (1985) *Encuesta sobre Condiciones de vida y de trabajo de las mujeres.* (Madrid: Cousejo de Iuvestigationes Sociales).

Comisión de Análisis y Evaluación del Sistema Nacional de Salud (1991) *Informe y Recomendaciones* (Madrid).

Council of Europe (1993) *Recent Demographic Developments in Europe and North America.* Council of Europe, Strasbourg.

De Miguel, J. and Guillén, M. (1990) 'La sanidad en España', in Giner S. (ed.) *España: Sociedad y Política* (Madrid: Espasa-Calpe), pp. 471–508.

Delgado, M. (1994) 'El proceso de formación de la familia en España', *Reis* no. 64 (Madrid).

Estivill, J. (1993) 'Social Minimum Income in Spain' in Moreno, L. (ed.), *Social Exchange and Welfare Development* (Madrid: Consejo Superior de Investigationes Científicas).

EU (1993) *Social Protection in Europe* (Luxembourg: Commission of the European Communities).

Eurostat (1992) *Demographic Statistics* (Brussels).

Fernández, F., Garrido, L. and Toharia, L. (1991) 'Empleo y paro en España, 1976–1990', in Miguélez, F. and Prieto, C. (eds), *Las relaciones laborales en España* (Madrid: Siglo XXI).

Elisabet Almeda and Sebastià Sarasa   175

Ferrera, M. (1994) 'Política social en Italia', in *III Seminario Internacional de Política Social 'Gumersindo de Azcárate'*, September – October (Madrid: IESA).

Flaquer, L. (1990) 'La familia española: cambio y perspectivas', in Giner, S. (ed.), *España: sociedad y política* (Madrid: Espasa-Calpe), pp. 509–50.

Freire, J.M. (1993) 'Cobertura sanitaria y equidad en España', in *I Simposio sobre igualdad y distribución de la renta y la riqueza* (Madrid: Fundación Argentaria), vol. 8, pp. 113–38.

Fuentes Quintana, E. (1993) 'Tres decenios largos de la economía española en perspectiva', in García Delgado, J.L., *España, economía*, pp. 1–142.

García Delgado, J.L. (1993) *España, economía* (Madrid: Espasa Calpe).

Gimeno, J. (1993) 'Cambios en la inciden cia redistributiva del Gasto Público', *Cuadernos de Actualidad de Hacienda Pública Española*, vol. 4, no. 5.

Giner, S. and Sarasa, S. (1992) 'Religión, política y modernidad en España', *Revista Internacional de Sociología*, no. 1, tercera época, pp. 9–60.

Iglesias de Ussel, J. and Meil G. (1994) 'Políticas de familia desde la transición' in de Ussel (ed.) *V Informe Foessa sobre la situación social en España* (Madrid).

Jiménez, A. *et al.* (1993) 'Impacto de las prestaciones sociales y su financiación en la renta familiar', in *I Simposio sobre igualdad y distribución de la renta y la riqueza* (Madrid: Fundación Argentaria), vol. II, *Sector público y redistribución*, pp. 173–228.

Labrador, C. (1985) 'El reto de la enseñanza en España', in C. Labrador (ed.) *Catolicismo en España* (Madrid: Instituto de Sociología Aplicada), pp. 215–32.

Lasheras, M.A. Rabadán, I. and Salas, R. (1993) 'Política redistributiva en el IRPF entre 1982 y 1990', in *I Simposio sobre igualdad y distribución de la renta y la riqueza* (Madrid: Fundación Argentaria, vol. 7, pp. 7–24.

Leal, J. and Cortés, L. (1993) 'Desigualdades en el acceso a la vivienda', in *I Simposio sobre igualdad y distribución de la renta y la riqueza* (Madrid: Fundación Argentaria), vol. 8, pp. 165–82.

Meil, G. (1992) 'La evolución de la política familiar en España, 1938–1990. Del salario familiar a la política de pobres', paper read at the Fourth Spanish Congress of Sociology, September (Madrid).

Ministry of Social Affairs (1992) *Gerontological Plan* (Madrid).

Moltó, T. and Oroval, E. (1990) *Estudio del Sistema General de Becas y alternativas para su reforma* (Madrid: Ministerio de Educación y Ciencia).

Moreno, L. and Sarasa, S. (1993) 'Génesis y desarrollo del Estado del Bienestar en España', *Revista Internacional de Sociología*, no. 6 (nueva época), pp. 27–70.

Naredo, J.M. (1993) 'Composición y distribución de la riqueza de los españoles', in *I Simposio sobre igualdad y distribución de la renta y la riqueza* (Madrid: Fundación Argentaria), vol. 3, pp. 7–42.

OECD (1988) *Ageing Populations: The Social Policy Choices* (Paris: OECD).

Ramírez de Arellano, A. (1993) 'Pension Policy in Spain During the Period of 1983–1993', Master's dissertation at the University of York.

Requena, M. (1993) 'Desigualdad social y dependencia familiar en España', in *I Simposio sobre igualdad y distribución de la renta y la riqueza* (Madrid: Fundación Argentaria), vol. 5, pp. 59–86.

Rivière, A. and Rueda, F. (1993) 'Igualdad social y política educativa', in *I Simposio sobre igualdad y distribución de la renta y la riqueza* (Madrid: Fundación Argentaria), vol. 8, pp. 7–34.

Rodríguez, M.; Murillo, C. and Calonge, S. (1993) 'Evolución de la cuantía y la naturaleza del gasto sanitario privado en la década de los ochenta', in *Hacienda Pública Española*, Monografía no. 1 (Madrid: Instituto de Estudios Fiscales).

Rodríguez Cabrero, G. (1993) 'Between Welfare State and Social Assistance State in Spain: 1980–1992', *Comparative Research Conference on Welfare States in Transition*, 9–12 September, Oxford.

Roll, Jo. (1992) 'Familias monoparentales en Europa', *Revista Infancia y Sociedad*, no. 16, July–August (Madrid: Ministry for Social Affairs).

Sarasa, S. *et al.* (1988) *Seguimiento de la gestión de los servicios sociales comunitarios* (Madrid: Siglo XXI).

Sarasa, S. and Moreno, L. (1993) 'The Spanish via Media to the Development of the Welfare State', working paper 93/3 (Barcelona: Universitat Pompeu Fabra/IESA).

9

The Demand for Welfare

VIC GEORGE

> The so-called crises of social protection, health and education all
> have something in common: an explosive demand from individuals
> and families. (EU, 1993, p. 20)

> Unemployment remains the major economic problem facing the
> Community – both now and for the rest of the decade. (EC 1994,
> p. 7)

All the evidence from the country chapters supports the conclusion
reached in Chapter 1 that the overall demand for welfare services has been
rising in recent years and will continue to do so in the foreseeable future.
How much of this demand should be met by the state or by voluntary or
private effort, or simply remain unmet, is a political question that has been
answered differently by different countries. This chapter is concerned
simply with the ways in which demand for welfare will rise or fall in the
future. It is not concerned with the question of how demand for welfare is
met by governments. This is the task of the chapter that follows.

Four main types of factors affect the demand for welfare services in
advanced industrial societies: demographic, economic and labour market,
familial, and social. We review and assess these factors beginning with
the implications of demographic changes.

The Rising Tide of Gerontophobia

Ageing is a normal physiological process that is the destiny of everyone.
Old age, however, is socially constructed and, as such, it can be perceived

177

differently from one country and from one period in history to another. Different theoretical approaches provide different explanations and hence different policy prescriptions for issues surrounding old age in society (Hugman, 1994). There is no one year which can be confidently claimed to be the beginning of old age in every country and at all times. Despite these very obvious observations, governments have used the year when people qualify for a retirement pension as the beginning of old age. Even this year, however, varies almost randomly from one country to another, from one period to another and it tends to be lower for women than for men. Labour market and economic circumstances, rather than health reasons, have been the major influences in the establishment of retirement ages.

As a result of labour market and economic pressures, governments in Europe have adopted two totally contradictory policies in relation to the retirement age and the financial provisions for retirement. In an effort to reduce their country's unemployment rate, most governments made it financially possible and sometimes inviting for employees to retire early. Thus schemes of flexible retirement, of invalidity benefits, of unemployment benefits and of full pension provision were introduced in several countries as exits from the labour market during the immediate preretirement years. Similarly employers, with and without the consent of trade unions, made older workers redundant, sometimes with generous financial terms, in order to deal with their labour costs. The end result has been that the proportion of people at work during the few years before the age of retirement has declined very substantially.

For men aged 60–64, France had the lowest employment rate in Europe in 1990 – a mere 14.4 per cent were in employment. A similar but less striking process took place in relation to men aged 55–59. For the same year, only 48.4 and 56.2 per cent of all men were in employment in Belgium and France, respectively – the countries with the lowest employment ratios for this age group. The same two countries claimed the lowest spots for the age group 65–69 – a mere 3.3 and 5.1 per cent, respectively, were in employment. In brief, employment for men in Europe has become a minority practice after the age of 60 and on present evidence it will become the same for the age group 55–59 (Walker, Alber and Guillemard, 1993, table 3.2, p. 95). All this has come about because of labour market reasons and it is not in any way connected with health or welfare considerations.

The policy of compulsory early retirement from work can have not only adverse financial but social status implications as well. For some, it can mean poverty for the rest of their lives. It also tends to reinforce the already existing belief that older workers are less productive than younger workers. To be considered less productive in a technological age can be a form of stigmatisation and a loss of social status. As the European Community's report on older people put it: *'Older workers, at younger and younger ages, have been as it were declared useless citizens, and stored away alongside all the unproductive members of society who must live on social transfers'* (Walker, Alber and Guillemard, 1993, p. 89; emphasis added).

The second policy adopted recently by several EU and other European countries has been aimed at reducing public expenditure on pensions and other social security benefits for older people. This has taken different forms in different countries: changing the indexation of benefits from gross earnings to net earnings or to inflation; raising the retirement ages of women and, less common, of men at a time when unemployment rates are high; altering the formula used to calculate the amount of pension that a person due for retirement is entitled to; applying stricter eligibility criteria for immigrant pensioners, and so on. Having encouraged and even forced workers to leave work early, governments resorted to the policy of reducing the cost implications of their policy by lowering the living standards of the very same group of people. Both these contradictory policies are evidence of the considerable dominance of economic over social considerations in government decisions affecting vulnerable groups in society, at times when the economy is not performing well. Weak groups always seem to bear an undue burden of the sacrifices needed to rectify the economic fortunes of a country. Vice versa, the top groups in society find ways of insulating themselves from the economic ill effects of recessions.

Despite the social construction of old age, official publications by governments, the EU, the OECD and others of necessity use standard criteria for old age: the year 65 as the dividing line between the old and the middle aged and the year 70 or 75 to divide the 'young elderly' from the 'old elderly'. The first dividing line has social security implications as increasingly more countries adopt it as their retirement age; the second is seen as the year after which demand for health and personal social services rises disproportionately.

Table 1.6 has shown that the proportions of people aged 65 as well as 75 and over has increased and will continue to increase in all European countries. Most of this proportional rise is due to declining fertility rates, though a minor but gradually increasing proportion is the result of the rising life expectancy. Women live longer than men so that while at age 45–49 their numbers are the same as those of men in the European Union as a whole, at the ages 70–74 there are four women for every three men, at the ages 80–84 the proportion rises to two women for every man and at later ages the ratio rises even further.

A pessimistic interpretation of these demographic facts and their assumed cost implications has given rise recently to a form of gerontophobia – the fear that too many people are living too long and are suffering from too many ailments, thus creating a 'demographic time bomb' threatening the future financial and social organisation of industrial societies. In these circumstances, it is argued, a guarantee by the state of a decent standard of living to all old people is inadvisable for it is unsustainable. No doubt, such a position reinforces the already negative image of old age in contemporary industrial society (Beauvoir, 1977).

Demographic predictions are always subject to varying degrees of margin of error. Nevertheless, there is general consensus at present that the number of people aged 65 and over as a percentage of the number of people of working age aged 15–64 will rise in the future. This is what is commonly referred to as the 'age dependency ratio'. On the other hand, the opposite is the case in relation to the young dependent, since fertility rates have fallen so substantially and no one forecasts a reversal of this trend. While in 1960 all twelve EU member countries had fertility rates above population replacement level, by 1990 all but Ireland had fertility rates below replacement level, with the two Catholic countries of Spain and Italy having the lowest fertility rates. The average fertility rate, that is the average number of children per woman of child-bearing age, for the twelve countries fell from 2.63 in 1960 to 1.59 in 1990 (Walker, Alber and Guillemard, 1993, table 1.2, p. 14).

Table 9.1 shows how the demographic picture has changed in recent years and how it is likely to look in the future for several OECD countries. The economic implications of these data has often been overplayed, ignoring the very simple point that the ability of a country to support its elderly depends on several factors some of which are more important than these dependency ratios. Let us look at these factors including the dependency ratios.

Despite the general use of these dependency ratios, their reliability and validity must be questioned. To begin with, we know from past experience that fertility rates are impossible to predict accurately, in the longer term. Moreover, the school age is being extended and more people are staying on in full-time and part-time education. On the other hand, the retirement age is being raised in several countries. The combined effect of all these trends is that it is not possible to predict accurately the future size of the population of working age.

TABLE 9.1 *Working-age population per (a) elderly person (15–64 years/ 65 years and over) and (b) per dependent person (15–64 years/ 0–15+ 65 years and over) (percentages)*

	1960 (a)	(b)	1990 (a)	(b)	2000 (a)	(b)	2020 (a)	(b)
Austria	5.4	1.9	4.5	2.1	4.3	—	3.3	—
Belgium	5.2	1.8	4.5	2.0	3.9	2.0	3.1	1.8
Denmark	6.0	1.8	4.3	2.1	4.4	2.0	3.3	1.8
Finland	8.5	1.7	5.0	2.1	4.6	2.1	2.9	1.7
France	—	—	4.7	1.9	—	—	—	—
Greece	—	—	4.9	—	—	—	—	—
Norway	5.7	1.7	4.0	1.8	4.3	—	3.6	—
Spain	7.6	1.8	5.0	2.0	4.2	2.1	3.7	2.2
Sweden	5.5	1.9	3.6	1.8	3.7	1.6	3.0	1.6
Switzerland	6.2	1.8	4.5	0 4	2 2	0 3	2 1	8
UK	5.5	1.9	4.2	1.9	4.1	1.8	3.5	1.8
USA	6.5	1.5	5.3	1.9	5.4	2.3	3.6	1.8
Japan	11.2	1.8	5.8	2.3	4.0	2.1	2.4	1.5

Source: OECD (1994), table 10a and 10b, p. 100.

Second, it is even more difficult to predict accurately the future size of the *active* working population, for it is this that really matters rather than the mere size of the working population. We do not know what the future level of unemployment or the degree of withdrawal from the labour market will be among older groups and among married women. The degree of withdrawal from the labour market among older groups of working age has been so high recently that it has been claimed that 'falls in the economic activity of older people have in general had a greater impact than demographic changes alone on the ratio of workers to pensioners in Europe' (Age Concern, 1992, p. 37). Experience shows that during periods of full employment many of those who withdrew from the labour market rejoin it. As Table 9.2 (on page 185) shows there are vast reserves of unused labour in all EU countries, particularly among women. When all this is taken into account, it is not very prudent to worry about the declining employment ratios shown in Table 9.1.

Third, there is the all important factor of productivity. Chapter 1 has shown that rises in overall productivity have been declining in recent years, though the decline was less severe in the manufacturing sector. If this continues it may create economic problems in meeting the cost of services not only for the young and the old but for the whole population. If this trend reverses itself, however, the opposite is the case. This decline in the rates of productivity growth must also be seen in the light of the international competition and particularly from South-East Asian countries. While all this appears rather worrying, we should not lose sight of the fact that productivity rates are still rising and that affluent countries possess the wealth to meet the welfare demands of their citizens, if they so wish.

Fourth, there is the issue of migration. Despite all the attempts by EU countries to close their doors to immigrants from Eastern Europe and from third world countries, immigration will continue and most immigrants are young and prepared to do the unpleasant and low-paid jobs. If the economies of EU countries improve substantially and there are labour shortages, then migration will play a larger part. Thus in the short to medium term, at least, and provided there is demand for labour, migration can only ease the demand for welfare provision.

Fifth, there is the vexed question as to whether older people are becoming healthier and hence their disproportionate demands on the health and the personal social services will not arise until much later in life. Most of the welfare cost estimates are based on the assumption that longevity will increase and, at its tail end, it will bring with it increased demand for services. The opposite view, however, is expressed most strongly by Fries who argues that 'the number of very old people will not increase, that the average period of diminished vigour will decrease, that chronic disease will occupy a smaller proportion of the typical lifespan, and that the need for medical care in later life will decrease' (Fries, 1980, p. 130). If Fries's views prove correct, the financial costs of old age will be considerably reduced. It is certainly a major challenge to geriatric medicine which has so far been the cinderella of medicine.

Finally, it is clearly incorrect to consider the old as totally unproductive for many of them provide useful child care and other services to their children, as well as other unpaid services to the community. With the right government policies, this could be extended further. Equally wrong is to imagine that older generations always make greater claims on the public purse than other groups in all areas of life. They make, for example, far fewer claims on education than younger age groups.

Debates on the implications of demographic changes for welfare provision sometimes tend to treat older people as a homogeneous group. Nothing could be further from the truth: there are as many divisions within old age as there are within working age. All these divisions emphasise the fact that great caution is needed in talking about the elderly as a group with common problems. In some aspects of life, there are common problems but in others only differences exist. These differences are not simply issues of academic interest but they could have substantial policy implications as well. Here we shall examine three of these: the young and the old elderly; men and women; the affluent and the impoverished.

It is generally agreed that the needs of the very old are greater than the needs of those who are only a few years past retirement. They are more likely to suffer from disability, to live alone and to have low incomes. While the proportion of severely disabled people in EU countries is 'below 5 per cent in the age-group 60–69, the proportion increases about five- or sixfold to around 30 per cent among those aged 80 or older' (Walker, Alber and Guillermard, 1993, p. 101). It is natural that with the advance of old age, both widowhood and living alone become more prevalent to compound the problems of ill health and of difficult financial circumstances. It is for this reason that the OECD report concluded its discussion on this issue by saying: 'While the frail elderly represent a challenge, the active retired constitute a potential resource' (OECD, 1988, p. 19).

The feminisation of advanced old age is as true as the feminisation of care and the feminisation of poverty. We pointed out earlier that women outnumber men considerably after the age of 75 and many have to live on incomes that are insufficient for even basic needs. This is the inevitable result of their inferior position in the labour market as well as in the state and occupational social security systems. It is not merely old age – it is that compounded by class and gender discrimination. Similarly, most of the care of dependent elderly and others is carried out by younger women whose relative numbers are declining, while their workload is rising by their greater rates of participation in paid employment.

In all EU member countries, excluding the Netherlands, poverty is more prevalent among the retired than among the younger age groups, using national poverty lines (Walker, in Age Concern, 1992, table 4, p. 177). Yet this should not conceal the fact that income inequalities among the old are as prevalent as among the young. Those with well paid jobs and with good occupational pension provisions are likely to become the affluent among the old. Vice versa' the low paid worker of today is likely to become the retired person in poverty. This is as true today as in the past despite the rise in living standards among all age groups in the population. On present evidence, it will also continue into the future.

Disaggregating the needs of different groups of older people provides a better basis for social service planning, though the ultimate decision of the nature and scope of these services is a political one for facts rarely speak for themselves. They are always interpreted politically in the policy-making process.

It is important to end this section by stressing a simple fact that can easily be forgotten in debates on the policy implications of demographic changes: the vast majority of older people live independent lives and of those who need help in order to manage their daily lives, the majority receive it from their families. This type of informal caring needs to be nurtured by the state in financial and other ways if it is to survive and thrive in the future. Without such state recognition, there is the danger that caring families may come to feel that state services 'will only be supplied to the elderly person when they have given up' (OECD, 1994, p. 41) and, if this happens, the pressures on public expenditure will increase further. Though it is very difficult to calculate in any precise way the value of informal family care in this area, estimates 'suggest that it exceeds by a ratio of at least 3 or 4 to 1 the value of formal services, even in countries with highly-developed social services' (OECD, 1994, p. 41).

The Disorderly Labour Market

X The most obvious and most powerful economic pressure for increased welfare spending today is unemployment. In mid-1994, 11 per cent – some 18 million persons – were unemployed in the whole of the European Union, that is they were out of work and were both available for, and actively seeking, work. This overall figure varied between countries and was higher among the unskilled than among other groups of workers. It was also higher among the very young – those below age 25 – than older workers up to the age of 55 when, as we saw earlier, people begin withdrawing from the labour market altogether in large numbers and are not counted as unemployed. In this and in other ways the official unemployment rate underestimates the proportion of people of working age who want to work but are not working.

Table 9.2 provides data not only for the official unemployment rates but also the ratios of employment to working age population for men and for women in EU countries. The table shows quite clearly that the level of labour force participation of people of working age is rather low. The problem facing most EU countries, therefore, is how 'to raise its *employment* rate, both by reducing unemployment and by increasing participa-

TABLE 9.2   *Employment indicators in EU countries, 1992 (percentages)*

	Employment ratios*			Unemployment rates			L/T unemployment		
	Total	Male	Female	Total	Male	Female	Total	Male	Female
Belgium	56.8	68.8	44.8	6.7	4.8	9.5	61.6	57.5	64.3
Denmark	76.1	80.7	71.3	9.0	8.3	9.9	31.2	27.9	34.3
Germany	67.8	79.1	56.2	4.1	3.7	4.7	45.5	48.9	42.0
Greece	55.4	74.9	37.2	7.8	4.9	12.9	47.0	37.0	53.7
Spain	48.8	66.3	31.7	17.7	13.6	25.1	51.1	42.7	58.8
France	60.5	69.8	51.5	10.2	8.1	12.9	37.2	34.8	39.0
Ireland	52.4	67.3	37.3	15.0	14.9	15.6	60.3	64.8	52.1
Italy	53.6	70.4	37.2	9.4	6.9	13.8	67.1	65.4	68.2
L/mbourg	62.0	76.9	46.6	2.0	1.6	2.8	30.4	41.7	18.2
N/rlands	64.2	77.0	51.2	5.6	4.0	7.8	43.0	50.2	36.7
Portugal	68.4	80.5	57.4	4.0	3.4	4.8	38.3	33.3	41.3
UK	69.4	76.9	61.8	9.7	11.5	7.3	28.1	32.2	21.1
Total EU	59.5	70.3	48.5	9.4	8.1	11.3	N/A	N/A	N/A

* Employment ratio = total number of people at work/ total population of working age, 15–64 years. L/T unemployment refers to unemployment lasting twelve months and over and the figures refer to 1991.
Source: EU (1994a), pp. 38–42 for employment ratios and unemployment rates. For long-term (L/T) unemployment, OECD (1993), tables P, Q and R, pp. 196–7.

tion' in the labour force from among those not registered as unemployed but who are not working either (EU, 1994a, p. 34).

Unemployment creates or increases both the direct and the indirect demands for welfare spending. The direct demands are in the form of benefits paid to the unemployed. They can be substantial at times of high unemployment, particularly when they are seen in conjunction with lost income tax and insurance contributions. As we saw in Chapter 1, however, most member countries reduced the generosity of their schemes during the 1980s in an effort to pressurise the unemployed back to work and to reduce public expenditure in this area.

The indirect costs of unemployment result from the fact that long-term unemployment can combine with other factors to bring about higher rates of physical and mental illness, of family break-up, of homelessness, of crime and of suicide (Brenner, 1980; Fagin and Little, 1984; Sinfield, in OECD, 1984). Long-term unemployment brings a drop in income and in self-esteem, a rise in feelings of inadequacy and inferiority and continual emotional stress in societies where the value of work is held supreme. Whether European societies will one day return to a full employment situation is a moot point but for the immediate future this is most unlikely. As the recent EU report put it: 'unemployment remains the major economic problem facing the Community – both now and for the rest of the decade' (EU, 1994a, p. 7). The globalisation of national economies makes it even more difficult for governments to deal with unemployment by simply pursuing their own initiatives.

The overall employment ratio for the whole European Union declined from 65.2 per cent in 1965 to 58.0 per cent in 1993, due entirely to the drop in the employment ratio for men. The need to create more jobs is overwhelming and all governments accept this. They differ on how best to achieve this between the majority which stress active employment policies – training for workers, financial incentives to employers who take on the long-term unemployed, direct government job creation programmes and other such measures – and the minority which favour labour market deregulation with its reduction of labour costs. Expenditure on job creation programmes thus varies considerably among EU countries reflecting not only availability of resources but ideology as well. Thus while Denmark and Germany spent 1.8 and 1.0 per cent, respectively, of their GDP on active employment policies, Greece because of resource constraints and the UK with its emphasis on labour market deregulation policies spent a mere one-half per cent of their GDP in 1992 (EU, 1994, p. 152). The room for expansion in expenditure on active employment policies is quite considerable, for even Denmark's relatively high rate amounted to only a quarter of its total expenditure on the unemployed – the other three-quarters were taken up by social security benefits.

There is now general agreement that future employment patterns will be very different from those of the past. It may well be that eventually some EU countries will achieve full employment for a while but they will not be providing full-time, secure jobs for life to most workers. Rather, there will be more part-time jobs, greater occupational insecurity, higher rates of labour turnover and most of the new part-time jobs will be for married women. In the UK, for example, 'Two-thirds of the new jobs created in the 1980s were part-time; 80 per cent of them went to married women, most of them with employed husbands' (Commission on Social Justice, 1994, p. 38). This pattern of job creation may force men to change their job expectations and their caring roles but the essential point for our discussion remains the same – the new employment pattern requires a new type of social security system. What is needed is a non-sexist social security system that takes full account of part-time employment and job insecurity. Such a system may well be more costly than the system we have had so far which was oriented towards men working fulltime in jobs with good security of tenure and in societies with full employment. It is a system that never reflected reality fully but in view of the high rates of unemployment, and the other labour market and family changes of the last two decades, it has now become obsolete.

All advanced industrial societies today are experiencing, to a greater or lesser degree, disorderly types of employment: high rates of unemployment, part-time work, temporary work, frequent job changes, job insecurity and income uncertainty. Some groups of workers are more vulnerable to this type of employment than others, black workers more than white workers and women with children are more prone than men. The fundamental question is whether European societies will return to full employment through the traditional economic policies discussed above or whether a much wider approach is needed that combines economic with political and cultural measures (Leadbeater and Mulgan, 1994).

The Arrival of Serial Monogamy

The traditional long-lasting monogamous, male-dominated, two-parent family is everywhere in retreat in Europe, though the pace and the timing of the retreat varies from one part of Europe to another. The move away from this type of family began in the Scandinavian countries, spread to North European countries and more recently to the Mediterranean countries of Greece, Spain and Portugal. Separation, divorce, cohabitation and remarriage rates have risen everywhere bringing about the institution of serial monogamy in many countries. These changes in family structures 'are being driven not by some isolated (and by implication reversible) "1960s permissiveness" but by profound economic and social forces' which renders them a permanent feature of industrial societies (Hewitt, 1994, p. 170).

Tables 9.3 and 1.7 on lone parents show that the traditional marriage, family and child-rearing patterns are gradually disappearing. Marriage rates have declined everywhere despite the rise in remarriages. Divorce rates have risen considerably and only countries where, until recently, divorce was not legally possible or difficult are the figures relatively low. Extra-marital births are the highest in Denmark accounting for one live birth to two. In the UK, cohabitation is now the norm among the young

TABLE 9.3   *Family trends in Europe (percentages*)*

	Mar. rates		Div. rates		Ex. births		Fert. rates	
	1965	*1990*	*1965*	*1990*	*1960*	*1991*	*1965*	*1992*
Belgium	7.0	6.5	0.6	2.0	2.1	10.7	2.60	1.56
Denmark	8.8	6.1	1.4	2.7	7.8	46.5	2.61	1.77
France	7.1	5.1	0.7	1.9	6.1	31.8	2.84	1.73
Germany	8.4	6.5	1.0	2.2	6.3	15.1	2.51	1.30
Greece	9.4	5.4	0.4	0.6	1.2	2.4	2.32	1.41
Ireland	5.9	5.0	—	—	1.6	16.6	4.03	2.11
Italy	7.7	5.4	—	0.4	2.4	6.6	2.55	1.26
Luxembourg	6.6	6.1	0.4	2.2	3.2	12.2	2.41	1.65
Netherlands	8.8	6.4	0.5	1.9	1.4	12.0	3.04	1.59
Portugal	8.3	6.9	0.1	0.9	9.5	15.6	3.07	1.48
Spain	7.1	5.5	—	0.6	2.3	9.6	2.97	1.23
UK	7.8	6.5	0.7	2.9	5.2	29.8	2.83	1.80

* Marriage rates refer to the number of marriages in any one year per 1000 eligible adults.

* Divorce rates refer to the number of divorces in any one year per 1000 existing marriages.

* Extra-marital birth rates are the number of such births in any one year as a proportion of all live births.

* Fertility rates are the number of children per woman.

Where divorce rates are shown to be —, it is because divorce was not legally possible.

Source: Hantrais (1994), table 1, p. 216; col. 6, and col. 8, CSO 1994, p. 39 and p. 40.

either as a prelude to marriage or as an end in itself (Alexander and Radford, 1994); divorce and remarriage is soon becoming a standard practice with 37 per cent of all marriages involving at least one divorced partner (CSO, 1994); one child in five is being brought up by a lone parent at any one time and a higher proportion are spending part of their lives in one parent family situations; and three babies in ten are born outside marriage but three-quarters of them to cohabiting couples in the whole country, while in some inner city areas the proportion of children born out of wedlock is one in two. As Table 9.3 shows, the position is similar in some other North European countries and only Ireland, Greece, Spain and Portugal differ substantially from this picture, though the trend even in these countries is in the same direction.

These family changes have three important implications for welfare demand. The first is the direct cost of maintaining or assisting to maintain lone parent families. Countries differ in the generosity of social security provision for lone parent families and they all try rather unsuccessfully to make the absent parent – usually the father – responsible for family maintenance. In addition to these social security benefit costs, there is the cost resulting from the greater risk that children of lone parents run for being in the care of the local authority than other children (Fisher *et al.*, 1986, table 1, p. 10).

The combination of state and other financial support for one-parent families turns out to be inadequate in all countries, with the result that a relatively high proportion of these families live in poverty particularly in countries with negative attitudes towards them. In the mid-1980s, the proportion of two-parent households in the USA in poverty (with incomes less than 50 per cent of the median income of the country) was 13.6 per cent, while the proportion of lone mother households was 56.5 per cent. In Germany, the corresponding proportions were 4.0 and 28.9 per cent, respectively, while in Sweden the figures were 2.7 and 4.9 per cent, respectively (Sorensen, 1994, table 1, p. 177).

The second demand implication of the changing family patterns is the provision of day care facilities for children either as an end in itself or as a means of encouraging mothers to take up employment. The traditional family pattern where father worked and mother stayed at home to look after the children has gone for good and it will never return. In many EU countries, the provision of pre-school child care facilities is seen as a state duty in the same way that full time education is. In others, the state is still reluctant to accept such a responsibility. It is for this reason that pre-school child care provision varies considerably among European countries though there is a trend towards increased provision everywhere.

Third, the new family patterns have implications for the nature of the social security system. As with the changing employment patterns, the requirement is for a system that responds to need irrespective of the individual's insurance contribution record. Under the present system, mothers who spend most of their lives caring for their children or for disabled relatives may find themselves with no pension entitlement in many countries; women who rely on their husbands' contribution record for pension entitlement will find themselves with no such cover if they are divorced. These and many other such injustices and anomalies make the current social security system based on the principle of 'derived' entitlements unresponsive to today's family patterns.

In recent years, the right-wing critique of state policies for lone parents has intensified accusing them of being part of the problem rather than part of the solution (Murray, 1984). Social security provision, it is claimed, encourages family break up, undermines self-reliance and breeds a culture of dependency on the state. Only its abolition can stem the growth of this type of family living and invigorate the spirit of self-support. Evidence from the USA itself provides no support for the claim that the rise in the numbers of lone parent families is linked to the benefit system (Ellwood, 1988). Research in the UK (Dean and Taylor-Gooby, 1992) and the Netherlands (Terpstra and Moor, 1994) does not support the claim for a dependency culture either. Nevertheless, Murray's ideas have influenced in punitive ways the social security policies of some governments, such as those of the UK, in a variety of ways. Such reforms, however, have only helped to increase the risk of poverty for the number of lone parent families has continued to grow.

Family social security policy is in a stalemate at present within the European Union. On one hand, the Commission recognises that 'derived' entitlements (entitlements based on the contribution record of the spouse) to social security benefits do not meet the realities of contemporary family life. The Commission's Recommendation in 1992 for the convergence of social protection cautiously suggested that 'social protection systems must endeavour to adapt to the development of behaviour and of family structures where this gives rise to the emergence of new social protection needs' (quoted in EU, 1994b, p. 121). On the other hand, it is feared that accepting the notion of 'individual' entitlement, particularly if it is not linked to the insurance principle, will result in a very different and more expensive social security system. Some governments have made a hesitant start with minor modifications to their social security systems, such as splitting entitlement to benefits in divorce cases but even these are within the insurance principle paradigm. Most EU countries have kept faith with the traditional social security system. As Hantrais observes, despite the growing convergence of family trends, 'the prospects of a more integrated family policy in Europe are limited' for both practical and ideological reasons (Hantrais, 1994, p. 229).

There is no reason to believe that the trends shown in Table 9.3 will not continue in the future. Indeed, as cohabitation, divorce and extra-marital births have become generally accepted among the young in all countries, including the Catholic and the Mediterranean, their incidence will grow at a faster rate in the future than in the past and, almost inevitably, the proportion of lone parent families as well. The clear implication is that demand for welfare provision will not decline and may grow in the future because of the changing family and sexual patterns.

The Social Dimension

The social factors making for more demand of welfare stem from both the successes and the failures of welfare capitalism. On the success side, welfare capitalism has raised not only people's living standards but their social horizons as well. As every public opinion poll shows, most people demand and expect governments to manage the economy in such a way that there are jobs and wages for everyone; and to provide adequate social services. Moreover, they are prepared to use their democratic right to vote governments that fail them out of office. In some countries, such as the UK and France, they also expect governments to maintain and even reduce taxation rates while pursuing these economic and welfare goals.

Beginning with education, it is generally accepted that children whose parents went to universities are more likely to do the same than other young people, even after controlling for such factors as class, income and intelligence. There is an understandable inbuilt generational mechanism that creates more demand for higher education. This is in addition to the wish of governments to expand higher education for they see it as a vital key to economic success. It is no surprise, therefore, to find that the proportion of young people going on to higher education has risen in all European countries so that in the 12 EU member countries the number rose from 3 510 000 in 1970–1 to 6 629 000 in 1986–7 (EU, 1991, p. 31). This rise was due more to the higher enrolment figures of women than of men. The number of female students grew by 138 per cent while that of male students by 60 per cent, even though men were still overrepresented in higher education in relation to women. Since the mid-1980s women have caught up with men in several countries and they will do the same in the others in the near future.

Though it is to be expected that the proportion of young people reaching higher education will continue to rise in the future, the actual numbers may not be higher than at present because of declining fertility rates. The desire of political parties to make higher education available to as many people as possible, however, will counteract the effects of declining fertility rates. Thus the Commission on Social Justice, advising the Labour Party in the UK, recently recommended for lifelong education, that is a system which in the long-run guarantees every citizen three years of higher education or its equivalent to be paid for by the state, employers and students (Commission on Social Justice, 1994, pp. 141–7). Some of this will be in the form of vocational training, for all EU countries now believe that a highly educated, trained and flexible labour force is a prerequisite to national economic success.

Demand for health care will increase in the future not only because of the demographic factors already discussed but also because of rising public expectations. As people become more affluent, the threshold of pain, discomfort and disability lowers and the demand for health care treatment rises. Moreover, the perception of good health widens to include conditions which previously were taken for granted. On the other hand, people's diet and living styles become healthier with the result that their need for medical care diminishes. On balance, however, increasing affluence makes for increased demand for health care because of heightened perception of health need.

The entire rise in public expectations for more and better health care has also been bolstered by the new medical discoveries that make effective treatment possible. There is general consensus on this although disagreement prevails on the cost implications. Some argue that the new medical technologies potentially reduce the cost of medical care, for example, laser treatment of cataracts and gallstones. Others, however, point to the fact that in areas such as heart transplants and cancer treatment, medical technologies are still very expensive even though far more successful than previous forms of treatment. On the whole, it does seem that so far medical technologies have raised both medical success rates and medical costs. Added to this is the effect of constant advertising by pharmaceutical companies for more consumption of drugs. In all advanced industrial countries the consumption of pills, tablets and drugs has gone up in recent years and it is difficult to see why this trend will reverse itself.

The number of health professionals per 1000 population has increased in all member countries of the European Union but with considerable variations between countries. Thus, in 1985, the UK had 1.5 doctors per 1000 population while the corresponding figures for Germany, Spain and Greece were 2.6, 3.0 and 3.3, respectively. For the same year, the corresponding number of dentists for these four countries were 0.4, 0.6, 0.1 and 0.9, respectively (EU, 1991, table 8.2, p. 88). Since salaries make up the biggest part of health expenditure, it is no surprise that health expenditure as a proportion of GDP has also increased. Within the limited national differences of affluence of the EU member countries, there is no correlation between country affluence and either expenditure on health or number of health professionals per 1000 population. Other factors intervene and one of the most important is the organisation of health care systems. Thus the UK with its National Health Service that controls the activities of both doctors and patients spends less on health care than countries such as France, where doctors have a financial incentive to treat people as frequently as possible and patients have the freedom to move easily from one doctor to another.

If, however, one compares the levels of health expenditures between, on one hand, third world countries and, on the other, advanced industrial societies then the link between affluence and health expenditure is all too evident. In 1985, for example, expenditure on health as a percentage of GNP in third world countries ranged from 2.1 in Chile, 1.8 in Malaysia and 0.3 in India (World Bank, 1990, table 3.6, p. 46). These were mere fractions of the corresponding expenditure in advanced industrial countries where the lowest figure was that of the USA, 4.35 per cent, because of its reliance on private provision, 6.17 per cent, making an overall figure of 10.52 per cent of GDP (OECD, 1994, p. 73).

Industrialisation brings with it not only economic growth and affluence but it also accentuates such social problems as crime, drug abuse and the destruction of the environment. These are social problems which cannot be solved by voluntary action let alone by private enterprise. They require government action on a planned national and sometimes international scale. Over the last few decades, all advanced industrial societies have seen an increase in these problems and the outlook at present appears to be more of the same in the future. In many European countries, crime rates have been escalating in recent years at alarming rates. People's welfare includes not only good health, housing and such like but also safety from violence against their person and property. One of the first duties of government is to maintain order in society not merely through repressive measures but also through wider preventive policies. Governments that refuse to acknowledge the connections between, on one hand, persistently high levels of social exclusion and, on the other, crime or drug abuse are failing their citizens. Creating the right conditions for the maintenance of order in society will require far higher levels of public expenditure than at present.

As for the destruction of the environment, we are not referring merely to the pollution of the earth, air, rivers and seas in an abstract way but to the implications of this for people's everyday lives. There is enough evidence, for example, of the potentially disastrous effects of the depletion of the ozone layer as well as of the link between air pollution and asthma. Greens and others feel that we may well in the future reap the whirlwind of the way we continue polluting our environment. All these problems demand more government attention than they have received so far for they are not going to go away. Neither the rate of environmental decline nor the rate of criminality or drug abuse shows any sign of abating in the near future. All these problems have implications for government expenditure in the future.

Finally, we come to the issue of social exclusion and its implications for government action. We have already covered several aspects in this area for

> the causes of exclusion are multiple: persistent unemployment and especially long-term unemployment; the impact of industrial change on poorly skilled workers; the evolution of family structures and the decline of traditional forms of solidarity; the growth of individualism and the decline of traditional representative institutions; and finally new forms of migration, particularly illegal immigration and population movements. (EU, 1993, p. 21)

The manifestation of social exclusion is equally multiple: insufficient incomes; inadequate housing conditions; insufficient access to education and health services; severe unemployment; and discrimination on grounds of ethnicity, gender, religion, age or any other such criterion.

The extent of social exclusion, in terms of insufficient incomes for basic needs, is shown in Table 9.4. It shows that in 1988, the poverty rate ranged from 4 per cent in Denmark to 26.5 per cent in Portugal. During the eight years covered by the table, Denmark experienced a substantial drop in poverty while Italy experienced a substantial rise. The other countries experienced only minor upward or downward changes. For the whole community, the largest group in poverty were people at work with low pay; the risk of being in poverty, however, was higher among those not at work through unemployment or retirement than among those at work. These are administrative explanations. In real terms, a person's disadvantaged position in the labour market is the fundamental reason for being in poverty both during working age and during unemployment or retirement.

The labour policies of deregulation, the restrictive social security policies and the worsening economic situation during the early 1990s can only mean that these poverty rates must have risen further in most countries. It is also more than likely that the situation will deteriorate even further in the near future for there is no sign of any bold anti-poverty programmes pursued or planned by any government at present.

TABLE 9.4 *Households in poverty* (percentages)*

	1980	1985	1988
Belgium	6.3	5.2	6.1
Denmark	8.0	8.0	3.6
France	18.0	14.8	14.0
Germany	10.3	9.2	10.8
Greece	20.5	17.4	20.6
Ireland	18.5	17.4	16.9
Italy	12.0	14.7	20.6
Netherlands	6.9	7.9	4.3
Portugal	31.4	31.7	25.2
Spain	20.3	17.8	16.7
UK	14.1	18.9	14.6

* The poverty line is set at 50 per cent of the equivalent mean national expenditure of adults. This tends to underestimate the extent of poverty for it assumes that expenditure equals income, ignoring the fact that some expenditure for some people is funded by debt.

Source: for columns 1 and 2, EU (1991), table 6.28, p. 78; for column 3, EU (*Poverty Statistics in the Late 1980s*), table 3.3, p. 63.

Excessive concern on poverty tends to obscure the wider issue of income inequality which is also relevant to both the demand for social services and the ability to pay for them. Trends in income inequality also help us to understand how the economy of a country has been working. There is now general agreement that economic and social policies are inseparable for they influence each other in many observed and unobserved ways. Table 9.5 gives the figures for the countries covered by this book, except for Greece, and for the USA and Japan. In the UK and the USA, income distribution widened during the 1980s no doubt partly because of the policies pursued by successive governments with New Right ideologies. But income inequality increased also in France that was under socialist rule and in Sweden under the social democrats for most of the time. In Germany, the picture remained almost the same, while in both Spain and Italy the distribution of income became more equal despite the fact that they were under very different party political governments. The overall conclusions from Table 9.5 and from data from other countries not included in the table are that the 1980s witnessed an increase in income inequalities and that this rise took place in countries with opposing political ideologies.

TABLE 9.5   *Trends in income distribution: Gini coefficients*

	Late 1970s/ Early 1980s	Late 1980s/ Early 1990s
France	36.4 (1979)	37.2 (1984)
Germany	25.4 (1978)	26.0 (1990)
Italy	33.8 (1979)	29.2 (1991)
Spain	32.9 (1980)	30.6 (1990)
Sweden	19.7 (1979)	24.7 (1991)
UK	24.8 (1979)	33.7 (1991)
USA	40.3 (1980)	43.3 (1992)
Japan	27.3 (1980)	29.6 (1989)

Sources: Ayala (1994); Atkinson (1994) from Canceill and Villeneuve (1990), Hauser and Becker (1993), Brandolini and Sestito (1993), Gustafsson and Palmer (1993).

Conclusion

Despite the difficulties involved in estimating future demand for welfare, most of the indicators examined in this chapter suggest that it will rise. At the heart of the network of factors making for the rise in demand lies the problem of high unemployment. In societies with full employment, the various population groups relying on the state for support can be reduced quite substantially: the numbers of the unemployed, of the early retired, of lone parents not at work can easily be reduced to manageable sizes. Added to this is the very real fact that the growth of the national economy will be larger, thus providing more resources for a smaller overall group of state dependents. The first major policy conclusion of the discussion on future demand for welfare, therefore, is that priority number one for governments is to reduce the current rates of high unemployment.

The second major policy conclusion – highly dependent on the first – is the need for governments to create socially cohesive societies where anti-social behaviour is reduced to the minimum and social concern for the welfare of others is raised to the maximum. The demand for certain types of welfare comes not only from those at the bottom of the economic pile but from others well above them for such problems as loneliness, mental illness and fear of crime cross financial boundaries. Trying to cope with increased demand through punitive and stigmatising measures will not reduce demand substantially, apart from the fact that many people will reduce demand substantially, apart from the fact that many people will suffer in the process and the social cohesion of European societies will be ripped further asunder. Similarly, the preoccupation with dependency ratios is largely misplaced for the problem facing European societies today is not shortage of workers but shortage of jobs.

References

Age Concern (1992) *The Coming of Age in Europe* (London: Age Concern).

Alexander, S. and Radford, T. (1994) 'Worry Clouding Home Life in the 1990s', *The Guardian*, 6 September.

Atkinson, A.B. (1994) *Seeking to Explain the Distribution of Income*, Welfare State Programme (London: London School of Economics).

Ayala, L. (1994) 'Social Needs, Inequality and the Welfare State in Spain: Trends and Prospects', *Journal of European Social Policy*, vol. 4, no. 3, pp. 159–79.

Beauvoir, S. de (1977) *Old Age* (Harmondsworth: Penguin).

Brandolini, A. and Sestito, P. (1993) 'La distribuzione dei redditi familiari in Italia, 1977–1991', *Servizio Studi*, Banca d'Italia.

Brenner, H. (1980) 'Mortality and the National Economy', *The Lancet*, 15 September, pp. 568–73.

Canceill, G. and Villeneuve, A. (1990) 'Les inégalités de revenus: quasi statu quo entre 1979 et 1984 pour les salariés et les inactifs', *Economie et Statistique*, 230, 65–74.

Central Statistical Office (CSO) (1994) *Social Trends* (London: HMSO).

Commission on Social Justice (1994) *Social Justice: Strategies for National Renewal* (London: Vintage).

Dean, H. and Taylor-Gooby, P. (1992) *Dependency Culture* (Hemel Hempstead: Harvester Wheatsheaf).

Ellwood, D. (1988) *Poor Support: Poverty in the American Family* (New York: Basic Books).

EU (1991) *A Social Portrait of Europe* (Brussels: Commission of the European Communities).

EU (1993) *European Social Policy*, Green Paper (Brussels: Commission of the European Communities).

EU (1994a) *Employment in Europe* (Brussels: Commission of the European Communities).

EU (1994b) *Social Protection in Europe* (Brussels: Commission of the European Communities).

Fagin, L. and Little, M. (1984) *The Forsaken Families* (Harmondsworth: Penguin).

Fisher, M., Marsh, P., Phillips, D. with Sainsbury, E. (1986) *In and Out of Care* (London: Batsford).

Fries, F. (1980) 'Ageing, Natural Death and the Compression of Morbidity', *New England Journal*, vol. 303, no. 3.

Gustaffson, B. and Palmer, E. (1993) 'Changes in Swedish Inequality: A Study of Equivalent Income 1975–1991', University of Gothenburg.

Hantrais, L. (1994) 'Family Policy in Europe', in Page, R. and Baldock, J. (eds), *Social Policy Review*, no. 6, SPA (Canterbury: University of Kent).

Hauser, R. and Becker, I. (1993) 'The Development of the Income Distribution in the Federal Republic of Germany during the Seventies and Eighties', University of Frankfurt.

Hewitt, P. (1994) 'Families in Flux', *Political Quarterly*, vol. 65, no. 2, April–June, pp. 168–79.

Hugman, R. (1994) *Ageing and the Care of Older People in Europe* (London: Macmillan).

Leadbeater, C. and Mulgan, G. (1994) 'The End of Unemployment: Bringing Work to Life', *Demos*, no. 2, pp. 4–14.

Murray, C. (1984) *Losing Ground: American Social Policy, 1950–1980* (New York: Basic Books).

OECD (1988) *The Future of Social Protection* (Paris: OECD).

OECD (1993) *Employment Outlook*, July (Paris: OECD).

OECD (1994) *New Orientations for Social Policy* (Paris: OECD).

Sinfield, A. (1984) 'The Wider Impact of Unemployment', in OECD, *High Unemployment* (Paris: OECD).

Sorensen, A. (1994) 'Women's Economic Risk and the Economic Position of Single Mothers', *European Sociological Review*, vol. 10, no. 2, September, pp. 173–88.

Terpstra, J. and Moor, L.G. (eds) (1994) *Normvervaging en sociale zekerheid* (The Hague: VUGA).

Walker, A., Alber, J. and Guillermard, A.M. (1993) *Older People: Social and Economic Policies* (Brussels: Commission of the European Communities).

World Bank (1990) *World Development Report 1990* (New York: Oxford University Press).

10

The Response of Government: Fragile Convergence?

PETER TAYLOR-GOOBY

> Governments are examining their social programmes, not only to alter any unintended effects, but also to use available resources more prudently ... Social policy has an obligation to ensure that resources are mobilised more efficiently and effectively ... for the credibility of the policies themselves as investments in society. (OECD, 1994c, pp. 7–8)

This chapter considers how European governments have responded to the pressures on social welfare systems discussed in the previous chapter. It consists of three sections which summarise the challenges to welfare, analyse the responses to them and consider whether there are common themes or trends in the responses which may nourish a European direction in social protection for the next century. First, however, we must review the possibilities open to governments in responding to changes in the environment of welfare, to provide a framework to the discussion.

Comparative analysis of social policy often deals with the question of how the interaction of political, economic and social factors generates different systems of social protection and how these evolve over time. The path-breaking work of the original comparative theorists (for example, Wilensky, 1975) sought to identify a small number of causal factors responsible for the development of welfare systems. Such perspectives were unable to account satisfactorily for the diversity of welfare and the stability of different arrangements under common pressures. Currently, the most influential approaches are concerned to construct typologies of welfare state regimes (Skocpol and Amenta, 1986; Esping-Andersen, 1990; Leibfried, 1990; Castles, 1993, chapter 3; Ferrera, 1994b). A regime is understood as a particular constellation of social, political and economic arrangements which tend to nurture a particular welfare system, which in turn supports a particular pattern of stratification, and thus feeds back into its own stability. Here our perspective is narrower. We are concerned not with the range of possible welfare systems, but with the range of courses of action open to European states in the current context – with the short-term future of welfare capitalism seen from the government's point of view.

The Scope of Political Action

Government responses to the problems identified in the previous chapter and Chapter 1 fall into three main groups. The state can *retreat* from its commitment to meet citizen needs, it can *redirect* demands towards non-state providers in market, family or community or it can pursue *welfare investment* policies which involve using social provision positively, as part of a strategy to overcome the problems of social and economic change. The first approach has been pursued by the political right, arguing for moves towards a minimalist state with a limited range of responsibilities. It is also put forward by those who argue that modern welfare systems encounter problems of political legitimacy, because governments are unable to satisfy the demands articulated by different groups. This results in a generalised retreat from the principle of state involvement in areas which provoke conflict, such as welfare policy (see, for example, Moran, 1988).

The second approach also assumes the contraction of the role of government in welfare, but places more emphasis on the transfer of responsibility to other agencies. Such a redirection of demand is allied to the Christian Democrat principle of subsidiarity. This approach, influential in much discussion of EU policy-making, for example in relation to the Social Charter, requires that power should reside at the lowest practical level (Spicker, 1991, p. 4). Consequently, the resources of family, local community and of the private sector should be exhausted, or be shown to be inadequate, before government is seen as having a strong role. The implications in the field of social care have been neatly conceptualised by Abrahamson in the model of the 'welfare triangle'. The triangle joins state, market and civil society as the three principal providers of welfare.

The West has emphasised the market, Eastern Europe, state solutions. 'In both East and West, the Southern countries ... have emphasized family, household and community assistance over both market and state programs' (Abrahamson, 1991, p. 239). According to Baldock (1993, p. 30), the European experience of the past two decades has been of a drift towards the market corner of the triangle, as the importance of civil society declines in the South and of the state in the East. The shift towards the market in welfare is seen as part of the inevitable process of modernisation, almost as a minor echo of the onward triumphal march of market liberalism that writers like Fukuyama celebrate (1989, p. 3).

The third approach is found in the EU's White Paper on Employment which calls for investment in physical and information technology infrastructure, training and environmental improvement in order to improve 'the effectiveness of the triangular relationship growth–competitiveness–employment and as regards the environment and the improvement of the quality of life' (EU, 1993b, p. 20). Similarly, the White Paper on Social Policy argues:

> the efficiency of our societies as a whole conditions how competitive they may be and the growth they can deliver. If economic growth is to increase human well-being, it must also take into account social and environmental concerns. Equally the pursuit of high social standards should not be seen only as a cost but as a key element in the competitive formula. It is for these reasons that the Union's social policy cannot be second string to economic development or to the functioning of the internal market. (EU, 1994, p. 2)

These approaches call for welfare investment, in training and employment policy in particular, but also in other areas, in order to enhance the quality of life and the economic competitiveness of the European Union. Similar arguments are advanced by parties of the left, and are neatly captured in the recent programme of the UK Commission on Social Justice (1994).

A variant of the approach is contained in a recent essay of Esping-Andersen. This points out that manufacturing can no longer provide mass employment and high-quality service jobs (banking, teaching, journalism) are scarce. The choice for mass employment lies between private sector junk-jobs, typified by such employers as McDonald's, or the state-led expansion of the social service sector, which can contribute to quality of life and can provide security and reasonable working conditions (Esping-Andersen, 1994a). State investment may improve the quality as well as the quantity of employment.

The different government approaches tend to be supported by claims about the impact of state activity on the performance of the economy. Despite extended debate, there is no compelling evidence to support any one of these approaches against the others (see Saunders, 1985; Pfaller, Gough and Therborn, 1991; and Esping-Andersen, 1994b) for assessments of the evidence). Table 10.1 contains OECD measures of the size of the state sector, the proportion of national income redirected by government through systems of taxation and compulsory social insurance, economic success as indicated by economic growth rates and competitiveness in terms of export price indices. The statistics cover the period 1984–94 which includes the recovery from the recession of the early 1980s, as well as the recession of the early 1990s, so that the effect of cyclical variations in activity is reduced.

The data in the table should be treated with caution. In particular, comparative measures of competitiveness through export prices expressed in a

TABLE 10.1   *State spending, investment and economic success, 1984–94*

	State spending (% GDP)	Total tax (% GDP)	GDP growth rate (%)	Export prices index
Denmark	60	50	2.2	99
France	52	44	2.0	101
Germany	47	38	2.8	98
Greece	45	37	1.7	N/A
Italy	52	38	2.2	93
Netherlands	56	46	2.5	100
Spain	42	33	2.7	91
Sweden	63	53	1.3	95
UK	42	37	2.3	96
USA	34	29	2.9	108
Average of above countries	49	40	2.3	98
OECD	40	38	2.8	N/A

Sources: State spending is general government total outlays, annual average, 1984–94, OECD (1994a), table 27; total tax is the total of tax and compulsory social insurance as a percentage of GDP, annual average, 1984–92 (most recent figures available) from OECD (1994b), p. 72; GDP growth rate is annual average, 1984–94, OECD (1994a), table 1; export prices is an index of relative export prices expressed in a common currency, annual average, from OECD (1994a), table 43.

common currency are vulnerable to shifts in currency values, which particularly affect Italy, Spain, Sweden and the UK during this period.

The state retreat approach would suggest a negative link between size of the state sector or levels of taxation and economic success, while the investment approach would imply the reverse. Neither supposition receives unambiguous support. In the period covered there are countries with relatively low spending and tax rates which are successful, such as the USA, and others with high spending and tax rates which are also successful, such as the Netherlands. Conversely, there are relatively low and high spending unsuccessful economies, such as the UK and Sweden respectively. The data indicate that the link between spending and prosperity is not simple.

None of the countries under review in this chapter has pursued a course that reflects one of the three approaches in pure form, although their policies mix them in different proportions. Analysis of the policies followed will enable us to identify whether there is a consistent trend in a particular direction among European welfare states.

The previous chapter approached the issue of pressures on provision on the basis of Europe-wide statistics. In this chapter we must sometimes descend to the detail of individual countries in order to focus on the relation between politics and policy. The countries to be discussed here are those whose policies have been analysed in the country-based chapters – Sweden, Germany, France, the UK, Italy, Spain and Greece. These form a convenient grouping to understand European patterns and to approach the main theories through which social policy has been understood in recent years. They include the five largest European countries (and EU member states), they offer a contrast between core and periphery, between Mediterranean and Northern, across the main dimensions of Esping-Andersen's, Leibfried's and Abrahamson's frameworks as these are present in Europe, between different political tendencies, levels of economic development and success, orientations toward the labour market, between Bismarckian and Beveridgean approaches and higher and lower levels of social protection and welfare spending. Most striking for our purposes, the countries contain different political traditions and orientations.

It is convenient to group the countries by level of welfare spending for purposes of discussion. Sweden, France and Germany spend substantially above the EU average, the UK and Italy spend at about average levels and spending in Spain and Greece is below average. This pattern has persisted through the 1980s and early 1990s although the last two named countries are moving closer to the average (EU, 1993a, table 1; Table 1.5).

The first of these groupings contains Sweden, with a history of Social Democratic government since 1932 (interrupted only in 1976–82 and between 1991 and 1993), with a strong commitment to state welfare and a highly effective and expensive system of social protection; Germany, governed by a centre-right CDU coalition through the 1980s and early 1990s, although with a declining majority, and with a tradition of Bismarckian, occupationally linked welfare, facing the pressures of reunification; and France, ruled by left coalitions from 1981 to 1986 and 1988 to 1993 and the right in the mid-1980s and from 1993 onwards, with a social insurance-based system, run at one remove from government.

The average spenders include the UK, with a self-consciously radical right government since 1979 suffering declining electoral support from the end of the 1980s, and a hybrid Beveridgean universal and social insurance/social assistance system, with a relatively large private sector; and Italy, governed by unstable Christian Democrat coalitions since the war, left-leaning in the 1980s, with a short-lived radical right coalition in 1994, and operating a social insurance-based welfare system.

The lower spenders have both been governed by left-wing parties for the recent past, Spain, since 1982, although the majority has been reduced in recent elections, and Greece through the 1980s and 1990s, with a coalition in 1989 and a radical right government from 1990 to 1993. Both have insurance-based welfare with little assistance and a substantial role for charity. Greece spends very little on unemployment benefits, and both countries have universal health care operating mainly through non-state agencies.

The only obvious political pattern is the predominance of left-wing parties in government in the lower income, lower spending countries who are also expanding provision. Other countries have pursued different pathways. We move on to consider the challenges that their systems of social protection have faced in recent years and their response to them.

The Challenge

The challenges have been discussed in the individual country chapters and at a more general level in the previous chapter. The main problems faced by European welfare states fall into six categories:

- demographic change, and in particular the ageing of the population;
- labour-market change, in particular high unemployment and subemployment, which not only increases the demand for social benefits but

also raises problems of entitlement and finance in systems based on the Bismarckian model of social insurance through employment;

● economic shifts, in particular the pressures on national competitiveness resulting from the increased salience of international markets in many fields;

● the pressures on national budgets produced by recession, rises in interest rates and high national debts;

● family changes, in particular the rise in one-parent families and the impact that serial and more complex patterns of relationship have on entitlement based on a stereotypical nuclear family;

● social changes, including the rising expectations for improved standards and for more responsive services, the continuing problems of industrial society, from rising crime rates to environmental pollution, and the increased importance of inequality and exclusion as a result of these changes.

In addition, the issues of population ageing, of the entitlement gap and of single parenthood have together reinforced the tendency toward the feminisation of poverty over the post-war period. A number of commentators have suggested that the structural problems of the welfare state may lead to a crisis of legitimacy and thereby to radical new departures in policy.

These pressures affect all European nations to some extent. The incidence of the various factors depends on particular aspects of national policy. Using the data discussed elsewhere in this volume (Tables 1.6 for demography, 1.3 for unemployment, 1.7 for family change, 1.10 for fiscal pressures and 9.4 for poverty rates), we may construct the following rough country profiles: among the high spending group, Sweden has relatively low levels of debt, unemployment and poverty, and no problem of entitlement has yet emerged. The proportion of elderly people is currently the highest in Europe, and is likely to remain high for the next three decades. There is also a relatively high proportion of one-parent families. Since Sweden's levels of provision are particularly high these pressures imply a considerable future burden. The recessionary pressures of the late 1980s and early 1990s have been experienced as a sharp contrast to previous success in assuring economic security. Uncertainty about the future of the Swedish model is reinforced by the economic problems of the early 1990s and the 1994 decision to join the EU.

Germany's levels of unemployment and poverty are not high, and its fiscal position is healthy. There are relatively large numbers of one-parent families, and a considerable proportion of elderly people, which is likely to rise to the highest proportion in Europe by 2020. The country has also undergone the fiscal pressures of reunification with the former East Germany and the added burden of supporting the integration of the social welfare systems of the two countries. Since German social protection is so heavily based on social insurance principles, the problem of providing for the needs of those who are not integrated into full-time work is felt with particular severity.

France has a relatively favourable demographic structure at present, although pressures on welfare will increase towards the second decade of the next century. Its unemployment levels are average, its debt level low, and the proportions of one-parent families and of low income households quite high. The problem of securing entitlement for those outside social insurance, sometimes referred to as the 'gap', is felt to be severe.

Thus in the richer higher spending countries there is a common concern about demographic pressures. In France and Germany, the problems of a social insurance tradition are emerging as the traditional pattern of household dependence on a male breadwinner is eroded by change in labour markets and in family structure. In Sweden, the impact of economic difficulties is keenly felt.

In the middle-spending countries, the pattern is rather different, with a contrast between Italy and the UK. In the UK, demographic pressures are currently high, but will improve compared to other European countries in the early years of the next century. In Italy, the currently favourable demographic position is likely to deteriorate abruptly. Unemployment rates are high in Italy and average in the UK, whereas the proportion of one-parent families is the other way round. Considerable numbers fall below the poverty line in the UK and very large numbers in Italy. Fiscal pressures are moderate in the UK, but substantial in Italy. The shift towards assistance provision in the UK blunts the problems of entitlement and finance, whereas the greater reliance on insurance in Italy means that these issues are hotly debated.

These contrasts have been reflected in very different policy stances. Demographic, unemployment and fiscal pressures pose a greater challenge in Italy, although benefits for those covered by the insurance scheme tend to be higher.

The lower spending countries have a number of similarities besides their tradition of left-leaning government. Both have relatively high poverty rates, low proportions of single parent families and severe entitlement problems resulting from insurance-based provision. Neither has a substantial assistance scheme. Both have expanded welfare spending substantially in the recent past. By way of contrast, Spain enjoys a relatively favourable demographic position, despite the low birth-rate, although this will deteriorate by the middle years of the next century. It has the highest unemployment rates of any EU country and substantial welfare spending for this group. The government does not carry a large burden of debt as a result of the rapid growth in the period of expansion after the emergence from international isolation at the end of the Franco era and, later, entry into the EU. Greece, on the other hand, is likely to experiences growing demographic pressures in the early years of next century, a particular problem since its welfare system is so heavily slanted towards the provision of pensions, but low unemployment. The level of indebtedness is extremely high by European standards and forced the government to apply for an IMF loan in the early 1990s. There is thus little similarity in the problems faced by the lower spending countries.

Welfare Futures and Public Opinion

So far we have considered the pressures that face the various countries from an objective statistical standpoint. However, political response is in practice influenced by how these pressures are understood and experienced. Public opinion does not immediately determine government policy, but is influential in relation to the political legitimacy and hence the long-run viability of a welfare system. The question of whether the citizens of European countries are concerned by the pressures on welfare identified in this book is difficult to answer without commissioning a Europe-wide survey. Material from the EU's *Eurobarometer* series (which unfortunately does not cover Sweden) provides a useful insight in relation to expectations and issues of political legitimacy (Table 10.2). The data enables us to examine both responses to the challenges of the future identified in demographic and fiscal projections and opinions about the adequacy of current levels of provision.

This table reviews answers to questions about popular concern for the future of welfare in the face of two of the most significant challenges to current patterns of provision. Round about half the population are concerned about the impact of costs on health provision in most countries – rather more in the UK and fewer in Spain, among the countries covered in our study. This is surprising in view of the relatively weak demographic pressures in the UK and may reflect the politicisation of health care debates

TABLE 10.2   *Expectations and legitimacy – Eurobarometer, 1992*

(a) 'In the future the health care provided to the average citizen of this country will be less good because of rising costs.'

(b) 'In the future there will be more elderly people than there are now. Do you think that people will get less pension for their contribution?'

	(a) Agree	(b) Agree
Belgium	54	66
Denmark	67	60
France	49	76
Germany	53	53
Greece	47	25
Ireland	65	36
Italy	55	36
Luxembourg	27	45
Netherlands	57	60
Portugal	55	23
Spain	39	37
UK	64	49
EU 12	53	50

Source: Ferrera (1994a), tables 10 and 30.

during the 1992 general election. In Spain, attitudes may be influenced by the relatively recent development of a universal system of provision.

Concern about the impact of an ageing population on pension provision is particularly high in France, and particularly low in Greece, Spain and Italy. Interestingly, there is little concern about future demographic problems in Germany, although these are likely to be severe. In France, there is a real deterioration in the demographic balance; Spain faces a relatively favourable future,. but Italy and Greece confront severe problems. Confidence may reflect the high level of commitment of the existing social insurance systems to pensions provision.

Thus attitudes do not appear to correspond to objective pressures in an obvious way, and are likely to indicate broad themes in political debate. Table 10.3 gives answers to questions about the degree of popular dissatisfaction with current standards of provision.

Levels of confidence in the protection offered by the system are relatively low everywhere, and markedly so in the Mediterranean countries, reflecting the recent development of their schemes, the lower levels of provision, and possibly the importance of clientelism and discrimination. In

TABLE 10.3 *Dissatisfaction with social protection – Eurobarometer, 1992*

Percentage who regard social protection in their country as inadequate for:

    (a)   Unemployed people
    (b)   Old people
    (c)   Sick and disabled people
    (d)   Poor people

	(a)	*(b)*	*(c)*	*(d)*
Belgium	33	69	59	78
Denmark	26	65	55	46
France	44	54	56	82
Germany	40	64	60	72
Greece	85	85	82	89
Ireland	50	66	66	76
Italy	74	84	79	84
Luxembourg	15	55	50	54
Netherlands	16	42	50	43
Portugal	79	87	85	90
Spain	69	73	72	84
UK	52	74	66	73
EU12	53	69	65	77

Source: Ferrera (1994a), table 5.

France and Germany, problems are seen as affecting the poor particularly, possibly reflecting the gap between social insurance and assistance welfare in those countries. Everywhere unemployed people are seen as being rather less vulnerable to poverty. This may reflect a lower priority for the needs of this group as much as the perception that they enjoy better provision.

    This section shows that there are real contrasts between countries in the pressures on state welfare systems and on how these pressures are perceived by their citizens. It is the condition of particular groups rather than concern about the prospective burdens identified in statistical predictions of the OECD that exercises public opinion most strongly. We go on to consider the policy responses of the various governments.

Policy Response

Inspection of recent policy developments reveals four main trends which are common to most if not all European countries and three developments that are specific to particular countries or small groupings. These developments have of course been followed at a different pace and with different thoroughness in different countries.

The common themes are: benefit cuts and cost savings; policies to generate additional income; managerial reform of the human services, especially the health care system, and decentralisation of responsibility. The commonest technique of benefit reduction is through adjustment to the formulae determining the level of pension entitlement. This is hardly surprising, since pensions are the most costly single welfare programme. In Sweden, early retirement, unemployment and sick benefit schemes were cut back in 1991 and pension increases pegged at 2 per cent below price inflation. In general, replacement rates have fallen from 90 to 80 per cent of relevant income. In 1994, proposals to restructure the entire pension system on actuarial lines, based on lifetime contributions, were agreed, so that the redistributive impact of pensions is reduced, and the problem of financing benefits in the face of an ageing population is resolved.

The German approach also involved pension reform and benefit cuts. In 1989, the pension formula was revised, with the effect of cutting benefits and increasing contributions. Commentators appear confident that the changes will achieve stability in pension funding as the population ages. In 1993, unemployment and other social insurance benefit rates were cut back and, more importantly, social assistance frozen for four years.

In France, a number of cuts in benefit levels have taken place through the late 1980s and early 1990s. Currently, pension reform proposals which will adjust the formula are under debate. Unemployment benefit has been revised in order to increase work incentives, with a fall in level of payment every four months.

Among the middle-spending countries, the UK has carried out substantial cuts in national insurance benefits, abolishing the link between the state pension and wage indices, and providing large incentives to shift to private pensions, transferring most sick benefit responsibilities to employers, and cutting back on entitlement to unemployment and disability benefits, In 1995, unemployment benefit is to be replaced with a 'Jobseeker's Allowance', with rigid behavioural conditions and limited to six months. As a result of these changes, claimants of working age have been shifted towards the large assistance scheme and retired claimants toward the private and occupational sector.

Italy adjusted pension levels downwards in 1991, but has not reduced the role of social insurance. Cuts in health care spending took place earlier, in 1989.

Among the lower spending countries, welfare expenditure has increased more rapidly from a lower base over recent years. In Spain, the pension formula was readjusted to increase qualifying contribution periods in 1985. However, political opposition culminating in general strikes in 1988 and 1992 prevented government from carrying through benefit cuts as originally intended, although the youth employment plan was shelved in 1988 and unemployment benefit rules tightened in 1992. In Greece, the pension formula was readjusted in 1991 and the large invalidity pension scheme cut back in 1992.

All the countries discussed have increased pension income by adjustments to contribution formulae. In addition, there are a number of specific measures. In France, a new tax, the CSG, levied on all income including corporate profits was introduced in 1983, then abolished in 1985, reintroduced at a higher rate in 1990 and increased in 1991. This tax is widely seen as a shift away from the basic principle of the finance of social benefits through social insurance. It is a response to the problem of meeting the needs of those who do not have a stable labour market record of entitlement. The solidarity tax and the extra subsidies to social insurance in order to maintain the solvency of the system in Germany, in the face of the additional pressures of reunification, have a similar role. There is a widespread demand to reject *Fremdleistungen* – the 'intrusion of alien principles', as the injection of subsidies from general taxation into the finance of social insurance is described – into the system. In addition a new social insurance contribution to finance social care has been introduced, a response to the extra nursing needs of an ageing population.

The reform of social and health care has generally involved the development of market oriented systems where there was previously a directly managed centralised state system. The clearest examples are Sweden and the UK. A recent study shows that in eight out of the twelve EU member states at the time, some form of overall budgetary control had been introduced (Abel-Smith and Mossialos, 1994, p. 89). In those countries where social insurance pays for independent medical practitioners or facilities, tighter controls have been introduced. In Germany, the imposition of drugs budgets and restrictions on the rate of increase in medical fees have turned a deficit in the statutory health insurance fund in 1992 into a surplus in 1993 and cut spending by nearly 3 per cent. In France, a number of minor changes to the regime of professional autonomy (*médecine libérale*) have been made and there are moves to establish full medical records and to limit consumer freedom of consultation. Some savings have been achieved, but there is widespread concern about the cost of the system and further reform is likely.

The process of decentralisation is sometimes linked to the introduction of market principles, but may have an entirely different rationale. Countries which have not taken this route have also devolved responsibility for provision and in some cases revenue raising powers downwards. In the Netherlands, decentralisation was initiated in the mid-1970s by the Den-Uyl administration with the primary objective of increasing popular participation in government. In Spain, the process is part of the settlement achieved by the Socialist government to the problem of the widely different interests and levels of development in different parts of the country after the return to democracy. In Italy, there are similar motives for decentralisation – as a way of creating a framework in which a large and disparate country with contrasting wealthy and impoverished regions can hold together. In France, decentralisation legislation in 1983 was directed at the improvement of efficiency and responsiveness. In the UK, decentralisation has taken place within a rigid framework of central spending control intended to undermine the independent revenue-raising and spending powers of local bodies and secure spending cuts.

The main theme in response to the pressures on social welfare has been the trimming of social benefits and the increase of revenues, most importantly through the readjustment of pension schemes. In addition there have been administrative reforms, especially in relation to health care. These policies have been pursued with more or less vigour and have met with different responses. In the richer countries, adjustments in social insurance systems have been achieved with little political resistance. In the middle spending countries, there has been more concern. In the lower spending countries, strike action prevented the government from pursuing their objectives in Spain, and in Greece the government has been unable to achieve a lasting pension settlement. There are tendencies in the direction of convergence as benefit levels are trimmed back. Those countries which rely on social insurance systems increasingly supplement budgets from general taxation, new methods of raising extra revenue and cutting benefits through readjustments to pension formulae are found, levels of spending are increased in the poorer countries and the most highly centralised administrations pursue decentralisation, but substantial differences still remain.

There are also real differences between countries in policy direction in a number of areas. The most prominent concern privatisation, the moral climate of reform and the role of assistance. Different countries have also pressed home their policies with different degrees of enthusiasm.

The UK has been most prominent in pursuing the development of private provision in relation to pensions. There has also been moralistic concern about welfare fraud in the UK, the Netherlands and Italy. The assistance system has become more important in meeting the needs of those of working age who are affected by changes in the labour market and family patterns (unemployed and one-parent families) – in Germany, where unemployment benefits have been cut back at the same time as assistance benefits have been frozen, in France, where solidarity benefits have been established, and in the UK, where insurance benefits have been curtailed, while assistance benefits are stringently regulated.

The combinations of policy in different countries have had rather different impacts on the welfare experience of citizens. In general, there have been real reductions in provision for some groups in the wealthier countries but the bulk of the welfare system remains untouched. The existing schemes have been revised in ways that seem likely to resolve problems. The UK stands out in that the reforms appear to add up to a regime shift in the direction of welfare minimalism. In the Mediterranean countries severe problems in welfare provision appear to remain, particularly in relation to support for unemployed people and those with a weak attachment to the labour market. None the less, social protection continues to expand in those countries.

Many of the policies currently being enacted will take some time to achieve their full effect. This is true of the changes in pension calculation throughout Europe. As time goes on the gap between those who have access to insurance benefits and those who are forced to rely on assistance welfare will become more pronounced in those countries which have not strengthened their assistance schemes. The development of assistance is one of the most significant issues across most of southern and northern Europe. The weakness and stigmatic nature of such systems in most countries generates particular problems for those not protected by stable employment records or attachment to work, especially single parents and those who have not successfully entered formal employment, have been forced to retire early or are subemployed.

These developments in welfare can be interpreted in two ways. On the one hand, there is a continuing process towards convergence in European welfare, albeit under somewhat harsher circumstances than in the 1960s and 1970s in spending levels, coverage and financial arrangements, especially the balance of tax and contributions. On the other, much of the response of the different European systems to the problem of squaring the welfare circle is at present unclear. The uncertainties about future directions particularly in the peripheral nations (Greece, Italy, Spain and the UK) suggest that it is too early to draw conclusions about whether the apparent stability of the solutions adopted in the north European mainland will be reflected elsewhere.

National Variations

In this section we attempt to relate the various responses to national politics. Are the approaches of left, centre and right-wing governments distinctive – does politics, as Castles puts it, 'make a difference' or are patterns of welfare to be explained primarily by economic and social factors (for example, Castles, 1981).

To put it simply, during most of the first half of the 1990s, the right has governed in the UK and Sweden, the centre in Italy and Germany, the left in France and Spain, and Greece has experienced a shift from right to left. The UK does exhibit a distinctive pattern of response which may be attributable to the political regime. Policy may be understood as a market-oriented restructuring of the system which is to some extent independent of objective pressures. In Sweden, the right have been weaker in government, forming a minority coalition. Attempts to cut back child benefit and the 'partial pension' system between 1991 and 1993 were blocked in parliament. The German solution has emphasised a shift towards assistance and benefit cuts for those of working age, within a Christian Democrat framework, in contrast to the development of new benefits for uninsured unemployed people (the RMI and solidarity benefits) by a left-wing government in France. Italy has not developed substantial social assistance despite the severe problem of unemployment. In Spain and Greece, left-wing governments expanded benefits in the 1980s, the former is beginning to develop a social assistance system and the latter has introduced assistance pensions and rent benefits. Programmes of retrenchment in the 1990s have been trimmed because they were unacceptable to supporters.

There is thus some evidence that politics has an impact, in the sense that different parties in government would have behaved differently. However, the impact of political complexion is not great when compared to level of development and the trend to convergence. Everywhere programmes of benefit curtailment and retrenchment are on the agenda, and the differences are of degree and of the vigour with which these policies are pushed home. Recession tends to reduce the significance of political differences in changing policy.

Esping-Andersen sums up some of the main themes in comparative analysis of social welfare systems in terms of their impact on what he terms commodification and stratification (1990, chapters 2 and 3). The former concerns the extent to which the system of social protection insulates the worker from the impact of market forces, the latter the extent to which welfare is differentiated by social class position. To this we might add the impact of policy on women's distinctive dependence in families – 'de-familisation' – to reflect the extent to which welfare systems allow women to resist dependency in traditional family forms, by supporting them as single mothers, as independent workers, with independent pension rights or substituting for familial care responsibilities.

Throughout Europe, the trend in policy has been towards greater commodification as stricter entitlement rules link the worker more strongly to the labour market. In those countries where real expansion in provision has taken place, such as Spain and France, access to the new benefits (Rentas Minimas and RMI) is determined in relation to work tests and tests for existing benefits have everywhere been strengthened. This process has perhaps moved most rapidly in the UK, but everywhere the trend is to reduce individual independence from the compulsion of the labour market. Those systems which traditionally base benefit on entitlements gained through social insurance are modifying their formulae to take account of the needs of those who do not have access to satisfactory work-based welfare, but the shifts are minor.

In relation to position in the class structure the picture is more complex. The extension of welfare coverage in the Mediterranean countries, particularly Spain and Greece, in areas like health care, and in France in the new solidarity benefits, and the introduction of new redistributive forms of finance in some countries, like the France CSG or the German solidarity tax, suggest a move away from a rigid pattern of class hierarchy. Clearly these tendencies do not undermine the Bismarckian hierarchy, but they do weaken the tendency of such an approach to grow more hierarchical in recession, as the lowest groups lose access to labour market welfare. By contrast, there have been measures designed to strengthen the stratification impact of welfare in some countries, most notably in the UK, where the redistributive aspect of state pensions and sickness benefits has been weakened and the pressures towards privatisation erode the capacity of government to moderate market inequalities.

A recent EU study points out that the social insurance basis of social security in the main Northern European countries (France, Germany and Benelux) penalises those with poor or interrupted work records, while in Scandinavian, Anglo-Saxon and Mediterranean systems, an interrupted working life makes less difference. Benefits tend to be higher in the

Scandinavian than in the Anglo-Saxon and Mediterranean countries (EU, 1993a, p. 129). A similar pattern applies to the impact of divorce from a spouse, who is the chief wage earner in a household, on a woman's entitlement to benefits. Social insurance-based welfare is particularly ill-suited to providing adequate benefits for women who are more likely to experience career interruptions than are men.

In relation to the needs of women – the feminisation of poverty among elderly people, single parents and unemployed people, and the problem of meeting the care needs of the elderly when these can no longer be devolved onto women in families – the policy response is generally weak. Programmes directed specifically at poverty among the poorest groups of pensioners and single parents, or to improve security for workers in the most vulnerable sectors of the flexible labour market, have not received a high priority. These are all positions in which women predominate.

While Germany has not developed programmes to deal with the poverty issue, it has produced a new benefit in the Christian Democrat tradition to tackle the care problem. No other country has so far gone down this route, although it is under discussion in most of the wealthier EU countries. Thus the specific impact of social changes on women is unlikely to be met by current developments in policy. Progress for women is most likely to result from better access to paid work and to the benefits that are achieved through it, rather than from a structure than respects specific needs.

Conclusion

Responses to the challenges to welfare vary between countries. The clearest general pattern is of retrenchment in benefits and of efforts to raise additional income, most commonly through adjustments to the pension formula. There is some indication of a mild tendency towards convergence as the lowest funded systems continue to develop and those most heavily based on social insurance expand their financial base to include taxation. There are also common tendencies in the direction of decentralisation and health care reform.

The trend towards convergence is fragile. The Mediterranean countries appear to have been least successful in achieving changes that will meet future demands. There is some weakness in the capacity of changes to adapt to the new pattern of needs resulting from family and labour market change. This is likely to bear most heavily on un- and subemployed people and women in countries without developed assistance systems. As things stand the impact of the new pressures on welfare is likely to be a worsening of standards, particularly for the weakest groups, set against the tendency to convergence in European welfare systems.

In relation to the three approaches set out at the beginning of the chapter, developments in Europe indicate little support for the strategies that imply either abandonment of the welfare state or the positive use of welfare programmes as part of a strategy of investment to aid future growth and social integration. None of the countries reviewed plans to excise whole areas of provision – indeed expansion of coverage, often with stricter detailed entitlement conditions, continues in many of them.

Conversely, the arguments developed at the end of the Second World War in the Beveridge and Laroque plans that linked social welfare with social investment and reconstruction, do not seem to find a powerful voice in national as opposed to EU political fora. The debate seems to lie between the restructuring of provision and the redirection of responsibility, mainly towards the market. The political right tends to be identified with the later approach, although its success in pursuing the strategy in Sweden was limited by coalition and in Italy by political weakness. Centre right governments as represented by Christian Democracy support a strong but stratified state sector, emphasising work discipline and the family. Only in the UK has a right-wing government succeeded in maintaining authority for long enough to achieve a redirection of provision sufficiently decisive to amount to a retreat from the welfare state.

Through most of Europe the emphasis is on restructuring in the face of the challenges to welfare. It is in the detail of restructuring, and particularly in the extent to which changes in policy meet the new needs generated by changes in work and family life, that the real debate lies. The indications at present are that European state welfare is not adapting with sufficient speed or imagination to meet the human demands of social change.

References

Abel-Smith, B. and Mossialos, E. (1994) 'Cost Containment and Health Care Reform: A Study of the European Union', *Health Policy*, no. 28, pp. 89–132.

Abrahamson, P. (1991) 'Welfare and Poverty in the Europe of the 1990s', *International Journal of Health Service* vol. 21, no. 2.

Baldock, J. (1993) 'Patterns of Change in the Delivery of Welfare in Europe', in Taylor-Gooby, P. and Lawson, R. (eds), *Markets and Managers* (Buckingham: Open University Press).

Castles, F. (1981) 'How Does Politics Matter?', *European Journal of Political Research*, vol. 9, no. 2.

Castles, F. (ed.) (1993) *Families of Nations* (Aldershot: Dartmouth).
Commission on Social Justice (1994) *Social Justice: Strategies for National Renewal* (London: Vintage).
Esping-Andersen, G. (1990) *The Three Worlds of Welfare Capitalism* (Cambridge: Polity Press).
Esping-Andersen, G. (1994a) 'Equality and Work in the Post-Industrial Life-Cycle', in Miliband, D. (ed.) *Reinventing the Left* (Cambridge: Polity Press).
Esping-Andersen, G. (1994b) 'Welfare States and the Economy', in Smelser, N. and Swedberg, R. (eds), *The Handbook of Economic Sociology* (Princeton, NJ: Princeton University Press).
EU (1993a) *Social Protection in Europe* (Luxembourg: Commission of the European Communities).
EU (1993b) *Growth, Competitiveness and Employment* (Luxembourg: Commission of the European Communities).
EU (1994) *European Social Policy – a Way Forward for the Union* (Luxembourg: Commission of the European Communities).
Ferrera, M. (1994a) *EC Citizens and Social Protection* (Luxembourg: Commission of the European Communities).
Ferrera, M. (1994b) *Welfare in Southern Europe,* International Seminar on Social Policy, University of Madrid, October.
Fukuyama, F. (1989) 'The End of History', *The National Interest*, no. 16, pp. 3–18.
Leibfried, S. (1990) 'The Classification of Welfare State Regimes in Europe', Social Policy Association Annual Conference, University of Bath, July.
Moran, M. (1988) 'Crises of the Welfare State: review article', *British Journal of Political Science*, vol. 18, pp. 397–414.
OECD (1994a) *Economic Outlook*, no. 56, December (Paris).
OECD, (1994b) *OECD Revenue Statistics, 1965–93*, (Paris: OECD).
OECD (1994c) New Orientations for Social Policy, *Social Policy Studies*, no. 12, (Paris).
Pfaller, A., Gough, I. and Therborn, G. (1991) *Can the Welfare State Compete?* (London: Macmillan).
Ploug, N. and Kvist, J. (eds) (1994) *Recent Trends in Cash Benefits in Europe* (Copenhagen: Danish National Institute of Social Research).
Saunders, P. (1985) 'Public Expenditure and Economic Performance in OECD Countries', *Journal of Public Policy*, vol. 5, no. 1, pp. 1–21.
Skocpol, T. and Amenta, E. (1986) 'States and Social Policies', *Annual Review of Sociology*, no. 12.
Spicker, P. (1991) 'The Principle of Subsidiarity and the Social Policy of the European Community', *European Journal of Social Policy,* vol. 1, no. 1.
Wilensky, H. (1975) *The Welfare State and Equality: Structural and Ideological Roots of Public Expenditure* (Berkeley: University of California Press).

Index

219